DEEP
HISTORY

SUNY series in Radical Social and Political Theory
Roger S. Gottlieb, Editor

DEEP HISTORY

A Study in Social Evolution and Human Potential

DAVID LAIBMAN

State University of New York Press

Published by
State University of New York Press, Albany

Printed in the United States of America

For information, address State University of New York Press
194 Washington Avenue, Suite 305, Albany, NY 12210-2384

Production by Judith Block
Marketing by Susan M. Petrie

Library of Congress Cataloging-in-Publication Data

Laibman, David.
   Deep history : a study in social evolution and human potential / David Laibman.
       p. cm.— (SUNY series in radical social and political theory)
   Includes bibliographical references and index.
   ISBN 0-7914-6929-8 (hardcover : alk. paper) — ISBN 978-0-7914-6930-9 (pbk. : alk. paper)
   1. Historical materialism.   2. Social evolution.   3. Capitalism.   4. Marxian economics.
5. Socialism.   I. Title   II. Title: Social evolution and human potential.   III. Series.

D16.9.L317 2007
335.4'119—dc22   2006002194

ISBN-13: 978-0-7914-6929-3 (hardcover : alk. paper)

10 9 8 7 6 5 4 3 2 1

CONTENTS

PREFACE

You sometimes hear: "History is a mystery. No one will ever get to the bottom of it. We shouldn't even want to." But years of reflection have convinced me that the human record *can* be unraveled, and that "for goodness' sake" (literally!) we should seek fundamental explanations—find the "deep structure" beneath the "surface structure" of our daily lives, and the history books. So—"Deep History." If you find this project intimidating, or off-putting, and are not willing to give it a try, read no further. But I hope you *will* give it a try!

A few years ago I was speaking on this theme, at the Brecht Forum in New York City. In the discussion following the talk, one listener conjured up the long list of adjectives that writers of the postmodern persuasion like to hurl, like missiles, against anything that smacks of systematic explanation. I was able to add to his list, although it is still undoubtedly incomplete: determinist, essentialist, teleological, linear, positivist, theoreticist, evolutionist, scientistic. There is one noun: metanarrative. And one nominative verb form: privilege. (Example: "We must refuse all *metanarratives* that *privilege* [the economy/the working class/science].") Now postmodernists usually do not sit still for definitions, but each of these verbal accusations needs precise characterization, so that I can enter a plea. In most cases, and against all legal protocol, I will plead both "guilty" and "not guilty" at the same time.

Take "determinist," for instance. Would an *indeterminist* position be preferable? Shouldn't we at least try to sort out the *levels* of reality at which *determinate* or causal claims can be made, against those at which there is too much variety and contingency for explanatory options to be meaningful? But this, of course, is "essentialism"—the distinction between essence (deep structure) and appearance (surface structure). Essentialism, incidentally, used to mean artificially separating essence from its outward appearances and deriving it independently of them; in short, essentialism meant *misuse* of the distinction between appearance and essence, not the distinction itself. The postmodern critique is directed against a crude parody of the original. Another example: teleology attributes will and purpose to things that do not possess them; it is not the mere perception of directionality, or progressive movement, in social or natural systems. This is why I want, for the most part, to plead guilty to embracing the appropriately subtle forms of these distinctions, but not the silly interpretations. I will want to get at the deep structure underlying surface appearances, but without losing hold of the connection between the two levels, or treating the deep structure as something that can be known independently of its outward manifestations. It's a question of using conceptual tools, like any tools, skillfully.

As you will by now realize, this book is not a work of "history," in the ordinary sense—not even a "people's history." I will not describe the details of movements, struggles, resistance; I leave that important task to others more qualified to carry it out. I will not try to broaden a people's history to include daily life, culture, forms of consciousness. I will not even offer yet another excursion into the stories of kings, wars, statecraft—the stuff of the standard history texts. My project is to reach behind the rich veins of human experience, in all its forms, through the entire time of our existence on Earth, and to seek out explanatory principles that might help organize our understanding of that record—our basic sense of ourselves, where we have been and where we are going.

The project implies, and assumes, that there is in fact a deep structure not apparent to our immediate perceptions and knowledge. To find that structure, we will have to use what Marx called the "force of abstraction," which replaces the laboratory experiment that is available to many natural sciences. In every phase of this inquiry, the reader will be asked to confront and master abstract concepts; these are the tools we use to *think beyond*, and *behind*, the endless detail and sensory overload of concrete experience.

Are we doing this correctly? Am I losing track of important elements, placing them into the category of fortuitous and accidental phenomena, only to focus on an incomplete set of basic principles? Possibly! That is for critics of my account to argue. But the proof of their pudding will be in the alternative *theory* proposed by them. To show how it can be done better is quite a different matter from abandoning the attempt altogether.

The problem of agency vs. structure looms large throughout this project. I will state immediately: nothing happens in human history that is not done by conscious, willing human beings—agents. Human will and action, however, never appear in a vacuum. Marx's famous formulation comes to mind: "Men make their own history. but they do not make it just as they please;

they do not make it under circumstances chosen by themselves, but under circumstances directly encountered, given and transmitted from the past" (Marx 1852, quoted in Cornforth 1954, 30). To sort out the ways in which the vast multiplicity of human individual consciousnesses and actions are shaped into stable configurations that reproduce themselves and persist— seemingly against and independently of those wills—and to understand how at crucial moments they converge into movements and struggle that eventuate in decisive transformations—all this clearly suggests that human will, indeed the complex of intersecting individual wills, confronts an objective framework and objective limits. "Objective" here means, quite simply, independent of subjectivity and consciousness. The natural environment, together with the accumulated state of knowledge applied to that environment and its transformation, is clearly one element in that objectivity. The structural interaction of multiple human wills, in which each individual is constrained by the desires and actions of others, is another.

Often, when I try to describe the objective side of this equation, as, for example, for the general theory of history in chapters 1 and 2 of this book, someone reacts by saying: "Aren't you leaving out class (or other) struggles?" And the answer is unequivocal: of course not. As you will find throughout this book, concerted struggles of large groups of people, whose consciousness and interests are aligned by the common situation in which they find themselves, are always the "motor" of history, and nothing in the positing of objective circumstances surrounding those struggles changes that fact. The point for the present is that structure and agency cannot be conceived independently of one another; each is necessary to grasp the concreteness and determinacy of the other. Agency, consciousness and purpose are central to every dynamic process described in this book. If anyone comes away with the perception that the subjective side has been somehow "left out" of my account, I can only wonder whether for that person subjectivity is only valid if it is taken out of its own context of possibility. In short, the point would seem to be that "men make their own history *only if* they can make it just as they please"—the opposite of Marx's contention.

So you will not find detailed history here; only an attempt to build up a set of tools with which we might be able to grasp its deep structure. Another thing readers will find missing is a systematic exegesis of Marx. From the preceding references, it should be clear that my overall standpoint is Marxist, in a general sense that anyone familiar with Marx will recognize. Nevertheless, I have not tried to present in detail the source material in the writings of Marx, Engels, or other classical or contemporary authors. There are three reasons for this. First, that material is already widely available in many places; see the bibliography. Second, publisher, author, and readers will all agree on keeping the length of this book down to manageable size. But, third, there is a, well, deeper reason. Some supporters and detractors of Marx show a pronounced tendency to treat his texts as a source of authority, on a scale not usually seen in discussions of other writers. Ironically, this deification of the text—I have sometimes called it "textualism," (as in Laibman 2002a)—is seen among Marxists with very different approaches to recent history (see chap. 7, on the Soviet Union), as well as among non-Marxists who expect the object of their critique to be textually oriented, and are often somewhat dismayed whenever they find that that is not the case. I cannot state too strongly my view on this. Marxists must work out for ourselves, from scratch, a theory of history in the tradition bequeathed to us by Marx, and we must drop the authoritarian impulse to validate our results by attributing them to Marx, or by "discovering" them in numerous extract quotations from his work. I like to imagine Marx himself kicking us fledglings out of the nest, saying: it is high time for you to sally forth on your own. Marxism has been the largest secular (nonreligious) mass movement in history, and I believe—because this is "objectively" needed, by all of us willing agents—it will eventually be even larger than it was in the past. All the more reason to try to avoid the old impulse to slide backwards into authoritarian-religious "quotology," rather than using scientific criteria for validity and acceptance.

This then raises a question: is this work Marxist? (My own favored definition of a Marxist is: anyone who sincerely believes her/himself to be one.) The question dissolves into a better one: is this work good Marxism or bad Marxism? But an even better set of questions may be these: is this work good social theory? Does it contribute to our toolbox for a politically fruitful and developing understanding of history? Is it scientific, critical, humane, open? Does it help orient people in the vast emancipatory projects of our time? I face the answers to these questions with considerable trepidation; my only consolation is that they must also be asked of all other efforts rendered along the same lines.

Deep History is organized into three parts. The first covers the most general level of the overall project: the principles regulating the evolution of human society as such, including its periodization—for which I use the quasi-neologisms "stadial" and "stadiality," referring to stages of development. The concept of *theoretical stages*, which have logical as well as empirical referents and are linked into a determinate ladder-like pattern, plays a large role. I suggest in part I that a "hard" (or "strong") historical materialist theory can coexist with a "soft" (or "weak") one; that these alternatives actually refer to coexisting, and complementary, levels of abstraction. This, of course, raises up a hornet's nest of questions about validity criteria: I must not appear to be "having my cake and eating it too," by setting up a "hard" level (the "abstract social totality") at which directional and progressive claims about history can be made without having to worry about mere matters of verification and historical variety; and a "soft" level, which can handle all of the slings and arrows of a rich historical narrative without having to worry about offering a determinate and meaningful account. The goal, of course, is to get the two levels talking to one another, and to establish solid logical, practical *and* empirical tests that can confirm or disconfirm the entire proposal.

Part II is about the most complex stage in the stadial structure of social evolution that has established itself in the historical record to date: capitalism. This part therefore has the most chapters, addressing, consecutively: (1) the structure of capitalism, how it functions as a system of surplus extraction (whether you believe it or not, I think there are still new things to say about this); (2) the logic of capitalist development (long-term trends and the taxonomy of crisis); and (3) the stadiality of the entire capitalist era, with the proposed system of stages subject to the same rigorous requirements as the stages of the Abstract Social Totality in part I.

Traditional Marxist accounts of capitalism have found the theory of value to be indispensable, and I have also labored hard in the value-theory vineyards, without—I must say—a tinge of regret (for the latest stage in this work, and full references, see Laibman 2002a). In order to keep the voicing of this book consistent throughout, however, I have decided to try to work out (in chapter 3) an account of capitalist reproduction and exploitation that does not require deployment of the value-theory armory, especially its quantitative aspects. I have stuck to my goal of keeping the presentation self-contained and accessible to the serious but inexperienced reader, and to that end I have tried to capture the essential elements in value theory, without succumbing to that theory's own language and quantitative expression. Time will tell whether, and to what extent, this tactic has succeeded.

Part III, the most speculative of the three parts, takes the story beyond capitalism, using the tools developed earlier to reformulate, refresh, and (I hope) reinvigorate the theory of socialism and communism: the projected transcendence of capitalist—and, simultaneously, all—class division and exploitation. If this part is successful, it should not be intelligible outside of the framework of the general theory of social evolution developed in the earlier chapters. Its goal is to present a non-utopian socialism; that is, to avoid arbitrary speculation and "recipes for the cook-shops of the future" while at the same time using the general stadial theory to reveal central features of social structures not yet in existence! A tall order, indeed.

I should mention briefly one feature of the text which, I hope, will turn out to be more of a help than a hindrance. This is the use of nonquantitative diagrams, what I call a "conceptual geometry" approach to working out relations among concepts. These figures appear in the first five chapters, and seek to give some visual determinacy to sets of interrelated concepts. Perhaps my training in economics is to blame for this, but I do hope that readers will find the figures more useful than otherwise.

There are too many influences on my thinking, over many decades, for me to properly acknowledge them; the bibliography will give some idea of the extent of this influence, but I am also painfully aware of the absence of sources that should have been included. Of all of the people with whom I have conversed and debated, and whose works I have benefited from, I must mention several people who read parts of the manuscript, in various stages of its development. Paul Blackledge, Renate Bridenthal, Alan Carling, Barbara Foley, Marvin E. Gettleman, Robin Hahnel, Derek Lovejoy, Gerald Meyer, Dimitris Milonakis, Deborah Mutnick, John P. Pittman, Tony Smith, and Paul Wetherly are among those whose comments and criticisms have been extremely helpful; they are not to blame for my not living up to their expectations. I have tried out many of the ideas in the book on several generations of students, and have gotten priceless feedback from them.

We need both the richness and variety of human life, and a grasp of its underlying deep structures. We need both a profound sense of the human spirit embodied in movement and struggle toward better futures, and a thorough grasp of the objectivity that limits possibilities in any period and reveals the stadiality of the path forward. Who says we can't have our cake and eat it, too?

DAVID LAIBMAN

Brooklyn, New York
Fall 2005

Acknowledgments

I would like to acknowledge, with gratitude, permission to draw upon some previously published materials. For chapters 4 and 5, and parts of chapter 7, to the editors of *Science & Society*, for my articles published in that journal: "Capitalism as History: A Taxonomy of Crisis Potentials" (vol. 63, no. 4, Winter 1999–2000); "Theory and Necessity: The Stadial Foundations of the Present" (vol. 69, no. 3, Fall 2005); and "The Soviet Demise: Revisionist Betrayal, Structural Defect, or Authoritarian Distortion?" (vol. 69, no. 4, October 2005). For chapter 6, to Brill Academic Publishers for my article in *Historical Materialism*: "Contours of the Maturing Socialist Economy" (vol. 9, 2001). A condensed version of chapters 1 and 2 appeared as "The End of History? The Problem of Agency and Change in Historical Materialist Theory," as part of a special issue on "Rethinking Marx and History" (*Science & Society*, vol. 70, no. 2, April 2006).

I.
THE GENERAL THEORY OF
SOCIAL EVOLUTION

Chapter 1

AGENCY, CAUSALITY, AND HISTORY

In thinking about human potential, we often encounter the view that the future is completely open; that "we can be whatever we choose to be." This contrasts with positions, at the opposite end of the spectrum, that rest on some sort of determinism—usually biological or theological, but sometimes encased in "natural law" or the inevitability of the "free market." These views place inexorable limits on human possibilities, with varying degrees of severity. Curiously, the two extremes complement one another. The open-endedness of the anything-is-possible attitude provides no sense of a foundation or platform from which movement toward a future of greater human achievement and quality of life might be launched, and the *probability* of decisive progress appears low-to-minimal; this then ironically reinforces the structural pessimism of the determinists. Historical materialism—the study of human social formations and the principles that regulate their evolution, transformation and supercession—is the best starting point for an inquiry into human potential that avoids the trap set by the convergent extremes of unalterable dystopia and incalculable utopia.

There has been a resurgence of interest in the historical materialist project in recent decades. The publication of G. A. Cohen's *Karl Marx's Theory of History* in 1978 sparked a wide-ranging debate, which continues today, concerning the nature of directional forces in history and the role of human agency and rationality in the historical process. My own work, developed independently of Cohen's, and published in 1984, also aroused some controversy, on a much smaller scale (see Sweezy 1986; Amin 1985; McLennan 1986). Subsequent work by Dimitris Milonakis (1993–94, 1997) and Claudio J. Katz (1994) sought to build, in different ways, on the inquiries into social evolution that in fact go back to the famous mid-century symposium on the transition from feudalism to capitalism involving Maurice Dobb, Paul M. Sweezy and others (*Science & Society* 1977; Hilton 1979). A related discussion of the work of Robert Brenner (1976) on the agrarian origins of capitalism in England (Aston and Philpin 1985) brought together historians, geographers, and demographers searching for answers to questions regarding the role of class (and other) struggles, population dynamics and markets in shaping the emergence of capitalism and the varied paths of that emergence. The focus shifted later to the world stage, with discussions of the world-system view of capitalism, and the larger historical themes in the work of Andre Gunder Frank and the Europe vs. China problematic (Wallerstein 1974, 1977; Frank 1998; Duchesne 2001–02, 2003; Wong 1997, 2003; Goldstone 2003). And most recently, a group of British social theorists has developed an approach to historical materialist theory that incorporates insights from Charles Darwin and natural selection (Blackledge and Kirkpatrick 2002). The list is undoubtedly incomplete.

In this chapter, I will first review and recapitulate the formalization of historical materialist theory that I originally developed some twenty years ago. This must of necessity be a self-contained statement that reproduces the theory "from scratch"; it would be unfair to impose on the reader the requirement to first read the original article (Laibman 1984, 1992a, ch. 13). At the same time, the reformulation arrived at here can only reflect many subsequent interventions and reconsiderations. In this chapter, the recent work of others will be addressed only implicitly. Chapter 2, with the model of this chapter fully on board, will then take up some of the recent trends and positions in more detail. Chapter 2 will return to the large themes in this discussion, above all the political implications of the several extant trends.

I. A GENERAL MODEL OF SOCIAL EVOLUTION

In theoretical approaches to history, the pendulum has continually swung between perception of commonality in the human experience, on the one hand, and insistence upon variety and the irreducible uniqueness of each historical situation, on the other (for a comprehensive survey, see Carneiro 2000). This has often been seen as a matter of classification and generalization: can "laws," in the sense of statements proposing observed uniformity among different historical experiences, be formulated? Do, for example, all societies pass through a uniform set of stages in their development? If these historical laws are to withstand scrutiny, it must not be possible to find exceptions to the generalizations, or at least no significant ones. In periods when the theory enterprise has been approached with confidence, law-governed development is postulated; when confidence ebbs, however, empirical research chips away at these conceptual structures, and passage from a "hard" theory to a "soft" one (e.g., Gottlieb 1984)—or, in some formulations, "strong" to "weak" (Wright, et al. 1992)—takes place. And the cycle repeats, enforcing continual alternation between a theory of evolution that appears to lack empirical foundations and to emanate only from its implied political implications, on the one hand, and a tangle of formless empirical material, acceptable to academia but with no useful broader implications, on the other.

The heart of my earlier proposal, which draws upon numerous sources in the literature (e.g., Marx 1913 (1859); Lange 1963; Dos Santos 1970) is my suggestion to overcome this dichotomy, by developing a theory that is *simultaneously* "hard" and "soft." I posit *levels of abstraction*, and arrange these into a hierarchy, so that at the "highest" level we find the *abstract social totality* (AST) and at a "lower" level the (more) concrete *social formation* reflecting geo-climatic and developmental variation. ("Higher" and "lower" are, of course, arbitrary metaphoric devices; "inner: and "outer" would work just as well.) At still "lower" levels numerous contingent and accidental factors, including the personalities and capacities of individuals, come into play and infuse variety into the picture, which thus approaches the concreteness of the actual historical record.

If this is to be believable, so that we are not "having our cake and eating it too," two requirements must be met. First, the higher level of the abstract social totality must inform the construction of the lower levels; it cannot operate in a vacuum, independently of the rich detail of the historical record. The "hard" theory must tell us what the relevant facts are, and help organize historical information into meaningful wholes. Second, the hard theory must be falsifiable. This is not to embrace some sort of "falsificationist" epistemology; it is simply to assert that there must be validity criteria on the basis of which the truth-value of the claims we make regarding the nature of the AST can be established. Rejecting any simple path from pristine facts to confirmation or disconfirmation of theory, I still accept the responsibility to support the theory from the evidence and experience of history. In other words, the theory cannot merely be useful, or fruitful; it must, in some sense, be true as well.

The central feature of human existence, as revealed at the level of the AST, is its *stadiality*. I use "stadial"—here, and throughout this book—as the adjective form of "stage"; it refers to the property of development through a series of well-defined stages. "Stage" and "stadial" seem easier to use than "periodization" and "periodization theory," which have come into common use (see Albritton et al., 2001); but "periodization" does not have an adjective form ("periodical" obviously does not serve), and "stage" and "stadial" do the job more concisely and clearly.

Terminology established, I proceed to the central property of the AST: social evolution proceeds through a series of stages, and at the level of the

AST these stages are (to quote myself; Laibman 1992, 265) an "*absolutely determinate* ladder." The stages are, in a terminology that I have developed more recently, *theoretical stages*, as opposed to *descriptive stages*. The latter are the familiar generalizations from observed temporal regularities: the empirical raw material for the derivation of theoretical stages, and—as noted above—the continuing basis for reconfirmation, disconfirmation, and development of the stadial conceptualization at the AST level. Theoretical stages, however, have logical as well as descriptive properties (this formulation, incidentally, suggests that logic is a category of ontology as well as epistemology). In a word, they are "chain-linked." Each stage in a theoretical sequence requires for its existence some crucial property of the preceding stage; contains within it a crucial contradiction, or progressive insufficiency leading to increasing tension and incoherence; and establishes a crucial foundation that defines the succeeding stage. The stages are therefore not arbitrary in character or number; they are not a recapitulation of "theoryless" history, "just one damn thing after another" at a higher level of generality.

This conception must clearly be squared with human agency; we are, after all, talking about *human* history, not natural history, and the element of human consciousness must be inherent in our account. Determinacy at the AST level does not exist *in spite of* human will and agency, but rather *because of* them; they are definitional for human, as opposed to earlier and coexisting nonhuman, life. I return to this major issue soon.

The central methodological implication of levels of abstraction can now be stated. The determinate ladder of theoretical stages—assuming it exists, an assumption that cannot be separated from confirmation of its ongoing extraction from the raw material of history—occurs *only* at the level of the AST. As soon as we depart from this level and examine social formations at more concrete levels, variety in external conditions and consequent variations in pace and detailed features of development are introduced. We might say that the AST would be directly visible only on a planet with one continent, with no mountains, rivers, narrow isthmuses, or any other barriers to communication and diffusion of cultural traits, and a common climate, flora, fauna, and so on. Our world clearly diverges in momentous ways from this abstraction, and that fact determines the enormous variety of paths and rates of development of human groups evolving in relative isolation from one another (see Diamond 1997, for a thorough treatment).

Distinct social formations come to embody varying combinations of traits associated with the theoretical stages. There are blockages and bypasses: social formations leap over stages in their own development by coming into contact with other formations in which those stages have already been completed—a "torch relay" effect (Semenov, 1980). Alternatively, external circumstances may create "low-level equilibrium traps" in which a given formation may stagnate. Conditions may even lead to retrogression and extinction along particular evolutionary pathways. In present times, when unprecedented levels of world integration have been achieved among human populations and technology contains hitherto unknown perils as well as promises, we must envision the possibility of the ultimate blockage: general nuclear or ecological extinction. A stadial evolutionary theory does not *predict* human survival! It may, however, point in the direction of the obstacles in the present that need to be overcome, if survival and progress are to be a reasonable prospect. To the extent that these obstacles, identified in theory and at the AST level, are actually effective in the lives of people, the ground or source is established for systematic agency—the consciousness-based movement that can eventually resolve a contradiction and initiate a new stage in sociohistoric evolution.

Building Blocks for a Rigorous Evolutionary Theory

To isolate the crucial elements driving the stages of the AST, we look at the most basic, and inevitable, requirements of social reproduction—what *all* societies must always do. And here we find the core of the insight that defines the Marxist tradition in social theory. Any human society that has ever existed—this is a synthetic *a priori* proposition, not an empirical generalization—has entered into a constant metabolic relationship with its external natural environment. The defining condition of human existence is *labor*: conscious interaction with nature to derive inputs and transform those inputs into forms that sustain life. In this process, since symbolic reference is inherently social and presupposes human interaction, there are two distinct but inseparable aspects: interaction of humans with nature, and interaction among human agents themselves. These are, respectively, the aspects of the social labor process that we call "productive forces" (PFs) and "production relations" (PRs). It is important to stress at the outset that the PFs and PRs are aspects of the same socially and stadially defining activity. There is nothing to gain, and much to lose, from reverting to a classificatory conception of this distinction and arguing about whether to "locate," for example, tools in the PFs and techniques in the PRs, or whether knowledge "belongs" in one or the other category. Labor activity is intimately connected to consciousness of that activity; ideas and action are in continual symbiotic interaction and tension. All technical activity is simultaneously social, and both forces aspects and relations aspects of that activity are simultaneously present in material practice and corresponding consciousness.

Two fundamental propositions characterize the relations between the PFs and PRs. The first of these will at first seem rather innocuous and obvious: the PFs and PRs of any society are not arbitrary and unrelated; on the contrary, they interact intensely and condition one another. As noted above (and below), social formations draw on elements of the AST in complex and combinatory ways, and all sorts of diverse PF and PR elements may be found coexisting within them. At the level of the AST, however, we find a well-articulated combination of a set of PFs and the PRs appropriate and congenial to that set. The PFs and PRs, therefore, form a consistent whole, to which we give the name "mode of production" (MP). Theoretical stadiality is based on a series of distinctions among the principles defining the MPs that make up the ladder of stages. For the present, the point is a relatively simple one: within a MP, the PFs and PRs are mutually shaping and conditioning. All I wish to emphasize at this point is that nothing in this formulation assigns causal primacy to one or the other pole of this relationship. I have come to believe that the quest for the basis of the "primacy of the productive forces," initiated by G. A. Cohen, places this inquiry on a wrong path. It is not that the PFs and PRs act equally within the model, as we will see; rather, the distinctiveness of the PFs will be found in a property they possess that is not present—or not as centrally present—in the PRs. Put this way, the question of the relation between PFs and PRs does not deteriorate into a sterile discussion of which pole "causes" which, or which has the "greater" impact, in some quantitative sense, on the other. The PF–PR model (the name I give to the formalization of historical materialist theory that I am proposing) need not struggle against the obvious insight that the relations of production always either assist or constrain the PFs, and significantly shape their qualitative characteristics.

The substance of what we may call the "correspondence principle" (of PFs and PRs) must still be established, of course. Why is it not possible to combine any set of PFs with any known or possible set of PRs? (One thinks of children's books with the pages cut horizontally in the middle, so that the upper torsos of people or animals can be combined with the lower torsos of completely different ones.) At this point, before we have elaborated the theoretical stages of the AST, we must be content with some general and illustrative answers. But the correspondence principle can only be finally confirmed (if at all) by means of the fully elaborated theory, including articulation among its different levels of abstraction.

The obvious starting point is to treat the PFs as establishing necessary (but not sufficient) conditions for a range of PRs. The coming into existence of a quantitatively significant and dependable surplus product beyond the subsistence needs of direct producers is a clear precondition for any elaboration of social structure—ruling strata, clergy, bureaucracy, ruling classes, and so forth—beyond the simplest horizontal relations among producers and dwelling or kinship units. Note that advances in productivity are not *sufficient* for a portion of the social product to take on the character of a surplus; for this to happen, there must be a lag in the evolution of needs among the producing population, together with development of means of coercion (surplus extraction). There is a chicken-egg problem here: the means of surplus extraction must exist prior to the surplus, but those means are themselves based on (supported out of) an existing surplus. Like all chicken-egg problems, this one does not prevent chickens and eggs from coming into existence; it only points up the complexity of the process, even at this rudimentary stage. What has been said, however, is sufficient to establish an obvious negative correspondence: complex institutions and stratification cannot be present in societies that do not generate a significant, dependable, and reproducible surplus.

The correspondence principle runs deeper than this, however. Certain forms of PRs are best adapted to any given level of development of the PFs, because the nature of production requires a specific form of *incentive and control*—whether these are democratic and socially solidaristic, or whether, as in the long period lasting from the earliest emergence of social classes until the present, they are antagonistic and involve coerced, exploitative extraction of surplus. In the long prehistory of human civilization, when people existed in small, nomadic bands hunting and foraging for bare subsistence, the absence of a reproducible surplus and the precarious nature of subsistence determine PRs that are communal, egalitarian, and solidaristic—although from much anthropological evidence, this did not preclude serious antagonism and warfare between groups. With the progress of the PFs (a concept yet to be elaborated), the problems of incentive and control become more complex. Once a surplus has been captured and a ruling class solidified on its basis, the means of coercion applied to the direct producers correspond to the level of productive development, and become progressively more sophisticated as the labor activity from which a surplus is extracted itself evolves. This periodic replacement of PRs by progressively more subtle ones—more sophisticated systems of surplus extraction, if you will—enables each stage in the growth of the PFs to proceed to its full potential, and to lay necessary foundations for subsequent stages in PF–PR development. This is the basis for the stadial conception, to be elaborated shortly.

The second proposition at the foundation of the theory is what I will call the "development principle," and it captures (more accurately, one hopes) what is intended by "primacy" in many formulations. The motivating question is: does the mode of production have an immanent or necessary tendency to change and develop, and, if so, where in the MP does this tendency reside? Proposition 2 assigns "developmentality" to the PFs, rather than to the PRs. More precisely, in the balance between stasis and transformation, the former is dominant within the PRs, and the latter within the PFs. Note that "dominant" in this wording does not require that the PRs can never acquire innovative momentum, or that the PFs must always be subject to a transformative dynamic. The assertion of the developmental property with regard to the PFs has often been countered by the claim that historical evidence does not bear it out: we know of many societies that languished, or even retreated, for long periods of time, in their technical capacities. There is also the question of the source of PF development. The view, often attributed to G. A. Cohen, that the PFs develop because people purposefully and intentionally develop them in order to reap the benefits of superior efficiency and productivity, is rejected on both empirical grounds, and on the basis of a methodological critique—that this "intentional primacy" of the PFs posits the existence of a super-historical "human nature" character-ized by rational choice. My presentation of postulate 2 should therefore have something to say about both of these issues.

Rational choice can mean the particular brand of quantified rationality that comes to characterize behavior of actors in advanced market economies; in this sense, projecting such behavior backward onto precapitalist institu-tions and times would indeed be a form of "presentism," and methodologi-cally unacceptable. However, a more general version of rational choice can be formulated, which in effect sees it as an expression of the unique human capacity (and necessity) to create symbolic meaning, manipulate symbols, and, in so doing, transform the external world (White 1969; Becker 1971; Deacon 1997; Harris 1979; Carneiro 2000). Conscious activity is purposeful activity. If there is a nonbiological human nature, involving cultural univer-sals such as symbolic reference, language, and labor, this must imply the ever-present potential to transform the environment, a potential that even-tually becomes actual. Humans thus have the capacity (and necessity) for *agency* in a way that other animal species do not, and this agency has gen-erally been effective in transforming the ways in which humans interact with the natural environment. Amidst periods of stasis, and periodic leaps from one level and/or rate of development to another, and given the inherent capacity for diffusion of knowledge and traits among cultural groups due to the superorganic, non-instinctual determination of human behavior, the historical generalization establishing the progressiveness of the PFs through-out history is well established—indeed, one of the few non-controversial and significant generalizations possible. I have always been amused by left thinkers who, even as they cast suspicious doubt upon all stadial theorizing on the grounds that such theorizing smacks of "determinism" and "fatalism" and amounts to a denial of human consciousness and agency, cannot see the immense role of consciousness and agency in the continual (if uneven) transformation of the productive forces.

But this transformation is indeed uneven. In fact, as noted, there are significant places and times at which it does not occur at all. Where it does not occur, however, pressure does not build up for corresponding transformation of the PRs; this scenario then describes cases of relative stagnation. For the AST all we need is the proposition that in the range of varied conditions in which production takes place throughout history, a significant number of situations will exist in which intentional action by individuals within classes or strata that have the power to act on the PFs will result in PF transformation, and that only rarely will PF changes result in *loss* of productivity or efficiency. Note that "intentional action" that *affects* the PFs does not necessarily mean action *with the purpose of* transforming the PFs.

With regard to the PFs, then, we have the following summary result. Certain societal configurations may or may not effectuate PF development. That development is the source of further progress, but this is not required or expected to appear in every historical circumstance. When the PFs do in fact develop, this is as a result of intentional action, but that intentional action may be for very different purposes than the improvement of productivity, which may in fact be an unintended consequence, and may be driven along pathways that are not intended. Rationality, in the sense of symbolic reference and the capacity for purposive action, is indeed inherent in the human condition, but its embodiment in behavior is historical and cultural.

If the PFs have the developmental property, the next question is: do the PRs similarly have this property? The PF–PR model answers this question with a qualified yes and an ultimate no! To begin with, there is a fundamental difference between the PF and PR aspects of productive activity. While the PFs are embodied in the continual practice of labor and are therefore subject to incremental change, the PRs are enshrined in a symbolic framework of meaning, including more or less complex ideological representations and the embodiment of those representations in institutions (state, church, school). In addition to the PF–PR dialectic, there is a *base-superstructure* dialectic (not adequately addressed, I think, in my earlier formulation of the model). As in the case of the PF–PR distinction, the base-superstructure distinction is not about classification of irreducible social elements; it is rather about the interrelated aspects of social processes and their reproduction in the consciousness of the actors who embody them and carry them out. We have, then, core institutions—the production relations—surrounded by a variety of supporting institutional structures (of which the triad state-church-school is richly, although not exhaustively, descriptive). The degree of integration of surrounding with core institutions varies significantly. Both sets of institutions have corresponding ideological structures: the forms in which they are reproduced in the consciousnesses of individuals. There thus arises a two-way "relative autonomy" dynamic: between core and surround, and between the practical and ideological instances of each. Aspects of this dynamic are frequently confounded together into the unidimensional base-superstructure dichotomy. For present purposes, I want to highlight only one aspect of this situation: the cultural framework of meaning that provides the structure of a society's ideological self-definition is strongly connected to the PRs, which after all embody the core interpersonal interactions of the society and are therefore inherently communicative, and symbolic.

The upshot of this is that the developmental property, working directly and incessantly (although unevenly) on the PFs, does not work in the same way on the PRs. Production relations tend more inherently toward stasis, for two reasons: culture, and class. Frameworks of meaning tend to preserve themselves; their very efficacy is bound up with their permanence, or with perception of that permanence infused into the consciousness of social actors. The contrast can be stated sharply: the PFs are (and are perceived to be) powerful precisely when and because they contain powerful impulses toward growth and transformation. The PRs, by contrast, are (and are perceived to be) powerful precisely insofar as they possess (and have an aura of) permanence. When the PRs are class-divided—are defined by the existence of antagonistic classes, on opposite sides of a surplus-extraction relationship—the impulse toward stasis and preservation of what exists, already immanent in the ideological and superstructural systems of definition that pervade any social system, is greatly enhanced by its functionality for the ruling class, which by definition is the site of the power to implement social policy.

Antagonistic and Non-Antagonistic MP Development

The two propositions—the "correspondence principle" and the "development principle"—work together very differently in the two cases of antagonistic and non-antagonistic modes of production, where the former sort contains antagonistic social classes and the latter does not. In Laibman (1984), I illustrated this difference with a pair of simple diagrams, reproduced with some adaptations alongside (Figure 1.1). The left-hand panel of this figure represents the non-antagonistic form of development. The development principle works (sporadically, but immanently) on the PFs; it is represented by downward movement, as shown by the heavy downward arrow on the left side of the panel. The correspondence principle is represented by the horizontal double-headed arrows. Correspondence between the PFs and PRs is (roughly) preserved as development proceeds, with dominant causality running from PFs to PRs (left to right in the figure). The tendency of the PRs toward stasis is *progressively* overcome by the need for institutional evolution to fulfill the potential of developing PFs, and the tension between development of the PFs and stasis of the PRs is therefore relative, and attenuated. We may think of this version of the model as describing social evolution over long periods of "prehistory"—the era of "primitive communism"—in which the low level of PF development dictates, in the negative mode of determination explained above, a regime of general equality and social solidarity in the PRs, and the absence of class formation. The fact of PF development, however, means the gradual emergence of a potential surplus, and where the circumstances of population growth, cultural diffusion and superstructural institutions facilitate this, the potential surplus is captured by emerging differentiated social strata—warrior castes, priesthoods, nobles and commoners. This process culminates in consolidation of ruling and exploited classes. The left panel of figure 1.1, needless to say, is a condensation of many thousands of years of (pre)history, taking place in a vast variety of forms.

When class division has been consolidated, the movement is then best described by the right panel of figure 1.1. Here, class conservatism is added to the general tendency toward stasis of the PRs, and PF development presses against a given system of class relations—embodied in and supported by legal and religious institutions and ideologies, specialized institutions of administration and coercion (the state), and other social structures. The resulting tension is represented in the figure by the wavy line connecting the static PR to the developing PF; it is a useful heuristic to think of this wavy line as a rubber band, which is progressively stretched as the PFs develop further and further within the existing PRs. Three aspects of this increasing tension are worth noting. First, the PRs, which have now come to embody a particular form of class power and domination, exert increasing pressure of a particular kind, forcing the development of the PFs along a characteristic path. The actual nature of technical development in a period described by this particular PF–PR tension (i.e., this particular mode of production) is determined by the social relations within which it takes place. I have always been surprised by the desire of some participants in the historical material-

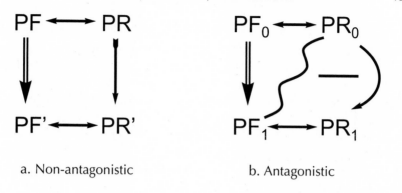

a. Non-antagonistic   b. Antagonistic

Figure 1.1. Social Evolution at the AST Level

ism discussion to characterize the PF–PR model as a form of "productive forces determinism" (which apparently means any conceptualization that takes the productive forces seriously), when in fact the model not only allows for the persistent shaping of the PFs and technical progress by social relations (the PRs), but in fact places that process at its analytical center.

The second aspect of the PF–PR tension is the clear implication that a given MP eventually and progressively restrains the PFs and blocks the ongoing development of productivity. The PRs turn from a form of development of production to "so many fetters," to be "burst asunder," in a classic phrase (Marx and Engels 1998 [1848], 11). The forcing of productive development along a particular line suitable for the existing PRs drives production in an increasingly problematic direction, in which the PRs are more and more revealed to be insufficient, even for existing levels and forms of output. This insufficiency may result in a crisis of surplus-extraction, that is, of the PRs; at the same time, potentials for further productive development along different lines are increasingly thwarted—although this effect may not be present in the consciousness of the actors within the existing MP, only being revealed in a subsequent departure.

The third implication of PF–PR tension is inherent in the rubber-band metaphor: when a rubber band is stretched, it eventually snaps. This is shown in the figure (right panel) by the horizontal bar blocking slow consistent development of the PRs, and the curved arrow representing (more or less) rapid transformation of the PRs. Since the PRs show a dominant tendency toward stasis, the set PF_0–PR_0 represents a well-defined mode of production (unlike the nonantagonistic form of development, in the left panel of the figure, in which no clear distinction between two discrete MPs can be discerned through the process of evolution depicted), and the breaking point represented by the stretched rubber band effectuates a transition to a similarly discrete, and more advanced, mode of production (PF_1–PR_1). This provides an analytical definition of *revolution*—the transition from one well-defined mode of production to another. (Needless to say, there is no simple association between this analytical revolutionary transition and the political revolutions that appear in more recent history, although some of these at least may be seen as embodying revolutionary transformation of the sort represented by a shift from one mode of production to another.) The revolution concept adduced here also serves as the basis for the *theoretical stages* that will be identified as constituting an inner model for historical analysis—the central dynamic of the AST. In this further development of the PF–PR model, we will be concerned not merely with underlying principles of social transformation, at the AST level, but rather with establishing the precise number of theoretical stages of development (modes of production) and the principles involved in their progressive supercession—what precise role each one plays in preparation for the one to follow, and how each precisely resolves the contradiction of the one preceding it.

Before we can trace out the stadial model in detail, however, a fundamental issue must be addressed: the precise nature of the break in the chain of biological evolution represented by the emergence of human, cultural existence.

The Biology-Culture Interface

The question of the precondition for human social evolution takes us to the interface between biology and the human sciences. In a masterful defense of science against postmodern nihilism, Barbara Ehrenreich and Janet McIntosh (1997) trace the valuable elements in the cultural and political critique of science—especially of the positivist epistemology and the presumption of scientific neutrality often adopted by the scientific establishment. They note and appreciate the substantial opposition to trends (sociobiology, eugenics, and, more recently, evolutionary psychology) that posit innate behavioral properties in human beings—from the territorial imperative to genetically determined drives for hierarchy and domination—with perverse political implications. Their concern is to decry the postmodern advance beyond this valid critique to the proposition that biology is *completely* irrelevant to human life; that we are culturally defined, and in that sense unique among life forms. The culturalist critics, they write, erroneously "dismiss the possibility that there are any biologically based commonalities that cut across cultural differences" (12). This attitude is dubbed "the new creationism"; with it, "we have gone, in the space of a decade or two, from what began as a healthy skepticism about the misuses of biology to a new form of dogma" (13).

In full solidarity with this attempt to rescue science as such and biology in particular as such (as distinct from their misuse) from withering idealist and relativistic criticism, I nevertheless point to a sweeping non sequitur that runs throughout the Ehrenreich-McIntosh argument. This is the linking of the binary biology/culture with two others: universal/particular, and necessary/contingent. It is seen in the phrase quoted above, referring to the denial of "*biologically based commonalities* that cut across *cultural differences.*"

The problem, of course, is that this completely ignores an entire dimension, and arguably a vital one: the *cultural universal.* It is intriguing to note that Ehrenreich and McIntosh come close to this concept in only one place in their article, and that is the one point at which they mention Marx: ". . . tacit assumptions of human similarity are embedded in the theories of even such ostensible social constructionists as Marx, whose theory of alienation assumes (in some interpretations, anyway) that there are authentic human needs that capitalism fails to meet." Marx's concept of *species being,* elaborated in the *1844 Manuscripts,* is a thrust toward precisely this cultural universal.

But the concept was best nailed down by the non-Marxist anthropologist Leslie A. White, whose contributions, I believe, have not been fully appreciated (White 1969; see also Becker 1971). White's term for the *unique* human quality that defines a cultural human nature is the *symbol* (see White 1969). More general than language, the symbol nevertheless finds its major expression in language. It is the capacity to create abstract meanings and bestow them on objects and relations (and not only to respond to signs created outside the organism, a property shared by many species). Symbols are an internal filing system, through which the flow of perceptions is restricted and regulated. The system of symbolic understanding is "dense"; it cannot be restricted to a limited sphere of perception or activity. (We cannot, for example, have symbols for plants, but none for animals.) It is, to use that currently despised word, a "totality." It provides both the possibility and the necessity of a framework of meaning, thus generating a "superorganic" realm, the realm of culture. Humans live in this realm, as well as in the external, natural world. Thus, our world is, and must be, mediated through symbols, which however do not *create* that world. This is the key to a materialist, as opposed to idealist, constructionism.

Symbols and culture are the basis for the planned, intentional action on the world that we call "labor," as indeed labor is the basis for the emergence of the symboling capacity. (White speculates on the organic basis of symboling, and considers this to be an open question. He does not use the category "labor" in the way done here, much less refer to Engels on this point.) Labor, in fact, may be thought of as having the same relation to human or social evolution as Darwinian selection does to biological evolution. The fundamental order of determination, however, is reversed: passive adaptation via natural selection in the natural realm, vs. conscious transformation of the external environment in the social. The social (symboling) process, of course, is far more dynamic and rapid than the biological, which requires the duration of biological time for random mutation and transmission of genetically acquired characteristics.

The concept of the symbol has a number of unifying features that cannot be explored here; I refer especially to the symbolic (abstract) conception of the self and acquisition of the ego, which occurs through language and is therefore necessarily social. Here I concentrate on the conjunction of two elements: the central role of intentional action, and the density (completeness of coverage) of the symbolic field. This conjunction carries a major implication for symboling behavior: to take effect comprehensively, the freeing of behavior from instinctual determination must be (almost) complete—leaving aside the autonomic nervous system, the startle reflex, the sucking reflex. These residues of genetically determined behavior are like the bare minimum of hard-wired programming built directly into a personal computer: the knowledge required to extract data from a disk inserted into the external drive.

Just as the existence as such of the symbolic, superorganic realm is not a matter of degree but of kind, behavior cannot be both instinctually (genetically) and symbolically (culturally) determined. The distinctively human superorganic form of existence cannot emerge until this release from biological determination is qualitatively complete. Here the massive evidence from cultural anthropology, showing the enormous variability of behavior, temperament and talents across human cultures, becomes relevant. Genetic differences in the strengths of certain generalized strivings or aptitudes among individuals, or clusters of individuals, certainly exist; these, however, remain vague potentials in the absence of cultural definition. It is noteworthy that instinctual governance of occasional behavior in other mammals, especially sexual behavior, is bound up in the transmission of pheromones through the sense of smell, and that it is precisely that sense which is highly attenuated in humans.

A Tale of Two Cats

It should be understood that symbolic reference refers to a qualitative distinction between human and (so far as we know) all other animal intelligence, and does not impugn or deny the effectiveness of the latter. A true piece of animal lore may help clarify this.

This is a tale of two extremely intelligent cats, Peri and Samir. Samir is the A-cat, and is clearly dominant—a behavior common not only to mammals, and clearly instinct-driven. (Hierarchy ensures discipline and order, and is therefore an adaptive trait.) As A-cat, however, Samir tends to monopolize the food supply, and his humans were concerned that B-cat Peri was not getting his fair share of the food they set out. The solution to this dilemma: put one of the food bowls on top of the refrigerator—a spot reachable by Peri in a single bound, something that Samir could not achieve.

Samir, however, learned to jump *first* to the kitchen table, and *then* to the refrigerator top. In their next countermove, the humans placed the kitchen door ajar, into a position blocking the space between table and refrigerator. But Samir tackled this challenge as well: he learned to push the door closed with his paw (a task requiring a fair amount of sustained effort), after which the path from floor to table to refrigerator top was again clear. So the humans then did what humans are good at: escalate. They propped the door open with a doorstop. And Samir again rose to the challenge: he worked at the doorstop until it fell away; then he worked at the door; and *finally* used the table to access refrigerator top and food. Our amateur ethologists thus witnessed a sustained sequence of actions, linking cause to effect repeatedly in pursuit of a goal. The proximate moral of the story: never underestimate the intelligence and creativity of animals.

The episode's deeper message, of course, is to question the claim that human consciousness and action have a distinctive quality not shared with other living species, which I have been calling "symbolic reactivity" or "symboling"; a more graceful term is "symbolic reference" (Deacon 1997). I would like to defend the claim, and explore its properties a bit further. The distinction itself is the central issue; human uniqueness in its possession is a distinctly secondary matter. But this is all the more reason to examine Samir's behavior with care, to see if human consciousness (including problem-solving ability) is indeed unique, in a way that has implications for directionality in social evolution.

At issue are the pathways that build upon the simplest form of an organism's interaction with its environment—the unconditioned reflex, or built-in (instinct-driven) response to a stimulus (in the case of Samir, the striving for food). The unconditioned reflex is genetically encoded, and therefore the result of natural selection of an adaptive behavior, a selection that takes place in biological time. Behavior and survival chances are enriched, as is well known, by the elaboration of this mechanism into the conditioned reflex: new behaviors not present in the genome can be created, and other behaviors extinguished, by associating an intrinsic stimulus with an external one. The external stimulus is arbitrary, as in the well-known behaviorist experiments inducing responses in animals to light or sound events, by associating these events with intrinsically pleasurable or painful stimuli (food, electric shock). The secondary stimulus is arbitrary, but the association must be imposed on the organism from outside.

In the next stage of this evolution, the last two properties are reversed: the organism itself makes the association, but between stimuli that are inherently connected in the environment. This is *learning*. Unlike the conditioned reflex, which can be observed or induced in many animal orders, learning appears to emerge only in mammals. It involves the (usually sudden) occurrence of insight: the moment at which a connection is established, between a simple tool and an outcome (chimpanzees inserting a stick into an anthill), or between a table and a refrigerator top. Learning greatly improves organismic reactivity: the organism makes the connection directly, rather than waiting for natural occurrences (or laboratory researchers) to impose it. With the underlying hunger (and, perhaps, dominance) drive in place, Samir learns one connection (table—refrigerator top); builds that connection into a conditioned response; then learns a new connection (move door—table) and builds the new connection into the conditioned chain; and finally learns a third connection (move doorstop—door), adding that one to the chain. In the absence of symbols—the exhaustive grid of meanings that enables the organism to do all this abstractly, independently of the sensory field, and prior to acting—this is an impressive intellectual achievement.

Symbolic reference completes the sequence. Symbols are arbitrary elements (constructed out of signs, largely but not exclusively linguistic) associated with objects or elements of experience by the organisms themselves. Here a shift in point of reference occurs: symbols emerge as elements of communication among individuals, and have an inherently relational quality. But with that understanding, they represent an alternative framework of meaning—a set of abstractions—that *intervenes* between *external stimuli* and *behavior*. Symbol processing thus precedes action; moreover, action takes place—and can only take place—on the basis of symbolic representations. "External" in this formulation refers to elements in the objective environment outside the organism (and cooperating organisms), but also, and crucially, to impulses coming from the genetic "interior." The inclusiveness and exhaustiveness of the symbolic field assures that *no* behavior of the organism, other than the most elementary reflexes and the functions of the autonomic nervous system, can result from an automatic triggering source. This "freeing of [from] instinct" is the central reproductive strategy along the chain of evolution leading through the primates to homo sapiens. We are driven by, for example, hunger, or sexual desire, but we cannot avoid translating these feelings into the superorganic realm of symbols *before* we act on them. We cannot grasp them purely emotionally, or in terms of picture-thinking; the symbolic reference field cannot be turned off.

In *African Genesis* (1967), Robert Ardrey—in total contradiction to his reductionist intentions!—provides a magnificent illustration of the distinction between symbolic and nonsymbolic reference. South African farmers, plagued by crop-stealing baboons, move into the planted fields and hide, while the baboons watch from the safety of the surrounding jungle. One farmer hides in the field while the rest retreat. The baboons will return to the field (to their peril), if they are fooled into thinking that *all* of the farmers are gone; this rests on their ability to count. Experience revealed that the baboons could count up to four or five, but got confused trying to distinguish quantities above those numbers. Imagine trying to "count" items by sheer perception, burdened with the necessity of receiving all of the rich extraneous particulars in the sensory field, that is, without *numbers* (symbols). A daunting task. By contrast, with symbols, they could, in principle, distinguish between 1,000,000 farmers and 999,999. Numbers clearly illustrate the *exhaustive* quality of symbols: n implies $n + 1$. There is no quantity for which there is *not* a number.

The schematic in Table 1.1 may help in nailing down the stages in the development of organismic reactivity, or reference. (This is my own construction, but it is based on Ernest Becker's conceptualization.)

What presumably distinguishes the dullest of human beings from the brightest of cats (Samir) is the distinction, often missed in casual discussions, between learning and symbolic reference along the bottom row of this table. The conceptual lacuna is illustrated in recent reporting on research by Frans B. M. de Waal at the Yerkes Regional Primate Research Center in Atlanta, Georgia. The findings consist of observations of behavioral variations among

Table 1.1. Classification of Levels of Reactivity/Reference

		Connection between Stimuli	
		Intrinsic	Arbitrary
Response of organism	Other-initiated	Unconditioned reflex	Conditioned reflex
	Self-initiated	Learning	Symbolic Reference

different communities of chimpanzees, as summarized in de Waal (2001). Summarizing work reported in the journal *Nature* in 1999, a reporter writes: "The researchers came up with 39 behavior patterns that fit their definition of cultural variation, meaning they were customary in some communities and absent in others, for reasons that could only be explained by learning or imitation" (*New York Times*, June 17, 1999). De Waal, in a commentary on this report, finds the evidence "so impressive that it will be hard to keep these apes out of the cultural domain without once again moving the goal posts." I can assure him (*a*) that, on my part at least, the goal posts will move no further than the distinction between learning and symbolic reference, a distinction that does not seem to have occurred to most members of the primatological community; and (*b*) that—as indicated above—should symbolic reference indeed be found to exist among primates the "uniqueness" of human beings can readily be abandoned, so long as the qualitative singularity and dynamic inclusiveness of symbols as such are grasped.

Terrence W. Deacon (work cited, ch. 3) develops a different conceptual hierarchy, in which the transitions are from iconic reference, to indexical reference, and finally to symbolic reference. Refer to this work for massive amounts of information about both human and animal behavior, and the crucial concept of co-evolution. The upshot is the defining insight that comes down to us in many forms, from Adam eating the fruit of the Tree of Knowledge in Genesis, to Marx's 1844 elaborations on human *species being*. This is, once again, the cultural universal—the missing link between biological universals and the cultural particularities so beloved of the "new creationists" targeted by Barbara Ehrenreich and Janet McIntosh. The universe of symbols imposes the ability (and need): to posit and manipulate contrary-to-fact situations; to be aware of space and time and their negations, that is, to know of nonexistence and death; to possess the acute self-consciousness that we call the Self, or the Ego, a symbolic abstraction that thus has language and culture as an unavoidable premise; to elaborate frameworks of meaning, cosmology, ideology; and much else.

Culture has thus effectively replaced nature, insofar as behavior and consciousness are concerned. This is a human universal, and its role is bolstered by the observation—which some may initially find surprising—that we are no longer evolving biologically. On reflection it should be clear that the built environment, the use of tools and machinery in labor, the massive medical intervention that takes place constantly, not to speak of such simple items as clothing, eyeglasses, prosthetics, hunting tools, etc., all ensure that survival of the (biologically) fittest is a thing of the past in human life (and increasingly, as we alter the physical environments and survival chances for other species, in all life). The gene pool is no longer being cleansed of nonadaptive traits; in biological time, we are in fact ceasing to be a unified species. When the crucial turn in evolution away from natural selection to culture takes place, therefore, it signals the *replacement* of biological with socio-cultural evolution, eventually including the progressive application of genetic engineering (something we quite rightly distrust at our current stage of *moral* evolution!). None of this, of course, should be taken to imply that humans no longer have a biological existence. Our biological functions are the foundation for social existence, and set limits to our physical possibilities in obvious ways. Culture does not transcend or eliminate the survival conditions that we share with all life, even though the environment from which we draw our sustenance is increasingly a cultural product.

McIntosh, in a subsequent reply (1998–99) finds my assertion that "culture . . . has *effectively replaced* nature, insofar as behavior and consciousness are concerned" too sweeping. I am inclined to agree, and now prefer a revised formulation: the natural influences on consciousness and behavior can only take place symbolically, and therefore culturally (in the sense of the cultural universal). McIntosh wants to argue against what she calls the "sponge theory" of consciousness—that the human mind simply absorbs (soaks up) anything that culture imposes on it. The transcendent-culture view that I am defending should be clearly distinguishable from any version of what was once called "Watsonian behaviorism," a position staked out at the "nurture" end of the "nature-nurture" spectrum. Like McIntosh, I believe that the spectrum itself should be transcended. She refers to studies that "suggest" the existence of certain universal psychological characteristics, such as a tendency (observed even in small children) to posit the existence of "insides" and "outsides" in other sentient beings (a form of "essentialism"), and a tendency to posit the existence of "unseen contaminative forces," presumably common to all or many cultures. These may be called "innate cognitive predispositions," as McIntosh does, but much turns on the interpretation of "innate." Essentialism is clearly impossible without symbols, as is the positing of unseen forces, contaminative or otherwise. Essentialism, in turn, is thought to be a basis for extra-group hostility, and prejudice; McIntosh is concerned to extract the implications of innate predispositions for the existence and exercise of power in social life. This is a complex subject; I will simply note here that even if we assume that there is an innate tendency for all human beings to produce essentialist (inner/outer) conceptions, there is no reason to link this to an inherent trope toward "racial or gendered thinking": witness the counterclaim of universal human goodness and worth, an *essence* posited by some religious philosophies, which would work against multiple "essences" that divide. The "innate" turns out once again to be symbolic, and to be "recruitable" for a full spectrum of ideologies buttressing different systems of definition and power, including ones that transcend domination and exploitation.

The claim that we—humans—are not now evolving biologically continues to be met with skepticism in many quarters. Some private communications received from biologists have referred to changes in the gene pool brought about by the humanly transformed environment—for example, the effect of the huge increase in sugar consumption in the last century, or in the presence of industrial pollutants. These could induce a form of "Baldwinian evolution" (Deacon, ch. 11), in which environmental changes brought about by human beings serve as the framework for adaptive genetic innovations— except for the fact that massive medical, technological and cultural intervention prevent these adaptations from becoming effective. The matter cannot be resolved by general pronouncements, such as: ". . . human phylogenesis has left its mark on the human genome" (McIntosh 1998–99).

So we are looking at a nonbiological universal. What would the "new creationists" have to say? They will have to speak for themselves, but in retrospect there should be nothing surprising in the moment of similarity between the old creationism, on the one hand, and a modern (yes, scientific) notion of a specifically human universal, on the other. The theological concept of the soul then appears as an early, and prescient, perception of the transcendent character of human consciousness that Darwin, fighting the battles of his day, was at pains to deny. The cultural evolution perspective provides solid ground for the projection of the political movement: after all, one inherent feature of symbolic reactivity (White) is the capacity to imagine contrary-to-fact scenarios and to project a vision of ongoing perfection.

Finally, the question must have occurred to many readers: how do we (claim to) *know* any of this? And: why does it matter? On the first, I have no simple answer, except to say that profound truths about the human condition are neither innate, nor simply empirical! On the second: if we can (legitimately) secure the understanding that human consciousness and action are qualitatively and irreversibly symbolic, the surest foundation is laid for the most central claim of historical materialism: the *conditional inevitability* of progress toward a society of equality, solidarity, and fulfillment. This is the (conditional) directionality of history: progress is inevitable—because it is possible. We have also the insight that an *intentional society* is the fullest embodiment of symbolic reference; that social evolution consists essentially of growth in the ability of human beings to bring their own development under deliberative, and in that sense symbolic, control. But this brings us back to the core project of this chapter: elaboration of the theoretical stages of social evolution at the level of the AST.

II. THE SYSTEM OF THEORETICAL STAGES

To understand the construction of the theoretical stages, a visual aid is useful. Figure 1.2, alongside, is my latest attempt to meet this need; it should be consulted regularly throughout the discussion in this section.

The model proposes five stages (modes of production), four of which are shown in figure 1.2. I have given them their traditional names: primitive communism, slavery, feudalism, capitalism, and (modern) communism. The problem of Eurocentrism emerges here, and I will address this issue at the outset. The model is intended as a universal distillation of the human experience, drawing upon all branches of social evolution in all corners of the globe. Certain exemplars of particular phases of development or transitions may (or may not) be unique to Europe, or to western Europe or even to Britain, due to unparalleled facts concerning the geography and climate in those regions, and the specific population and societal dynamics resulting from these specifics. It should not be necessary to state that this is a matter of chance location in time and space, and not of any innate intellectual or cultural superiority. Still, the Euro-specificity of certain embodiments of the model must be established, not assumed; in the past, many European scholars, with access mainly to European data, unwittingly biased this search in favor of the familiar. While I cannot resolve this enormous issue here, I am responsible for seeing that the PF–PR categories themselves are not tethered, intentionally or otherwise, to any specific geographic experience.

The problem lies with "feudalism." The other MPs have worldwide referents. Slavery, not necessarily as the designation of a mode of production but rather simply the fact of personal subordination and servitude in production, enforced by direct restraint and coercion applied to the human subject (the slave), appears quite generally in early history, from the Northwest Coast of North America, to Mesoamerica and South America, China, India, and Africa, as well as the ancient Mediterranean. Capitalism, in turn, by virtue of its inner tendency to diffuse outward, has achieved global reach (but see the qualifying argument concerning the global dominance of capitlalism in chapter 5). By contrast, the category "feudalism" is essentially European (with perhaps a Japanese variant). The question therefore arises: as the name of a mode of production (a theoretical stage), is it adequate to bear the full weight of generality required? I have sought long and hard for a replacement concept, and have not been able to find one; "feudalism" will

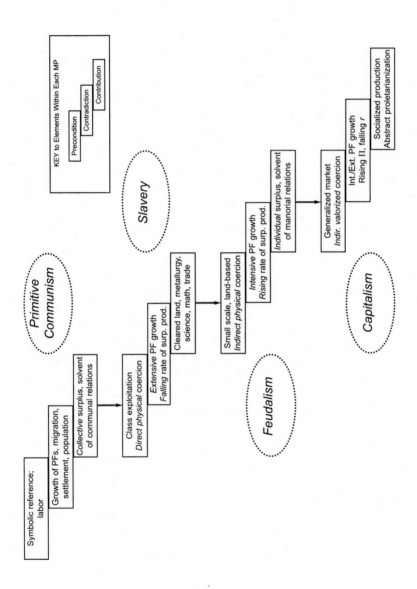

KEY to Elements Within Each MP

Precondition
Contradiction
Contribution

Primitive Communism

Slavery

Feudalism

Capitalism

Symbolic reference; labor

Growth of PFs, migration, settlement, population
Collective surplus, solvent of communal relations

Class exploitation
Direct physical coercion

Extensive PF growth
Falling rate of surp. prod.

Cleared land, metallurgy, science, math, trade

Small scale, land-based
Indirect physical coercion

Intensive PF growth
Rising rate of surp. prod.

Individual surplus, solvent of manorial relations

Generalized market
Indir. valorized coercion

Int./Ext. PF growth
Rising II, falling r

Socialized production
Abstract proletarianization

Figure 1.2. The PF–PR Model: Stages in the Development of the Abstract Social Totality

thus have to stay for the present. I will address the question of the ubiquity of the elements usually associated with European, or western European, feudalism below, in context. Note, for now, that it is *possible*, within the requirements of a universal theory, that *in historical fact, on this planet*, the MP with the chain-linked middle role in the sequence of class-antagonistic MPs arose nowhere else than in Europe, for strictly geo-climatic reasons, and that the European origin of the terms and concepts defining it is therefore justified.

Figure 1.2 is a sequence of sets of three juxtaposed rectangles, each set characterizing a MP. The meaning of the three boxes is given in the key at the upper right. We are concerned to identify, in each case, the precondition, contradiction, and contribution (in an obvious meaning of each of those terms) associated with the MP in question.

Primitive Communism

This is the name for a vast stretch of prehistory, in which antagonistic class formation has not yet occurred, and therefore the analytically precise correspondence between PFs and PRs that characterizes the antagonistic MPs does not exist. The precondition is simply the defining characteristics of human society, against the background of the biological evolution of species. The two defining and separating qualities are labor—in the sense of conscious, symbolic transformation of the environment—and the symbolic faculty itself, elaborated in the preceding section. The two are clearly closely related. There is an enormous literature from symbolic interactionist social psychology and cultural anthropology behind these insights, which I associate to the Marxist tradition through Marx's remarkable prescience on this, often cited ("the architect and the bee"; see *Capital*, I—Marx 1967, 178). The symbolic faculty, as we have seen, with its condensation and abstraction of information from the sensual field, contains within itself the capacity to envision contrary to fact (counter-sensual) situations, to imagine perfection, to doubt, to require frameworks of meaning that suspend doubt. All of this comes about through social interaction and communication. As humans cannot do otherwise than perceive and act on the world through a "superorganic" realm of symbolic understanding, they cannot forego the constant reproduction of the symbolic field—language, culture, ideology— through participation in and reproduction of social relations. Labor, consciousness and sociality are interdefined and interdefining aspects of the essential human whole. The reproduction of this whole presupposes its continual transformation. This is the fundamental ground of the development principle: the immanent tendency for the PFs, human power over nature, to expand. Labor and its continual transformation are the defining mode of evolution for human life, in a parallel relation to biological evolution through natural selection for nonhuman life.

Successful migration, population growth, early settlement, mastery of tools and weapons, flora and fauna, domestication of animals, horticulture, and then (decisively) the emergence of grain agriculture around 8,000–7,000 BCE create the foundation for "civilization" (literally, the emergence of cities: settled concentrations with unprecedented density of population). All of this culminates a process going back to early homo sapiens, several millions of years. The very success of human dispersion, based on growth of the PFs, is the contradiction of primitive communism, as it leads to the eventual emergence of the *collective surplus* (or, perhaps more accurately, the transformation of this surplus from potential to actual). The grain agricultural revolution is crucial for this, as it made possible storage of a relatively nonperishable food source, without which any significant rise in population density would lead to mass starvation in bad harvest years. The emergence of dense human settlement, in turn, is the basis for differentiation in institutions, the rise of political structures, the capture of the surplus by a leisured class that forms the basis for scientific development, written languages—in short, indispensable preconditions for further PF development.

Note the qualifier "collective" on the surplus that serves as the *contribution* of primitive communism to the next stage of development (and class-antagonistic MPs generally). The PFs in the vast prehistory of primitive communism are meager; continual struggle for subsistence is the defining characteristic of human life, a situation well described by the word "scarcity." In these conditions, of course, social differentiation and stratification can only be minimal. The surplus, once captured and therefore defined, is based on *collective* production: the coordinated, simultaneous effort of the direct producers, which must therefore be consciously directed, either by cultural tradition or by enforced command. The qualifier is important; much further development is required before a very different kind of surplus, on *individual* isolated and uncoordinated production, can arise. Once the collective surplus exists, however, potentially or actually, it *can* result in the progressive dissolution of long-established communal structures. This erosion of clan or tribe solidarity takes the form of progressive stratification of societies into higher and lower castes, perhaps the evolution of stratified political or theological institutions (governing councils, priesthoods), whose membership at first may be rotating or determined by merit, but slowly becomes hereditary with the emergence of differentiated (non-communal) property. This long, slow evolutionary differentiation culminates in full-blown antagonistic classes; this is the transition to slavery, the first of the class-antagonistic MPs in figure 1.2.

Again, the interplay between accident and necessity must be stressed. Is this transition inevitable, either in any concrete social formation or at the AST level? The question is rhetorical, and the answer is clearly "no." The emergence of a potential surplus depends on the growth of productive capacity ahead of population—shades of Malthus emerge here—and this may require a series of fortuitous circumstances; for example, the existence, in a particular area, of geographical opportunities for outward migration, which would limit population pressure on the emergent surplus at any one site. The possibility of a surplus may be present, either as a result of productive development or simply the fact that the culture under observation inhabits an especially provident environment protected from inmigration and conquest by natural boundaries, as in the case of some islands in the South Pacific. Peoples in this position may choose to take the surplus in the form of leisure, or evolution of an unusually rich ceremonial culture—and some have done precisely that. There is an irreducible probabilistic element in the emergence of precise cultural-ideological conditions, population dynamics. and the natural environment (and perhaps even fortuitous events associated with particular historical individuals) that "spark" the capture of the collective surplus and creation of its directed use in formation of a coercive machinery that can compel collective exploitation and further PF development. We can imagine circumstances in which these conditions do not exist anywhere, so that all intelligent life (on the imaginary planet in question) settles into the culturally rich but materially restricted leisured existence akin to life on a South Sea Island. (Some readers may actually find this a not too dismal prospect!) But given the variety of circumstances in which the inherent pressure of a potential collective surplus emerges around the globe, the probability of a breakthrough to class division and a new form of PF dynamism is high. Inevitability, however, is always conditional.

Slavery

Given the emergence and capture of the potential surplus in collective production, the foundation is laid for class-antagonistic MPs. Now the forms of these MPs may be thought to be arbitrary, determined only at the level of the social formation by random and contingent factors. If there is an ordering to successive forms of class-exploitative MPs, that must be shown; it cannot be assumed.

The ordering given in figure 1.2—slavery-feudalism-capitalism—is not determined from historical observation as such. Slavery, for example, appears in different places concurrently with the period of high feudalism in western Europe, perhaps later in some cases, and has a resurgence in connection with primitive capitalist accumulation in the sixteenth century CE. Capitalism, in turn, has roots going back into the ancient world. The ordering is theoretical, not empirical, and it is based on the concept that the development of the PFs through the entire period of class-antagonistic MPs requires periodic replacement of PRs, in an order revealing progressively more sophisticated and powerful means of coercion, incentive, and control. This ordering must now be explained.

Slavery is direct subjugation of the producers (slaves), by physical force. Population is relatively sparse; land is widely available for communal subsistence (if not for collective surplus extraction, which requires gang labor in clearing forests, establishing systems of irrigation, etc). Under extreme duress in their condition of forced labor, with simple tools and methods of production, the direct producers would quickly leave the site of their exploitation, migrate and revert to communal subsistence production were it not for their direct forcible confinement and coercion in labor—that is, were it not for their status as slaves. The first form of systematic surplus extraction, then, is the first because it emerges when it becomes possible— when collective coercion of slaves is sufficient to extract a surplus large enough to support the necessary apparatuses of coercion and control—and necessary—*only* direct, physical subordination and coercion will suffice for surplus extraction.

The nature of slave PRs determines many aspects of the slave MP. Slaves cannot, in general, be given sufficient personal autonomy to have families; internal increase of the slave population is therefore absent. A slave's life expectancy is very short, owing to the brutal captivity in which she/he exists. Together, these features compel a viably self-reproducing slave MP to continually search outside its own territory for new sources of slaves, and to devote an increasing share of the surplus to supporting this activity. Slaves also perform labor in conditions of extremely weak personal incentive, for obvious reasons. Any development of labor productivity, such as would be afforded by the use of tools, draft animals and machinery, would place inordinate power in the hands of slaves, undermining the crude and rigid system of control (chains, overseers, whips), or placing undue strain on this system. Slave PRs, therefore, propel PF development away from productivity growth (intensive development) and toward increase in the size of agricultural holdings (latifundia), or construction projects (roads, aqueducts, etc.).

The power of each member of the slaveholding ruling class is increased in proportion as the size of his estate grows; the surplus he acquires is roughly proportional to the number of slaves under his control. The slave MP, therefore, produces immanent pressure toward *extensive growth* of the PFs. This is our first example of the conditioning of the path of PF development by the PRs associated with them.

The slave contradiction is the crisis associated with this extensive growth. I take it as axiomatic (the point does not appear to yield to further decomposition) that growth in the scale of slave production is associated with more-than-proportional growth in the means of coercion and control necessary to extract the surplus and reproduce the slave system. The very success of slavery in achieving extended reproduction (where it actually achieves this, of course) results in ever larger proportions of the surplus being devoted to both internal control and external expansion. The *net* surplus product, available to support the slaveholding class and its retinue, falls relatively, and perhaps absolutely, as a general crisis of control looms. This is the emergent tension between PFs and PRs in the slave MP (as symbolized in the right panel of figure 1.1).

The contribution of slavery, to complete the description of this stage, lies in all of the developments in the PFs, including the rise of science, mathematics, mechanics, knowledge of natural raw materials, and so forth, all afforded by the prior existence of a leisured ruling slaveholding class. To this should be added, crucially, the clearing of land, making varied forms of agricultural production possible on a wide scale; the discovery of metallurgy—only possible on the basis of extensively coerced gang labor of slaves in mining, especially of iron—whose application in agriculture is forestalled in the slave MP owing to incentive/control problems but will emerge as central in the feudal MP; and the rise of population density, again a crucial element enabling the more powerful feudal PRs.

It should, perhaps, be noted that the slave MP emerges against a backdrop of small-scale peasant production and communal subsistence production, both in varying stages of decomposition. These elements, along with rudimentary market relations, form the inert medium within which the slave dynamic occurs. The transformations brought about by the surplus and by extensive PF development are decisive for further progress, as we will see; this fact, however, in no way suggests that the slave relation ever involves more than a distinct minority of the population in the territory where the slave MP is situated. The surrounding regions react passively to the slave empire, sometimes managing to mount resistance to it; they emerge as a crucial destructive element at exactly the moment when the internal crisis of surplus extraction reaches a critical level. If we take the Roman Empire as the paradigmatic case for this transition, we have in the PF–PR account a theoretical underpinning for the historical observation of the overrunning of Rome by Germanic and other peoples around the fourth century CE. This example shows how the analysis at the AST level can advance the treatment of history as such from description to explanation. It should, however, be remembered that the succession of MP stages at the AST level leaves out many more concrete determinations of the historical record, such as factors that break an MP stage, even in one region of the world, into phases based on the rise and fall of particular social formations. These processes in turn reflect other dynamics: for example, the challenge-response dialectic of Arnold Toynbee (Toynbee 1972), according to which a particular sociopolitical formation, or "civilization," rises to prominence by its energy and creativity in ousting incumbents, only to then become the incumbent and subject to bureaucratization and decay. A special instance of this is the nomadic invasion cycle described for (what we call) the Middle East by the fourteenth-century Persian scholar, Ibn Khaldun (see Gettleman and Schaar 2003, 54–58). Particular historical experiences, such as the Roman Empire for the slave MP and nineteenth-century England for capitalist industrialization, can be cited to give some concrete flavoring to the regularities adduced in the PF–PR model, but it should not be thought that the model can be used to give a direct account of even these "pure" cases, let alone the much more involved and complex majority of social formations through which the principles of the AST work themselves out.

Feudalism

Each stage in a theoretical stadial model must be validated, by demonstration of its necessity. The necessity of *slavery* lies in its unique capacity to realize a surplus on a societal scale, and to develop the PFs extensively, laying required foundations for subsequent development. To understand feudalism in a similar way, at the AST level, we will need to establish *its* necessity; this can be done by showing why capitalism cannot develop directly on the basis of the slave MP, even though the great slave civilizations, in all parts of the world, had developed markets, money, and financial institutions.

The crisis of the slave MP is the crisis of large-scale extensive production, with the attendant difficulties of incentive and control (as summarized above). The solution, arising on the ruins of slave empires whose surplus extraction has become problematic and whose centers have therefore collapsed under external invasion, is a set of PRs based on small scale and using indirect forms of physical subjugation and coercion to produce a surplus. Production relations are so central to the life experience of people in a society, so "elemental" (i.e., like the elements, or the weather: foundational and therefore unquestionable), that they are rarely the object of conscious contemplation or design. The PFs embody an instrumental relation between humans and the tools and natural environment in which they act, and are therefore inherently reproduced in *instrumental* consciousness. By contrast, the PRs, through most of history, are grasped in ideological forms that render them "natural" or "inevitable," and they are not generally seen in instrumental terms—until, of course, the development of socialist consciousness (see chapter 6). Emergence of the feudal "solution" to the problem of slavery, then, must be seen as an instance of a nonconscious functionalism: remnants of the ruling elites from slavery evolve forms of subordination and dependence that enable surplus extraction to proceed, and a system involving these forms gradually emerges. We need not imagine that feudal PRs, or any PRs prior to those of socialism for that matter, were first conceived in the minds of individuals and then implemented by intentional design, or that they were "produced" by choosing some point on an "PR production function" which is shifting through time (so that the temporal sequence of institutions, and especially the late "discovery" of the market, can be explained).

The feudal solution rests on the confinement of class relations to the small scale of the manor: a self-contained and territorially enclosed social system based on agricultural production (although it also incorporates handicrafts and other nonagricultural activities). The ruling function rests in the Lord of the Manor, with a retinue of retainers and a caste of military functionaries (the knighthood). The subjugated producing class consists of serfs, who are held in service to the lord (vassalage) through their connection to the land. Unlike slaves, serfs are not owned outright by the lord; they cannot be bought and sold. Tied to the manor by birth, they also have a right to that connection, which cannot be taken from them. They have rights within the legal system of the manor, a political status that is foreign to the slave, the *instrumentum vocum* (Cicero) of the slave MP. They also have household rights within the manor: they own and control their own tools and animals, and have families (thus ensuring internal biological reproduction of the subject population). Surplus extraction takes a variety of forms, along a spectrum running from demesne serfs, who work full time cultivating the lord's estate, to cotters, working part of the time on the lord's account and the rest on their own plots, whose produce they keep for themselves, to those who work entirely on their own land, paying rent in kind to the lord.

The surplus-yielding coercion in the manorial system is much less direct than the sheer physical subjugation and confinement of the slave, and has a number of related aspects. The presence of physical coercion in the form of overseers and the warrior caste is one of these, and punishment in the lord's courts and prisons could be harsh. But physical constraint is buttressed by an ideology of servitude and obligation. (This, again, is something that was absent from the slave experience; no one was concerned with what went on in the *minds* of the slaves.) Feudal ideology imposed not only the requirement to labor for or pay rent to the lord, but also the latter's obligation to protect and provide. A crucial element in this provision is allocation, out of the manor's surplus, of certain collective means of production: seed, irrigation, use of milling facilities, use of common lands for grazing livestock. Surplus extraction is also buttressed not only by the scale of the manor—small enough so that the imposition of personal obligation is credible—but also by the multiplication of manors across a significant and densely populated territory. One tolerates the "contract" with one's lord because there is nothing over the next hill except—another lord (and one with whom one has no privileges by right of birth). A certain development of population, residing on contiguous cleared land, is therefore a prerequisite for the manorial system. A final component in this mix is the concept of "infeudation"—the system of hierarchical obligation in which the subjugation of the serf is just one instance of vassalage, which extends upward in a pyramid of subject–master relationships exemplified by the sequence of noble titles: Lord, Baron, Duke, King. This hierarchy establishes the "right" of the lord as part of a larger system over which no one presides, a system that therefore acquires the force of elementality or "natural law."

The small scale ("parcelization of sovereignty"), ideological infusion, exhaustive territoriality and feudal hierarchy all work to buttress and enable surplus extraction. But a central feature of production, in contrast with the slave MP, is the serf's ownership and control of means of production (other than the land itself, by definition owned by the lord). With fixed labor obligations or rent in kind, the serf has an incentive to care for tools and animals, and to find ways to increase productivity on his personal plot, and the manorial system thus gives a major boost to agricultural productivity and productivity growth, relative to the inherent trope of slavery toward their repression. Contrary to the classical image of the feudal era in Europe as the "Dark Ages," a time of stagnation, the millennium beginning in the fourth century CE was a time of intense innovation, especially in agriculture: introduction of draft animals, the iron plow, systematic manuring, the open field system, crop rotation, contouring of land, irrigation, wind and water power in threshing and milling, mechanical tools, and many other elements (a summary of this technological history is provided in Laibman 1984; cf. Lilley 1966; Childe 1969; Milonakis 1993–94). While the later transition to capitalism raises productivity and productivity growth to still higher qualitative levels, the progress of the PFs in the feudal MP, relative to slavery, cannot be discounted.

Generalizing, the feudal MP gives a dominant direction to the development of the PFs within it: feudal PFs develop *intensively*. The parcelization of sovereignty (Anderson 1978) prevents further development in the extensive direction, while the increased incentive to the direct producers cultivated within the manor makes possible, and therefore eventually actual, intensive growth: increasing output per unit of labor. Note that as an aspect of the personal obligation that drives the feudal process, individual production must be dominant; the serfs work separately on isolated plots, a quality that spills over into demesne cultivation as well. The forms of productivity growth then come to reflect that individualized locus of production. But the manor also involves surplus extraction and the application of the surplus to production, in the form of land clearing, irrigation, milling, storage, and provision of workshops, tools, and other elements of production. The manor unwittingly provides resources to serfs that are not available to freeholding peasants, who surround the manors and in fact constitute significant proportions, often majorities, of the populations of countries in which the feudal MP is dominant. It is, in fact, a subtle combination of individual production and the benefits of surplus extraction, and this combination serves as a hothouse or incubator of a historically new kind of surplus: a surplus in *individual* production, or *individual surplus*. Without this incubator, individual peasant production remains subsistence production; the struggle for bare existence precludes the implementation of incentives for productivity improvement that one might think are inherent in the peasants' private ownership of land. Private ownership is neither necessary nor sufficient for productivity incentives to operate; this requires also the stability and infrastructural support afforded by the insertion of individual control at the point of production within a system of surplus extraction.

The individual surplus, product of the feudal incubator that in turn rests on extensive PF development within the slave MP, is then the essential ground for the spread of market relations. Markets are not an idea waiting to happen, or an invention of the Western European seventeenth century. Trade is present in all known periods of human existence, either in the "interstices" of social production, as in the European high Middle Ages, or flourishing, as in the trading civilizations of the ancient Mediterranean and China, or the modern capitalist world. The potential of markets to encompass ever wider segments of the PRs, via the emergence of a "home" market in means of production and consumption for the majority of the population, however, rests on the individual surplus occasioned by intensive PF development, which occurs specifically under feudalism.

The possibility to produce for the market weakens the hold of lords over their serfs, as it gives them an incentive to commute feudal obligations, either labor or in-kind, in favor of payment of money rent. Thus begins a period of depopulation of the manors and migrations, including the rise of cities in which production and markets are increasingly centered. The period of the late Middle Ages in western Europe is defined by this long, slow shift in the balance of economic and political power away from the manor and the landed nobility to the commercial and craft economies of the increasingly independent cities and towns. Once the rise of market relations acquires the critical mass to be self-sustaining, the market becomes the solvent of the feudal PRs, just as the collective surplus played this role in the earlier transition to slavery.

The story of this transition is familiar: the rising power of the merchant class, which promotes (and eventually dominates) absolute centralized monarchies to oppose the retrograde resistance of the feudal nobility; the progressive dispossession of the serfs and freeholders, and enclosure of the commons; creation of a landless, propertyless mass that can serve as the basis for what will become a capitalist proletariat. This is Karl Polanyi's "great transformation" (Polanyi 1957)—although, as I will emphasize later, it is important to see it as the *third* great transformation. The PF–PR model does not interfere with the richness of this story, which is at the heart of modern historical and social exegesis (e.g., Anderson 1978, 1979a, 1979b; Moore 1966). What it adds is an explanation for the theoretical timing of the transition to capitalism: for the fact that it did not occur, say, one thousand years earlier, but required an intervening evolution under the feudal MP. The usual story, from Henri Pirenne (1939), to Max Weber (1998), and R. H. Tawney (1926), to Paul M. Sweezy (1977), cites and documents the role of trade and markets in the dissolution of precapitalist social forms and the emergence of capitalism. Trade itself, however, is a deus ex machina; its sudden significance is not explained. The PF–PR model removes this deus-ex-machina quality and supplies the necessary and sufficient preconditions for market relations to move to center stage.

Other explanations for the transition to capitalism in western Europe, and especially in agrarian England (Dobb 1947; Brenner 1976) look to internal factors: the rising need of lords of revenue, and class struggle. The "need" of lords for revenue is the pretext for increasing pressure on the serfs, often cited as a source of their migration and revolt in the late Middle Ages, as well as a *dis*incentive for productivity enhancement. This disincentive is the reverse of the central feudal dynamic, but it is precisely a sign of the *crisis* of the feudal MP, and emerges in a period in which the contribution of that MP to PF development is shown to have largely been exhausted. Insofar as increasing exactions upon the peasantry are concerned, they are a deus *intra* machina, an unanalyzed internal causal factor. It is not explained why the lords' "needs" increase when they do; the impact of this change in needs, in any case, must depend crucially on the ability of the peasants to resist, and that ability is decisively conditioned by the presence of an urban and market-based alternative to the manorial economy, which, as we have seen, had to wait for the intensive PF development of the high feudal era.

The key role of "feudalism" for the AST is its provision of a protective environment for the incubation of the individual surplus; this is its theoretical necessity (much like the chrysalis stage, mediating the transformation from caterpillar to butterfly). With this conception on board, we can ask, again, whether the specific institutions of feudalism in England and western Europe—the manor, the feudal hierarchy—were necessary for this purpose. If one thinks of the entire precapitalist, postcommunal epoch in terms of a general "tributary" mode of production (Amin 1985), with regional variations, it is still necessary, in the approach exemplified by the PF–PR model, to distinguish situations in which direct producers are sufficiently protected against the brutalities of nature and competition, and sufficiently supported by collective structures outside of their own individual labor environments, for the intensive PF innovations to be achieved and applied in production. Could this eventually have happened within the Chinese communal villages overlain by the Mandarin bureaucracy, had western European capitalist imperialism not arrived and altered China's course of development from outside? The same question can be asked of the Islamic civilizations that flourished precisely in the period of western European production's "confinement" in the chrysalis of the manor, from around the seventh century CE. In both cases, the evident answer is that stagnation and blockage are never absolute; that of course the stadiality of preparation for the transition to capitalism might have taken other forms, including those that could only be described in terms of some sort of "combined development." Empirical confirmation of the PF–PR proposal requires demonstration that intensive PF development and the formation of the individual surplus in fact do not occur in the areas of the world that did not give rise to capitalism; this is, incidentally, an important site for potential falsification of the PF–PR hypothesis, and corresponds to a challenge issued in my earlier work on this theme, never (to my knowledge) taken up. But the present point is that it is not only possible, in the spirit of the PF–PR model, but very much appropriate to that spirit, to develop—terminological difficulties aside—a version of the "middle" theoretical stage that does not have any residual Eurocentric holdovers.

III. A PROVISIONAL CONCLUSION

The discussion to this point, as readers will by now realize, has been a table setting exercise: to put in place a conceptual structure that can be used to address the intricacies of the "great transformation" to the capitalist present. We are now ready to apply the PF–PR proposal to the second-most-difficult of the revolutionary transitions: to capitalism. The increasing complexity of labor involved in PF development, of course, makes each successive transition in the theoretical chain of transitions more involved than the last. In the next chapter, we continue our investigation of the model represented in figure 1.2, by applying that model to the emergence of capitalism— a process that is often more vaguely referred to as the emergence of the modern world. Then, with this thumbnail sketch of the entire PF–PR proposal in place, we will be in position to address some of the wider questions concerning social evolution, as raised in some recent interventions in historical materialist theory.

Chapter 2

TRANSITION TO CAPITALISM

The PF–PR Model and Alternatives

L ike childbirth, transitions (revolutions) are always difficult. They involve chicken-egg problems (as we have seen). They also get increasingly problematic and protracted, as the PFs evolve to higher levels of complexity and the new PRs, with more sophisticated functionality, require ever more intricate conjunctures of elements to become firmly established. The transition from feudalism to capitalism—in which surplus extraction and the market form of PRs, instead of being in conflict, come to be symbiotic—is particularly subject to blockage and equilibrium traps. Its historical embodiment in the "great transformation" in western Europe, therefore, is a long-drawn-out process lasting some six centuries, and itself involving distinct phases of development.

In this chapter, to complete the discussion of figure 1.2 from chapter 1, I will consider some aspects of the feudalism to capitalism transition. We will want to see whether the PF–PR framework remains robust as we come to examine this most complex historical period, which has of course been the subject of an enormous exegetical literature, coming from both social scientists and historians. This transition, in fact, has played a large part in recent discussions in historical materialist theory, and thus serves to frame my consideration of some of these interventions. Section II of this chapter considers a range of recent contributions, beginning with Jared Diamond's monumental work, *Guns, Germs and Steel*—perhaps the most sophisticated statement of a "geographical determinist" view of social evolution over a long time horizon. Later sections consider Dmitris Milonakis' work on feudalism, the Darwinian historical materialist proposal of Paul Nolan, and Alan Carling's "competitive primacy" position. The chapter concludes with an overview of the debate, and points to a central tendency uniting many of the participants: a deep identification of market-driven rationality as the enduring source of social change, and of technical progress. This then leads smoothly into the topic of chapters 3–5: the capitalist mode of production.

I. THE PF–PR MODEL AND THE TRANSITION TO CAPITALISM

As suggested in the "capitalism" segment of figure 1.2, the key to resolving the insufficiency of feudalism—its incapacity to unleash the tremendous forces of PF development inherent in its own application of intensive factors in production—lies in "marketizing," or *valorizing* the PRs. From indirect physical coercion of serfs, buttressed by superstructural systems of ideological control, the progression is to an even more indirect system of coercion: through the complete takeover by commodity forms of the core social relation between subordinate and ruling classes. The capitalist relation of exploitation is unique within the AST sequence of exploitation relations in that its key elements, labor-power and capital, both assume the form of commodities—things that are produced for exchange. This enables a structure of domination and surplus extraction to assume an outward form of personal (individual) equality and voluntary (rational) choice, a form that is not merely a disguise or illusion, but is objectively present in the social experience of the actors in this drama. Understood in this way, the capitalist market is a uniquely powerful engine of coercion and exploitation, whatever other properties it possesses as such or shares with markets in general. Full understanding of this process is the subject of the core theory of capitalism, initiated by Marx in *Capital*, volume I, where it takes the form of the *theory of value and surplus value*. I will not say more about this here, except to note that valorization appears as a necessary condition for dependable surplus extraction (viable social reproduction), when PF development is at a level at which *extensive* and *intensive* forms of progress can (and must) be combined. The value form is at the heart of capitalist PRs, which provide the basis for the industrial, fossil fuel, electrical, and electronic revolutions that characterize the capitalist MP and bring new potentials into existence.

Figure 1.2 suggests that the core contradiction of capitalism can be conceived in terms of a combination of a rising *share* of profit in the net social output (π) and a falling *rate* of profit on capital stocks owned and advanced (r); the former is a measure of the degree of surplus extraction, or exploitation; the latter of the system's capacity to expand. The rising/falling trends are implicated in capitalism's increasing tension and insufficiency, in ways that cannot be elaborated here (see chapter 4). I note, in closing this initial survey, that an outcome of the capitalist accumulation process is the advent of fully socialized production, in the sense that the separation and isolation of individual producers, so central to the progress of the PFs in the feudal MP, is transformed into its opposite: intense intra-production and market division of labor. (This is so, I would note, irrespective of the degree of concentration of production in one site, vs. outsourcing and "flexibiliza-tion.") Finally, the valorization process—the progressive adoption of the commodity form throughout the social field—creates an abstract working class or proletariat, one that has the negative universal attribute of being stripped of particularizing social and cultural attributes ("identities"). This negative universal has the potential for transformation into a positive uni-versal: the embodiment and pursuit of human interests as such.

The protracted character of the feudalism-capitalism transition may reflect the contingent circumstances imposed by the historical and geo-graphical conditions in which it took place, mainly in western Europe. I believe, however, that it also contains a dynamic that exists at the level of the AST, one resulting from a particularly severe chicken-egg situation. Markets and trade act upon the manorial economy as a solvent (as noted), and a class of merchants and craftspeople emerges, along with a rising sector of individual peasant proprietors in agriculture who are producing for the developing home market. In order for *capitalist* surplus extraction to take root, however, direct producers must be dispossessed; this requires force, which in turn requires support by a surplus. As always, in a rigorous his-torical materialist theory, the nature of surplus extraction must be carefully and fully explained; it cannot simply be assumed, or "established" by rich historical description. So, for example, it is not sufficient to say that mer-chants were "able to" exploit direct producers, through the putting-out system in which merchants deliver raw materials to the homes of workers, pick up the finished products, and sell them at a profit. This capacity to extract a value surplus must be established, presumably by referring to the specific conditions—legal, cultural, physical-geographical—making it difficult for direct producers to gain access to markets for raw materials and finished products themselves. These conditions, however, must themselves be ex-plained, with reference to a general capacity for surplus extraction at a much deeper level. The question returns: what is the source of the surplus that is used to *create* a capitalist working class?

An obvious answer is that feudal surpluses are turned toward this purpose. It should, however, be remembered that new PRs rarely emerge as a result of intentional action; this possibility is greatly limited by the im-possibility of the relevant actors thinking instrumentally at the required level for this to occur. Lords can only be lords; their intentionality is devoted to protecting and fortifying their power, to the extent this is possible. Merchants can only be merchants; they seek ever greater enrichment through trade and finance. Who "finances" (materially supports) the enclosures and forcible dispossessions that occur at intervals from the fifteenth through the eighteenth centuries in England and northern Europe? Who supports (and out of what surplus?) the colonial plunder so well described by Marx? If this is being done out of feudal surpluses, the question is, why? Why would the embattled and diminished landed aristocracies lend their wealth and power for these purposes? If it is being done out of surpluses derived on the basis of merchant's capital, the question is again one of chickens and eggs: that surplus is precisely what needs to be explained, and cannot be part of its own explanation. In sum: there is an inherent low-level trap in this transition, one in which the surpluses that are needed to transform merchants and artisans into capitalists is lodged in a reduced, but fortified feudal sector (the manorial economy will, of course, have first thrown off its weakest links). This is, I think, sufficient to account—theoretically—for the protracted character of the Great Transformation, and for its apparent division, in England at any rate, into separate phases, well described in the original transition debate (Hilton 1979).

Before taking final leave of figure 1.2, I should reemphasize the methodological limits within which it operates. The premise of the entire stadial conception is that it characterizes the abstract social totality, and it alone. The AST is then to be used as a relevant tool for the study of social history at ever richer and more elaborated ("lower") levels of abstraction. To repeat a metaphor that I have used before (Laibman 1984): the PF–PR model is the set of primary colors, out of which the diverse hues of history are (re)created. Diffusion—learning and adoption of technical and social practices and knowledges by one social formation from another with which the former comes into contact—is *central* to human reality; symbolic reference makes this both possible and inevitable, given continual contact among peoples that have evolved in different ways and at different rates due to divergent natural and accidental circumstances. This gives rise to the coexistence of two or more MPs within a single social formation, with one of these usually achieving dominance. Any society, therefore, will bear within it traces of many internal and external pasts, and these can only be sorted through using a theoretical searchlight.

Given social formations may skip stages, or phases within a stage, by coming into contact with other formations that have evolved certain elements to a higher level. The extensive PF development and scientific achievements of Greco-Roman slavery, for example, serve as a platform for the feudal structures that emerge throughout western and northern Europe in the first five hundred years of the present era, including in areas where the social formations on the ground had not achieved the class division that was the essential foundation for the PFs they now absorb and build upon. Japanese capitalism evolved as late capitalism directly out of feudalism, without passing through long phases of early commercial precapitalism and early capitalism.

Blockages also confound the direct, unmediated appearance of the AST in the historical record. The "Asiatic mode of production" (misnamed, in my view) is a blockage of the long transition to a class MP. China's ancient communal villages—still a factor to this day—have survived over the centuries, perhaps largely as a result of rigorous natural conditions that require communal irrigation systems in agriculture. This is the famous "hydraulic society" (Needham 1969; Wittfogel 1957; Krader 1975). The surplus resulting from China's remarkable PF development—here the opponents of Eurocentrism make their case by showing, convincingly, that China's technological development was equal or superior to Europe's, in many relevant time periods—supported a luxuriant bureaucracy and much scientific and cultural achievement, but failed in the crucial respect of being successfully employed to dissolve the old communal PRs at the foundation. This, in turn, precluded extensive PF development and the individual surplus—the two key developments, in slavery and feudalism, respectively, that grounded the surge of commercialization and the transition to capitalism in Europe. In the Euro–Sino discussion (Frank 1998; Duchesne 2001–02, 2003; Goldstone 2003; Wong 1997, 2003) the fact that the Industrial Revolution did finally occur in the West and not in the East must be explained; if we are not to rely on arbitrary geographical determinist explanations (Diamond 1997; Blaut 1993), the problem must be solved at the level of the AST. The elements are, I believe, in place to do this.

In my original presentation of the PF–PR model (Laibman 1984), I suggested that either excessive scarcity or excessive abundance in the external environment might create a condition that would block one or both of the crucial transitions leading out of communal prehistory: the capture of the collective surplus and subsequent extensive PF development; and the emergence of the individual surplus out of intensive PF development. The "scarcity blockage" results in what comes down to us as the "Asiatic Mode of Production" (a misnomer, of course, in terms of the PF–PR categories). The "abundance blockage" has no corresponding counterpart in the literature, but it can be said to occur in parts of the world where nomadic or settled communal PRs resist dissolution, owing to the *provident* character of the natural environment; this might be thought to characterize parts of sub-Saharan Africa, the North American northwest coast, perhaps also the Meso-American civilizations. (We should resist compounding confusion by designating these as an "African" or "American" "mode of production.") If, in this perspective, western Europe, owing to its particular geographical,

climatic, and agricultural conditions, presents an environment that is between the scarce and abundant extremes, that fact would serve as the basis
for an answer to the perennial question, why did the crucial breakthroughs
occur on that continent rather than elsewhere? Attempts to assert European
"superiority" in terms of aggregate economic ratios (output per capita, e.g.)
are likely to fail, as R. Bin Wong and Jack Goldstone have pointed out.
Sufficient conceptual clarity, however, may help us to get beyond a gross
ratio approach to comparison, and to focus on qualitative types of PF development and the associated social relations.

As a final observation, I cite the example of the *ultimate blockage*,
mentioned earlier. The key to the "ladder" of social evolution is, at bottom,
the erratic but ultimately unidirectional growth of the PFs, passing from a
general level of scarcity that dictates egalitarian and communal organization,
through a middle range in which development can only be secured by means
of the antagonistic class principle, and on to a higher level of abundance at
which only a return to egalitarian and solidaristic organization, but now
based on individuation and conscious democracy, can assure continued technical and social development. Within their class-antagonistic shell, however,
modern productive forces are also *destructive* forces—a fact that has often
been emphasized. Unless humankind gets a hold on these forces, removing
them from control by a capitalist class bent on private accumulation of
wealth and power and placing them instead on a principled and universal
foundation, they contain a potential for nuclear or ecological destruction.
Should the destructive potential of capitalist PRs overwhelm the capacity of
the PFs to develop, and even to sustain human life at levels previously
achieved, social evolution could enter a low-level trap of scarcity and strin-
gency from which it may not be possible to recover. As stated in chapter 1:
historical materialism does not predict that the transitions identified in the
PF–PR model, and in particular the "greatest of all," the transition to communism, will actually occur. All of the transitions are potential only.

If a new scarcity emerges between the nether forces of population
growth, on the one side, and social and ecological deterioration, on the
other, this can become a permanent blockage. Progress of intelligent life
toward a principled, egalitarian and fulfilling form of social organization
may then have to wait for some other planet, in some other galaxy (perhaps
this all happened "long, long ago and far, far away"?), where biological
evolution only gives rise to cultural evolution after a longer period of time,
enabling a much greater build up of fossil fuels to support transition to a
democracy of abundance. In this case, the Earth will enter the galactic
history books as a prime example of scarcity blockage, perhaps mislabeled
by extraterrestrial social scientists "the Terran Mode of Production."

This too, of course, is not inevitable. We do, however, have our work cut out for us.

II. ALTERNATIVE APPROACHES, ISSUES, AND CONTROVERSIES

The original presentation of the PF–PR model occasioned a round of comments (Amin 1985; Heller 1985; Hoffman 1985–86; McLennan 1986; Sweezy 1986; Rudra 1987; Gottlieb 1987), and received a brief reply (Laibman 1987). Concern was expressed in these exchanges concerning "productive forces determinism" (although the core principle of distinction between higher and lower levels of abstraction as such was not challenged), Eurocentrism, and rationalism. I have chosen to incorporate these concerns into the continuing development of the PF–PR conception. I acknowledge the need to avoid (*a*) conceptions of productive forces primacy that posit a direct link between rational action and PF development, unmediated by culture and by social relations; (*b*) any biasing of the conceptual toolbox by undue influence from the specifically European experience; and (*c*) detaching the logic of the AST from continuing reconfirmation by the empirical record and by practice, as though the model could be derived by reason alone from nonempirical truths about human existence. I have pointed to the set of broadly conceived facts on which the model's explanatory force depends, as the potential site of its disconfirmation.

The discussion of G. A. Cohen's *Karl Marx's Theory of History* was lively, and, like most such discussions, did not lead to closure (see, e.g., J. Cohen 1982; Cohen, ed. 1988). The attempt to provide ever-greater qualification and precision to primacy claims, stated abstractly, produced a sort of logical bog, in which participants wallowed for a while and, sensing that it has no bottom, tired of the exercise and moved on. Something similar on the empirical side happened in the (Robert) Brenner debate, around the same time (Aston and Philpin 1985).

In the meantime, several new approaches to feudalism-capitalism transition have been suggested, with new attempts to address, and improve upon, the Cohen problematic of PF primacy and intentional agency as history's driving forces. I will address three of these positions below: the view of feudalism and feudal crisis put forward by Dimitris Milonakis; the "Darwinian historical materialism" proposal of Paul Nolan; and Alan Carling's "competitive primacy" thesis—the latter two appearing in a recent collection, *Historical Materialism and Social Evolution* (Blackledge and Kirkpatrick 2002). But it will be useful to begin with Jared Diamond's influential work on the long view of history, which proposes a rational, and broadly functional, explanation for the sweep of social evolution without developing the specifically historical materialist categories of the AST/PF–PR model.

The Long View: Jared Diamond's Geographic Determinism

Jared Diamond's *Guns, Germs and Steel: The Fates of Human Societies* (1997, 1999) offers a fresh perspective on history from the longest possible point of view: from the emergence of the hominids some 4–5 million years ago and homo sapiens 100,000–200,000 years ago to the present, but focusing on the migrations and conquests in the thirteen thousand years since the last major Ice Age. Diamond's goal is to explain the broad patterns of diffusion and domination: the rise of chiefdoms, and then states, in the supercontinent he calls Eurasia, especially the Fertile Crescent of the Middle East and in northern China. From these centers, conquests, both military and epidemiological, spread to all other inhabitable parts of the globe. Diamond concentrates and summarizes massive amounts of archeological, anthropological, historical, and linguistic evidence to trace both major and minor population movements: the migration throughout the Americas; the Austronesian expansion that populated the Pacific islands, Hawaii, and New Zealand; the various conquests of and within Europe; the Bantu expansion through sub-Saharan Africa; and others. He is preoccupied throughout the work by a need to go beyond description to explanation; the central question, asked in many different contexts, is, Why? Why did expansion and conquest take place in the direction it did, rather than the reverse? Why did Pizarro conquer Peru and capture the Inca Emperor Atahuallpa in 1532 CE, rather than the latter coming to Spain and capturing Charles I? Why did North Chinese civilization expand into South China and the rest of Southeast Asia? Why did Europe conquer Africa, rather than vice versa? And so on.

Diamond's basic position is self-identified as geographical determinism. The broad movements of human history are to be explained by variations in shapes and sizes of land masses; climate; presence or absence of domesticable plants and animals, and any other physical conditions affecting possibilities of hunting and gathering; the transition to food production; the subsequent emergence of a surplus and the possibility of science (guns and steel); the increase in population, of both humans and domesticated animals, and the consequent emergence of deadly viruses and resistance to these viruses among peoples with long exposure to them (germs). Diamond's concern is to counter, once and for all, all racist, xenophobic and "centric" theories of cultural or intellectual superiority of any one people or peoples compared with others. He shows vividly, in multiple contexts, how the differences in historical outcomes and patterns of dominance are completely unrelated to differences in intellectual capacities and achievements of peoples.

Here he echoes a large literature from cultural anthropology. The genre can be represented by this story, from Clyde Kluckhohn's *Mirror for Man*

(1950). A team of French anthropologists studying one of the most "primitive" peoples ever encountered, the Kaingang "Indians" of the Amazon Valley in Brazil, found an abandoned infant lying on a path in the jungle. A married couple, part of the team, took the boy back to Paris and adopted him as their son. This pure-"blooded" Kaingang grew up in the City of Light as a full-fledged French intellectual; thirty years later, armed with a doctorate in anthropology from the University of Paris, he returned to Brazil as part of a new team in a new generation to study his biological forebears.

Eurasian, and eventually western European, dominance in today's world thus have everything to do with differential geographical opportunities for food production, leading to increasing complexity in social structure, technological development, population, and military power; they have nothing to do with any presumed "innate" qualities of any given peoples or cultures. This is indeed evidenced by instances of independent achievement of major steps in human evolution—food production, animal domestication, metallurgy, written languages—in different isolated parts of the world, rather than their diffusion from a single site.

Diamond develops his account with remarkable erudition and exquisite detail. The conceptual interrogations that follow should be taken in the spirit in which they are intended: as encouraging efforts to develop further the insights achieved in Diamond's study.

I would note first that the geographical determinism perspective studies the outward growth and movement of civilizations, to the comparative neglect of their internal structure. Diamond focuses on conquest, but does not address internal division, social class in particular. His conception of social evolution, shared with many non-Marxist cultural evolutionists (e.g., White 1959; Harris 1979; Carneiro 2000) is dominated by a linear progression from simplicity to complexity, passing through stages that are not clearly defined and that may overlook crucial qualitative distinctions. Thus, human groups, in this view, pass from a tribal stage to chiefdoms, with settled villages and a political structure emerging above them, to states, and finally to empires. If one treats complexity as an undifferentiated quantitative measure of the degree of progress of civilization (here "civilization" is used without the invidious or moralizing overtones that sometimes accompany the word) one might conclude that the Xia Dynasty in China, around 2000 BCE, represented a fuller social development than did later societies with smaller populations, less complexity, fewer "moving parts." As soon as we ask, complexity of what?, we are led to the qualitative dimension of social structure: class, production relations, property, forms of internal incentive, and control. Bigger and more complex may not mean more advanced or potentially developmental. We would want to inquire into not only the directionality of conquest, but also its nature in different times and situations.

Comparison of the Roman and Norman conquests of Britain may serve as an example. The Roman incursion, which came to an end around 400 CE, was experienced by the aboriginal inhabitants of that island as an unpleasant but manageable occurrence: the Roman legions advanced, feeding themselves by means of a lengthy pipeline to the slave economy on the European continent, and the local peoples gave them wide berth. They came, they conquered, they left; things then returned (more or less) to the status quo ante. The Normans, by contrast, coming about seven hundred years later, brought with them a new *mode of production* involving small-scale manorial organization and a servile hierarchy. Food production was organized locally on the basis of feudal production relations. The Normans, in short, came equipped to stay. Some attention to internal social relations adds explanatory power to a model based simply on food surpluses, complexity, and conquest.

Diamond's main argument concerns the vast land mass he calls "Eurasia," stretching from Ireland to Taiwan. The multiplicity of reasons for Eurasian dominance at first seems impressive: a horizontal axis, rather than the vertical orientation of Africa and the Americas (uniformity of climate over large areas makes diffusion of plants and animals easier); absence of major obstacles to diffusion and population movement (mountains, bodies of water, narrow bridges such as the Isthmus of Panama in the Americas, deserts), variety of domesticable plant materials, variety of domesticable animals (and their survival; cf. Australia, where the original human population dispersions destroyed the large mammals that originally inhabited that continent). Multiple reasons, however, raise suspicions. One must wonder why the entire set of conditions favorable to social evolution happen to be present on one continent, rather than, say, some being present on one and others on others. Is there a danger of a tautological reading backwards from the present, that is, from the *fact* of Eurasian predominance? For example, Diamond points to the importance of the horse for both agriculture and warfare, and the fact that the horse was available on the Eurasian continent, but not elsewhere. Africa, however, had the zebra. But the zebra is not domesticable; even modern zoologists have failed in efforts to achieve domestication of this species. (Domestication, as Diamond points out, is more than taming; it means breeding under human control and development of traits that are advantageous for humans.) The problem lies in the possibility that modern scientists have not, in a comparatively short period of time, domesticated the zebra because there is no reason to do so; the horse, imported from Eurasia into Africa as into the Americas, already exists. Diffusion eliminates the necessity which would have been the mother of domestication. The failure of animal domestication in Africa over the 12–14 millennia since the (second) human dispersion out of that continent may have much more to do with the absence of an *internal* impetus toward intensive food production in the societies existing there than with inherent qualities of the local fauna.

The argument concerning continental axes (see the map in Diamond 1997, 177) is powerful, but may be exaggerated. The longest axis on the African continent is, of course, vertical, stretching from temperate to tropical to temperate, north to south. But the continent is still more than 4,600 miles wide at its widest latitude—the distance from "California to the New York Island" and half way back again. Plenty of room for diffusion there. More important, the connection drawn in the continental axis argument between an unbroken diffusion path, on the one hand, and societal expansion, on the other, seems arbitrary. One might counter that a north-south axis, which imposes challenges for movement of plants, animals, and technology, would better reward diversity and creativity—a sort of Toynbeeian "challenge-response" approach to early human dispersion. To put the matter differently, an easy diffusion path may mean conquest and population growth in some circumstances, or expansion to the point of stasis in others.

The Roman Empire may again serve as example. Here, culminating a series of empire-building events (the Persians, Alexander the Great, Egypt) an empire based on the surplus generated by a central slave economy spread outward, without geographical obstacles, into the then "known" (by the people designated as doing the "knowing") world. It eventually, however, stopped, never expanding eastward into central Asia and China, for reasons unrelated to geography: the expansive energy of this social formation was bounded by the method of surplus extraction and its inherent limits, and an equilibrium trap occurred, in which the given extent of the empire consumed the surplus on which it was based, making further expansion impossible. Geography is necessary, but not sufficient, to fully explain historical outcomes.

One is troubled by the "Eurasia" category that dominates discussion throughout Diamond's book. This supercontinent is finally broken up in the last chapter ("Epilogue: The Future of Human History as a Science"), where the question is finally posed: why Europe, and not China? Here Diamond at last connects with the Eurocentrism discussion, most recently occasioned by Andre Gunder Frank's *Re-Orient* (Frank 1998). Diamond's answer to the question, Why did China not conquer Europe, instead of the other way around?, is weak and inconclusive. Uncharacteristically, he refers to fortuitous historical events—in particular, a decision made by the unified leadership of the Chinese state in 1433 CE. A power struggle between two factions, the eunuchs and their opponents, ended with victory of the latter, which then reversed a standing policy of sending forth "treasure fleets," thus bringing to an end China's pursuit of maritime supremacy. This is contrasted with the diversity of Europe. Christopher Columbus, turned down in his funding request by one European head of state after another, finally found Ferdinand and Isabella of Spain. "The real problem in understanding China's loss of political and technological preeminence to Europe is to understand China's chronic unity and Europe's chronic disunity" (413–14).

Against this, there is the obvious point that an arbitrary decision by a ruler, or ruling faction, which throttles technological development or economic expansion creates a *material political basis* for opposition to and overthrow of that ruler/faction. But the further question arises: when is geographic variation conducive to political disunity? And, in turn, how does societal development depend on the balance between unity and disunity? In some circumstances, natural barriers (deserts, mountains, oceans) may produce isolation and inhibit diffusion; *or* they may serve as a challenge to develop unifying political structures and ideologies (thus the crucial role of Christianity in the early spread of west European precapitalist monarchies eastwards—the so-called Great Crusades). Moreover, the unity-disunity polarity conceals crucial qualitative variation—in particular, the *unifying-differentiating* quality of the peculiar institution of the market. (See chapter 3, for a full discussion.) The *law of value*, or the central positioning of commodity exchange in capitalist or near-capitalist social formations of recent centuries, changes the terms of the analysis entirely; Diamond, however, is not able to incorporate this dimension into his theory.

To fully grasp the broad shape of recent history, geographical determinism must be supplemented by historical materialism. Large-scale states in East Asia, Africa, and the Middle East failed not in the development of politics, art, and science (China, in particular, from about four thousand years ago, has been at the forefront in all these areas and the Islamic empires were the sites of much early scientific and cultural development), but in the geographically determined capacity to transform the primary tribal, or communal, social units into subaltern *classes*—something civilizations elsewhere than in western Europe and Britain, for different reasons, were not able to accomplish. The incentive/control structures that we customarily call "slave" and "feudal" (Eurocentrically, in the case of the latter) are, as we have seen, at the heart of this evolution. The sudden disappearance of large-scale, slave-based empires in Europe in the first centuries of the Common Era, and their replacement by a *dis*unified (but intensively organized) patchwork of manorial units facilitated small-scale technical development in a way broadly not present in other large centers of civilization; this contrast is the source of the ironic observation that Europe was visibly outstripped by African, Fertile Crescent, and Asian civilizations in the first millennium CE. The expansion of the Islamic world around 700 CE eastward into Persia and westward into North Africa and Spain did not transform production and internal class relations in those regions. By contrast, the European *in*volution, seemingly a regression from earlier stages of high civilization (when measured on a simple quantitative scale), served precisely as the cocoon-stage of capitalism. All of these insights, if borne out by further empirical investigation, are unavailable to the perspective of geographical determinism, with its unilinear stages of complexity and its failure to distinguish among different qualitative class structures.

Milonakis and PF–PR Parity

In two articles (1993–94, 1997), Dimitris Milonakis addresses the chasm, as he sees it, between Cohen's mechanistic PF determinism, and Brenner's class-struggle voluntarism. He proposes instead a view that rejects assignment of primacy to either pole of the PF–PR relationship. Forces and relations are mutually conditioning, and the driving force for transformation of both is class struggle. Here is one summary formulation:

> The proposed framework has the advantage of avoiding the one-sidedness and voluntarism inherent in the "class conflict" approach, while not dispensing with class conflict altogether as in Cohen's (and Laibman's) analysis. At the same time the mechanistic causality that characterizes the productive forces/production relations framework is replaced by a dialectical causality, where the two basic coordinates of the FMP [feudal mode of production] provide the fuel for each other's movement through a continuous dialectical interactive process mediated by the conflict between lords and peasants. (Milonakis 1993–94, 416)

We will leave to one side, for the moment, the perception that my PF–PR analysis "dispens(es) with class conflict altogether." The problems of incentive, coercion, and control are, of course, central to the definition of class conflict as the inherent and ever-active core of the PRs in any class-antagonistic MP.

Milonakis proposes a rich definition of feudalism. More than simply "production for use," feudalism entails a complex relation between lords and serfs, in which ownership by lords and possession by serfs creates a unique incentive for the direct producers to develop the PFs. (Despite his dismissal of the "productive forces/productive relations framework," Milonakis uses these terms, and their acronyms, throughout his articles.) He is also sensitive to the need to explain feudalism as such before explaining the *crisis* of feudalism. If we see only crisis and insufficiency, we can't understand why feudal PRs led to healthy PF development in its earlier phase, and crisis in its later phase.

When one looks for a usable theory of the feudal dynamic in his work, however, one comes away disappointed. Milonakis does not accept my concept of intensive PF development; he cites this, but then uses its opposite, "extensive," to refer instead to population growth and the outward spread of feudal PRs. (Why use one set of words for two different purposes?) Productivity growth is part of the feudal dynamic, as in my approach, but Milonakis does not want to link this to an intensive surplus as a new foundation for market relations. What, then, undermines feudal PRs? The answer is not clear. Perry Anderson (1978) is cited for increase in grain cultivation and neglect of animal husbandry, resulting in inadequate manuring and agricultural crisis (Milonakis 1993–94, 413); why this should result from specifically feudal PRs is not explained. Milonakis then argues that "both the intensive and extensive development permitted by the feudal social system reached their limits." How? "For the direct producers to acquire an extra interest in their work, their feudal burdens and restrictions had to be lightened. Such a development, however, was not possible without threatening the very existence of the feudal social order" (414). This is followed by a circular invocation of "the requirements for further growth of the market," which "would require nothing less than the destruction of the feudal social edifice" (ibid.). Milonakis' effort to create a third option between PF determinism and class-struggle voluntarism thus does not appear to meet the requirements of theory, as elaborated for the PF–PR model: to rise above description to the level of explanation.

Is class struggle missing from the PF–PR model? (I cannot, of course, speak for G. A. Cohen's formulation, only for my own.) Class struggle is *a* motor of history, but I think it is time to acknowledge that it is not the *only* one. When a MP enters into its crisis phase, so that reproduction of its basic structure and surplus extraction are threatened, the ever-present conflict between its fundamental classes takes on new possibilities. Slave revolts and peasant uprisings appear with greater frequency and effectiveness in certain historical periods, not because the idea of revolt suddenly occurs in the minds of the oppressed, but rather because the existing social structure has been weakened to the point at which internal and external challenges can be effective. "Class struggle," in fact, has multiple meanings. It is the largely unconscious and informal daily reproduction of the balance of class forces within antagonistic MPs, and as such is an ever-present, immanent aspect of the PRs. It is an occasional and intermittent process of resistance, sometimes individual, sometimes collective; often encased in ideological and organizational forms (especially, in many periods, religious ones) that do not directly reflect class position. Finally, it means organized (i.e., ideological) consciousness and struggle, based on class (Marx's "class-for-itself"); this level of *political* class struggle characterizes modern capitalist society, and again only intermittently. In the deepest sense, then, class structure and class relations are inseparable, and class conflict is inherent in social reproduction. In the sense of conscious (political) action, class struggle is only occasionally present, and constitutes a central dynamic of social change in some periods but not in others. The feudal crisis has a unique "choreography" (Nicolaus 1967): the class dynamic involves interposition of a new dominant class between the defining classes of feudalism, the urban "middle class" or bourgeoisie. The transition from slavery is essentially the transformation of the existing ruling and exploited classes. Only the transition from capitalism shows polarization and depletion of middle strata, and full agency embodied in the exploited class, which must therefore organize and act politically. In a sense, the slogan "class struggle is the motor of history" is inexact; it should be replaced with: "class struggle *must become* the motor of history if the transition to communism is to be realized." But I cannot see why Milonakis thinks that the PF–PR model, and affirmation of the uniquely developmental capacity of the PFs, means "dispensing with class conflict altogether."

In fact, class struggle is not separate from the PRs; it is a defining characteristic of the PRs in antagonistic MPs. There is no "third term" between PFs and PRs, therefore, that can force development, and this raises the question: is a theory that refuses to assign (in some sense) causal primacy to either the PFs or PRs an adequate one? Evidence from Milonakis' enterprise suggests otherwise. He refers often to dialectical qualities as characterizing his model, seeing its alternatives as one-sided or "mechanical." Dialectics, however, refers not simply to mutual interaction, but to interaction between unequal poles. In a dialectical interaction, *dominant determination* runs from one pole to the other; without this, the dialectic characterizes the mutual conditioning of the poles, their relational consistency, but does not reveal a dynamic movement in the system that they constitute. Taking class struggle outside of the PRs and treating the PRs and PFs as codetermining amounts to implicitly reverting to the autonomy of class struggle, the Brenner position (cf. Katz 1994), especially in the absence of any demonstrated link between PF development and crisis of the PRs.

Nolan and the Darwinian Moment

G. A. Cohen's work contributed to the perception that a new school of "analytical" or "rational choice" Marxism had come into being (Roemer 1982; Elster 1985)—although Cohen, in personal communication with the author, cast some doubt on the existence or uniformity of this "school, to which I supposedly belong." The central commitment of methodological individualism to the rational individual as building block for any sufficiently rigorous analysis seems most consistent with an interpretation of historical materialism in which the PFs develop as a result of intentional human action to raise productivity and efficiency—whether this is the immediate goal of those with power over the PFs and the sources of their development, or an unintended consequence of other goals, especially those involving fortification or extension of class power. This position provoked a strong counterreaction, citing cases in which ruling-class interests block productive development, and pointing to general cultural variation in the extent of PF dynamism (described above, in chapter 1). One aspect of this countermove has been the recent elaboration of an interpretation of "PF primacy" that ascribes this to the unintended impact of productive development on population growth. Paul Nolan (1993, 2002, 2005) is a major proponent of this "Darwinian historical materialism." This section briefly examines his proposal; I will draw on his 2002 essay for this purpose (in Blackledge and Kirkpatrick 2002).

The Darwinian aspect of Nolan's reconstructed historical materialism is his borrowing, from the received doctrines of biological evolution, the mechanism of spontaneous selection of advantageous traits. These traits, however, are cultural, not genetic; Darwinian historical materialism must not be confused with biological reductionism, as in, for example, the Social Darwinism of the nineteenth century or some more recent resurgences of biological determinism (e.g., Herrnstein and Murray 1994; Wilson 2000). Here is the basic position, in Nolan's words:

> If we make the simplifying assumption that offspring usually adopt the cultural traits of their parents, only occasionally making relatively minor cultural innovations, then cultural traits that enhance survival and reproductive success are likely to spread through human populations from generation to generation, at the expense of traits that do not confer a reproductive advantage. This process could perhaps be described as a natural selection of cultural variation. . . .

If . . . cultural traits have a tendency to be inherited within groups rather than between groups (perhaps because of the relative proximity of members of the same group, or geographical, linguistic or cultural barriers between groups) and this tendency is significant enough to allow between-group variation in cultural traits to persist, variation that gives rise to systematic between-group differences in reproductive success, then a selective process can take place in which reproductively advantageous characteristics can spread in successive generations of human populations (or the human species). (Nolan 2002, 79, 80)

Nolan then goes on to argue that the cultural trait that matters most, in the long run, for reproductive success is "power deployed in production"—essentially the PFs. "To the extent that offspring adopt . . . the productive techniques of their parents . . . then differential reproductive success will ensure that improved productive techniques will tend to spread" (85). Superior PFs then come to predominate, not because they are intentionally chosen—Nolan thinks that humans generally cannot know "with any degree of certainty *which* cultural variables would increase" (82) efficiency, well-being, or longevity, and therefore cannot consciously choose them—but because they exist, for random reasons, in populations that are therefore expanding at relatively rapid rates.

Nolan is aware of a crucial difficulty with his theory; in fact, he mentions it repeatedly, almost from the start of his essay. This is the possibility that *diffusion* of cultural traits, most importantly productive techniques, from one cultural group to another might constitute a "threat" (76); it must be assumed that selection "is not subverted by diffusion" (83), and so forth. There are other difficulties, such as the possibility that forces other than production—especially military forces—may take over the role of chief progenitor of reproductive success and population growth; these, however, take second place to establishing that growth in productive power will lead to population growth, rather than diffusing across cultures and societies via adoption and imitation. To this end, Nolan postulates the existence of separate human groups: "Let us think of the human species (and human populations?) as divided into groups that constitute (to some extent and for some significant period) *discrete reproductive lineages*" (79; emphasis added; parentheses in original). Random improvements in technique thus enable a given lineage to have differential reproductive success, and the improvement is carried forward into a larger relative population group. Thus, the PFs develop, without intentionality. Social forms that help increase productive power are then also indirectly selected (in this quasi-Darwinian sense); aside from a pair of unrelated—and, in this author's view, problematic—

examples regarding irrigation systems and optimal family size for foraging success (87–88), there is no systematic discussion of the actual evolution of social forms.

The diffusion problem is indeed central. Diffusion, in fact, is not a "problem"; as I have elaborated in detail in chapter 1, it is a central category of cultural existence, based on symbolic reference (White 1969, ch. 1; Deacon 1997). There are simply no instinctual, or genetic, barriers to manipulation of symbols, acquisition of knowledge, spread and sharing of cultural traits. Moreover, symbolic consciousness implies an immanent drive to improvement in control over the external environment. While the PRs are of course subject to ideological petrification, and therefore only dimly perceived by social actors in most periods of human evolution, so that Nolan's strictures concerning inability to set rational courses of action with fully intended consequences do apply to them, it is hard to say the same for the PFs, where intentional action to transform nature—labor—is in fact the *definition* of the human, as distinct from nonhuman animal, relation to the environment. There is no such thing as *non*-intentional labor! Massive anthropological and historical evidence attests to the rapid diffusion of productive traits; witness the speed with which the indigenous peoples of North America mastered horses, firearms, and written languages when these benefits (or dubious benefits) of civilization were introduced into their environment by Europeans.

In fact, Nolan's quasi-Darwinian historical materialism contains a major contradiction; one may almost speak of a crucial flaw. It needs *parallel* but *noncommunicating* human groups ("reproductive lineages"), so that nonintentional advantages spread in the combined population. But the advantaged group then becomes, tendentially, the sole group. Where, in that group, do new improvements in technique come from? Once there is only one group, either globally or in some isolated region, its population growth cannot be explained in a Darwinian manner; one must then assume either that no PF development occurs, or that human intentionality is at work in the selection and improvement of techniques, with effects on population growth, among many other variables.

In effect, if groups come into contact, diffusion will play—and undoubtedly has played—the key role, undermining the population/selection mechanism. Contact among peoples—often, to be sure, of a violent nature—is constant throughout history, and borrowing of knowledges, practices, and beliefs is always present: intentional, though often with unintended consequences along with the intended ones, and usually mediated by class-based and ideological, rather than directly productive, motivations. If one wishes, however, to propose noncommunicating groups or lineages, then random variation in productive technique will cause relative population growth now in one group, then in another, with no trend. Unless it is suggested that random *regressions* in productivity will be adopted by a group, leading to population *decline*, an intentional element is clearly at work. In any case, the quasi-Darwinian proposal does not have a clear explanatory role to play.

Nolan's essay is very thin in describing production *relations*, other than the two brief examples mentioned earlier. If some conception of historical modes of production were present, it would become apparent that each MP has its own "law of population," as Marx in fact suggested with regard to capitalism (1967, I, ch. 24). Perhaps this is a bit epigrammatic, but I would suggest that the slave, feudal, and capitalist MPs, respectively, are characterized by the following distinct immanent population tendencies. In the slave MP, the constant extraction of slaves from the surrounding social formations and the early death of slaves lead to population decline, or (at best) stasis. Feudalism, by contrast—both because of the emerging intensive surplus and the drive, noted by Milonakis, to territorial expansion and colonization (the earliest serfs were, in fact, "*coloni*")—creates pressure toward population growth whenever income is above subsistence, precisely the dynamic on which Adam Smith, Malthus, and Ricardo based their thinking. Feudalism also evidently generates population *cycles*, in which overpopulation causes subsistence crisis and depopulation, with associated swings in the balance of class power between lords and serfs (Postan and Hatcher 1985; Bois 1985; Federici 2004). Capitalism, finally, produces the well-known demographic transition associated with the Industrial Revolution, decoupling population growth from the subsistence wage.

I return to the question: why do Cohen's critics distrust intentional human action to the degree they do? Mediated goals and unintended consequences notwithstanding, intentionality is still at the heart of what separates us from other species, and prevents any direct application of evolutionary biology to the social-cultural context.

Carling's Competitive Primacy and the Transition from Feudalism

Alan Carling (1991, 2002, 2005) has developed his own proposal to draw upon Darwin to escape from the straitjacket of "intentional primacy" of the productive forces. As with Nolan, I will concentrate on the formulation given in his essay in Paul Blackledge and Graeme Kirkpatrick 2002 (Carling 2002).

Carling begins by setting forth G. A. Cohen's Development Thesis. In its most ambitious form (the Full Development Thesis), this asserts that the

PFs have an "asocial," or supra-historical, tendency to develop, as a result of human rational choice and action. The Primacy Thesis asserts dominant causality running from PFs to PRs. The problem with this, for many participants in the discussion, is that the PRs demonstrably shape, and at times curtail, PF development. The argument is then either inconclusive, or circular. Carling sees Cohen's next move as an attempt to get beyond this riddle, by postulating that the correspondence between PFs and PRs is not merely functional, but, more strongly, intentional. People *consciously* choose the PRs, to correspond with the intentionally chosen PFs. Carling finds this position to be "beyond credence," "massively implausible" (104). It is not clear what Cohen might think of this interpretation of his position, in either its earlier form (1978) or in his later response to the discussion (1988); he has not been active in the more recent discussions.

Carling's own proposal is to replace the strong position attempted by Cohen—a *general, directed* theory, which determines or explains the directionality of historical change in all times and contexts—with something less ambitious: a general, *undirected* theory, based on what he calls "Competitive Primacy of the forces of production":

Primacy of the forces of production will certainly obtain when:

(i) there has been a competition between two different systems of production relations with higher and lower levels of development of the forces of production

and

(ii) the differential in levels has caused the system with the higher level to prevail over the system with the lower level. (108)

While there may be cases in which no productive differences exist between systems that are in contact with one another, or cases in which systems are not in contact, or in which a society with lower productivity prevails over one with higher productivity, Competitive Primacy still holds as a general rule. It says that "superior forcehood confers a competitive edge on its associated production relations which is tendentially decisive" (110).

Competitive Primacy may not apply to many periods of history, and where it does apply it may do so in only a qualified, potential way. "Perhaps all that can be said is that history exhibits a *bias* imparted by Competitive Primacy; a bias weaker than a tendency but considerably stronger than nothing at all" (114). This general, undirected result, however, can be supplemented by a theory of transition from feudalism to capitalism that *is* directed—it refers to a result occurring with (almost) inevitability, and is a transition with only one direction—although it is special, not general, referring to only one historical episode, the emergence of capitalism.

European feudalism (Carling does not try to distinguish between "European feudalism" and "feudalism as such") had two characteristics: it was politically decentralized (the "feudal fission thesis"), and it was characterized by a demographic cycle of "population boom and slump." The first of these made Europe an ideal social laboratory, with a large variety of systems of production relations. (It is, again, not clear why all of these are appropriately called "feudal.") Population slumps (depopulations) then create vacant land, and a degree of freedom concerning the outcome of the struggle for control over land. Schematically, these outcomes range from one extreme, at which the direct producers (peasant households) have a large degree of autonomy, amounting to virtual private property rights (the "French outcome"), to the opposite extreme, reimposition of serfdom (the "Polish outcome"). In between is the "English outcome," "wherein the lords prove strong enough to control the land but insufficiently strong to cow the peasantry." This "establishes the class structure of agrarian capitalism, and such a structure leaves its two sides no choice but to negotiate the labor market relations which 'comprise a world's history' " (116).

Thus, we arrive at a "composite Marxian explanation":

> . . . it was almost inevitable that an economic regime would emerge from feudalism which as a matter of fact had a higher propensity than feudalism to develop the forces of production (Feudal Fission Thesis) and . . . it was very likely that this propensity would lead to a differential development of the forces which would in turn prove decisive in the competition between the two regimes (Competitive Primacy). (116–17)

This is essentially a probabilistic theory of the emergence of capitalism. An event that occurs with only a small probability in any one region, and in any one population cycle is all but sure to happen somewhere and sometime within the matrix of cycles and regions of Europe. Carling jokes: "There will always be an England." And once the birth event occurs somewhere, the superior PFs kick in and spread, first to the rest of Europe and then around the world. We thus arrive at a significantly qualified, but in Carling's eyes much more defensible, version of a Marxist theory of history.

Carling, like Nolan, wants to replace intentional action with a nonintentional competition, after the fashion of Darwinian selection. Both

face a similar core problem: humans transform the environment, rather than
being transformed by it, so the Darwinian analogy is, to say the least, not
well established. Ironically, one wants to say, in the spirit of analytical
Marxism: superior PFs do not "prevail," or "spread"; real people make them
prevail, or spread them. In his zeal to distance himself from Cohen, Carling
tells a story that invites analytic deconstruction, in the classic A. J. Ayer
fashion, or following the dictates of Jon Elster (cf. Elster 1985). He does not
tell us *how* one MP "prevails" over another, or "spreads."

Carling's feudalism is not richly described; the characteristic relations
of hierarchy and subservience, and the all-encompassing enclosed world of
the manor, are not present in his account. It is not clear why Europe is the
site of the action he unfolds; European specificity seems to reduce to variability in regional conditions, much as in the work of Jared Diamond (1997).
The population cycle is not itself explained. Given the cycle and the moment of feudal control crisis, it is not clear why any particular set of environmental conditions leads to a position on the spectrum between the "Polish"
and "French" outcomes; why the intermediate ("English") outcome does not
lead simply to an intermediate position in the feudal balance of power
between lords and serfs, rather than to a transmutation of their relationship
into a capitalist-worker relation on the land; why the English path involves
increasing prevalence of market relations in, say, the seventeenth century,
rather than in the seventh, and so on. It is certainly not indicated in the
historical record that English lords became agrarian capitalists, while serfs
correspondingly evolved into workers. If anything, agrarian capitalism in
the British seventeenth century formed via differentiation of the freeholding
peasantry into tenant farmers, paying rent to the lords, and hired agricultural laborers who were part of the evolving proletariat formed by the successive enclosures of common lands and dispossessions of freeholds.

Carling's feudalism does not have its own inner developmental tendencies; all we learn about it is contained in its two named features: unex-
plained decentralization and population cycles. It does not evolve from young
to mature phases; it does not display an internal contradiction. And,
significantly, it appears as a static, low-productivity system of production for
use, with little internal technological dynamism. I must leave an authorita-
tive examination of this claim to others, but there is a large "revisionist"
literature (e.g., Postan 1975; Lynn Townsend White 1964) that questions
the view of feudalism as "The Dark Ages," in which production was primitive and stagnant. This view characterized eighteenth-century Enlighten-
ment thinking: the bourgeoisie was anxious to declare the "beginning" of
history at the start of its reign, and the "end" of history nearer to its demise

(e.g., Bell 1965). The upshot of Carling's proposal is that prior to capitalism, which he equates with "market forces" (110), there was essentially stasis; precapitalist MPs are not importantly distinguished from one another, and laws of motion concerning their stadiality and succession are not sought. Feudalism, in this structure, appears simply as a branch of precapitalism in which, due to special regional factors, decentralization and variety are present; this gives the market an opening at some juncture (England), and when this connection is made, Competitive Primacy takes over and the spread of capitalism is under way. Since there is no possibility of a general directed theory of history, there remains only the one transition to explain, and it is explained essentially as the occurrence of a probabilistically certain event: the planting of the market (capitalist) seed into suitable soil.

Carling invokes the case of the Soviet Union and its demise in support of the Competitive Primacy Thesis, and against Intentional Primacy. The Soviet demise represents the failure of the most significant intentional social experiment in history, and thus casts doubt upon whether intentional action ever has (or ever can) bring about social change. At the same time, it offers "a new, if unfortunate, endorsement to the doctrine of Competitive Primacy—for why has the Soviet experiment failed, if not for its failure to compete economically and militarily with a system of production relations that has proved itself technically superior?" (124). I will leave discussion of the Soviet experience until chapter 7; this passage is cited only to reinforce my sense of the direction in which Competitive Primacy takes us: it is primacy of a superior MP *in competition with* others, but it is also the superiority of *competition as a component of the MP*, that is, "market society" or capitalism. There is only one "great transformation," and that one leads to capitalism; as Carling himself notes, somewhat ruefully, in his most recent paper (2005), his composite theory, based on Competitive Primacy and Feudal Fission, suggests that *capitalism*, or at least some form of market economy, is the ultimate end of historical evolution, in the sense that the prevalence of the most productive form leads to it.

A BRIEF DIGRESSION: CARLING ON LAIBMAN. Carling (2002) contains a short discussion of Laibman (1984), for which I am grateful. Carling wonders about my attempt to distinguish among levels of abstraction; "it is difficult to see how the theory could be hard at the level of the totality while remaining soft at the level of all, or some or most of the historical events to which the theory applies" (122). I am not certain what the difficulty is; the "hard" level points to certain key underlying logically required steps in the unfolding of an evolutionary process; the "soft" level then locates these transitions in the variety of contingent forms in which they occur (or do not occur).

"Laibman introduces a characterization of feudalism's effect on the forces of production which is at variance with the understanding of every other contributor to the debate" (ibid.). This refers to my concept of intensive PF development. Carling's point is that feudal PFs are "sluggish" in comparison to those of capitalism; this is not in doubt, and I certainly do not claim otherwise. He also agrees that feudalism advances the PFs beyond their state in the slave MP—his only reference to a precapitalist MP other than feudalism. My point is that not only do the PFs develop in the transition from slavery to feudalism, but that they also develop in a characteristically different way, given the PRs of each system.

Carling's final point addresses a passage in my earlier work in which I am trying to account for the protracted character of the feudalism-capitalism transition. There (as earlier in this chapter) I note the difficulty of accomplishing the coercive separation of direct producers from the means of production, which requires use of the feudal surplus (the capitalist one is not yet being extracted). The question is, how are feudal surpluses turned to this purpose? By what agency? It is a difficult question, and one passage (quoted and criticized by Carling) in my earlier discussion, I now believe, is indeed inaccurate. It reads: "The feudal lords therefore not only can, but must, turn feudal surpluses to the task of primitive accumulation, if the logic of commodity production is to unfold" (Laibman 1984, 279; quoted in Carling 2002, 123). As Carling points out, this is historically inaccurate; the lords in general did not develop the productive forces or turn them to capitalist purposes, but rather fought a retrograde battle to preserve their privileges and antique methods of surplus extraction. I still insist, as argued earlier, that feudal surplus extraction, regardless of the lords' consciousness or intentions, is necessary to create the infrastructure within which intensive PF development by relatively autonomous serfs can occur. I regard as still open the question of how, and by whom, the feudal surplus is enlisted in the task of capitalist class formation; it is not necessary or useful to suggest that capitalist PRs were consciously created by anyone, and least of all by the feudal lords.

Carling's critique, however, returns to the issue of intentionality—whether the lords, or anyone else for that matter, are "agents of a conscious transition to capitalism." This again refers to the rejection of the project, which in some sense I share with Cohen, of adducing a rigorous historical materialism in which human will, consciousness, and agency are the basis for a determinate yet open-ended theory of historical evolution, one that is precisely (in Carling's terms) both general and directed. I have argued that the Carling composite of Competitive Primacy and Feudal Fission is not a successful replacement for the general theory that Cohen and I both seek. It fails to grasp the specificity of feudalism, to isolate a prime mover in that MP or any other; it collapses the entire historical experience into one great transition, and therefore casts doubt on the core Marxist project of scientifically envisioning the transformation beyond class-antagonistic society that awaits us. In concluding this chapter, I will address the question: can anything be derived from the Darwinian/analytical assault on the PF–PR model that holds promise of a "general directed" theory, one that is not open to the challenges thus far made against such a theory? Where do things stand?

III. CONCLUSION: TWO HISTORICAL MATERIALIST TRAJECTORIES

We can, I think, reject two extreme positions that emerge from this extended discussion. One is a general, directed theory (Carling's terms) that is based on *extreme intentionality* (my term): rational agents consciously choose the PFs, and the PRs corresponding to them. They presumably do this along a PF–PR production function, which shifts (exogenously?) over time; thus, the human race wallows along in various forms of tradition or command economies, until "the market" ("capitalism") is discovered. The rest is—the end of—history. This view, which could be extracted from Cohen's attempted systematization of historical materialism—I do not for a minute attribute it to him—clearly converges with capitalist orthodoxy in social science, the core of which is neoclassical economic theory.

The alternative is the several anti-intentional proposals, which appeal to a broad analogy with Darwinian evolution in the nonhuman lifeworld. This approach sees history as essentially undirected; the only directed component—arising (almost) inevitably in probabilistic fashion as the precapitalist social environment affords varied spaces within which it may at some point be ignited—is the transition to capitalism. Remarkably, this position converges with its hyper-intentional nemesis: capitalism emerges as the *final* outcome of the only *directed* historical process.

With notable consistency, the "Western" Marxist enterprise arrives at this fundamental conclusion. ("Western"—see, e.g., Anderson 1979b—is a nongeographical designation that appears to include all Marxisms outside of the twentieth century's Communist parties.) Both the intentional and the Darwinian–competitive poles support directionality *toward* capitalism, and *within* capitalism (at least to the extent that market relations presume an autonomous "economic" sphere in which objective social laws exist; see Gottlieb 1984), but not *beyond* capitalism. This is an outcome of seeing the formation of the modern era as *the* Great Transformation; the neglect of earlier "great transformations," and of the entire stadial structure of the PF–PR model, is thus symptomatic, not accidental. I would also note that this bias is consistent with other practices and schools within Western Marxism. World System Theory, for example, is a hyperextension of capitalism, now projected as a world system going back to the sixteenth century, or even perhaps to antiquity, whose separate components and the social relations within them are relegated to the background (Wallerstein 1974; Arrighi et al., 1999). This again converges with mainstream social science, for which "capitalism" is conflated with all rational thought and instrumental behavior. Another example is afforded by the Uno School in political economy, for which capitalism—indeed, the isolated abstraction of the Pure Capitalist Society, in which the valorization (commodification) of social relations is complete—is the unique lens through which objectivity in society can be grasped (Uno 1980; Sekine 1984).

We have, in sum, a profound tendency to construct a historical materialism in which *all roads lead to capitalism*. The clear implication is that contemplation of transition beyond capitalism cannot be theorized; it exists inherently in a utopian, speculative mode.

The J. Cohen–Nolan–Carling critique of hyper-intentionality does not, I argue, touch the PF–PR version. In the conception outlined in this chapter and the preceding one, intentionality is pervasive in human life; it is central to the defining human activity, labor, and is the ground for the Development Principle that drives the PFs in a single direction: toward ever greater human power in the transformation of the external environment. This development, however, is *never not* mediated by culture—by social relations, especially class relations. Even when people consciously act on the PFs with a view to greater efficiency and productivity, the symbolic field through which this is carried out is a social, and therefore historical, product. More often, transformation of the PFs—always intentional at some level—is based on an intentionality related to fortification and expansion of surplus extraction capability, religious obligations, military requirements, or any other social or conceptual source that may exist. The PFs are *never not* profoundly shaped by both structural and superstructural social relations and their ideological counterparts. In any given circumstance, the PRs may completely block PF development. Even at the AST level, it is conceivable (though, perhaps, not likely) that absolute blockage may occur; the PF–PR conception has no need to deny this possibility a priori. Should this occur, life on a given planet in our universe would indeed experience the "end of history," however prematurely this notion was foisted upon us, during the cold war, for ideological reasons.

Until the advent of modern socialism, the PRs have generally appeared in human consciousness in nonsystematic, heavily ideologized forms. We may assume, then, that the PRs, unlike the PFs, have only rarely been the focus of intentional action. The efficacy of a given set of PRs in enabling a new stage in PF development is a property of historical materialist understanding, not ordinarily shared by the actual historical actors. It is unreasonable—"wildly implausible," to use Carling's phrase—to assume that, e.g., feudal lords "reasoned" that giving some autonomy to serfs in the disposition of land and tools would lead to intensive PF development and therefore enhance the possibility of surplus extraction; indeed, if they were to "reason" to that extent, they most likely would see a bit further down the road, and note that intensive PF development will then ground the extension of market relations that is their (the lords') undoing; they would then consciously block feudal PF development, and try to revert to some form of slavery, reducing their serfs to the status of demesne slaves. All of this, of course, is ridiculous. Feudal relations emerge spontaneously, not intentionally, out of the variety of situations produced in the wake of the collapse of the slave civilizations (or, given the proximity of those civilizations, of whatever tributary social formations were present). This is the important core of truth in the Darwinian–Competitive position. Once feudal relations come into existence, they solidify and spread, because they are effective in using and developing the PFs—without anyone being conscious of this fact. If the lords do anything intentional, we may assume that this is for grand purposes such as: to enforce the Will of God, to serve their superiors, to destroy their rivals, to please their ladies and enhance the dignity of the court, and (not incidentally) to suppress and contain any rebelliousness or indiscipline that emerges among their subordinates and inferiors. Also, of course, to acquire ever-greater material wealth, especially in the form of precious metals, jewels, cloth, spices, ivory, hardwoods, weapons, and other blessings of long-distance trade. The Correspondence Principle works "behind the backs of" the social actors who embody it. Problems of incentive, control, quality of work life, social organization only become matters of conscious intentionality at the social level when the possibilities of further human development through antagonistic, alienated, and ideologized PRs are increasingly problematized, and class polarization has proceeded to a point at which only intentional, political action by the subordinate, increasingly universal class can challenge the now-pervasive (because valorized) power of the class that rules.

Competitive Primacy focuses on the PFs, and implicitly assumes that *competitive* PFs—the "market"—will ultimately prevail. The stadial PF–PR model, by contrast, focuses on the PRs that in each MP enable further PF development. Market relations are therefore always mediated; they are always forms of expression of underlying production relations. The possibility therefore emerges of evolution of market relations beyond their capitalist form, and of evolution of social relations more generally beyond the market form. A full, stadially elaborated model of social evolution, then, points squarely beyond the present: it is a form of historical materialism in which *all roads lead to communism*. (Here I use "communism" in the classic sense given to the term by Marx, as the general name for the MP that transcends capitalism, and therewith all class-antagonistic MPs. Communism as a twentieth-century political movement is a separate matter, requiring separate analysis.) It should not be necessary to add, after what has already been said, that progress along this road is *always* a matter for conscious human agents, never automatic; and that it is *never* guaranteed. To extend the metaphor, an avalanche could create a blockage that closes the road to communism, perhaps even permanently. The AST conception sketched here is, as I have repeatedly emphasized, about the distillation of potentials only. Embodiment of these potentials in human agency and achievement is the continuing work of the makers of history.

II.
CAPITALISM:
STRUCTURE, LOGIC, STADIALITY

Chapter 3

THE ELUSIVE ANATOMY OF
CAPITALIST SOCIETY

With a general theory of social evolution—the PF–PR model—under our belts, we can now examine the most complex and difficult of the class-antagonistic modes of production. This is a monumental task; in the spirit of the PF–PR model, we understand that "history" is "searching" for ways to bring about surplus extraction and PF development that are consistent with the qualitatively advanced level of productive forces unleashed by capitalism. The task is complicated by special cognitive problems. The reader must, for example, be wondering how anything could be said in this regard that hasn't been said a thousand times already. We have analyses of "capitalism" too numerous to summarize. The word itself has become an almost empty catchphrase, and indeed many people on the left use it as a pejorative, to characterize anything they do not like. The word is also combined arbitrarily with any number of descriptors, as in terms like "consumer capitalism," "monopoly capitalism," "financial capitalism," "Pentagon capitalism" and "rentier capitalism," to the point where the core concept all but disappears. We face the classic dilemma of the fish in the fish bowl: we are too close to *this* MP to see it whole.

There is an additional problem. In the classical Marxist literature, following the pioneering work of Marx in *Capital*, vol. I, the categories of the *theory of value* have been the lens through which this problem is addressed. To the uninitiated, *theory of value* sounds like either an ethical inquiry, or one that concerns relations of exchange among commodities—the foundations of price. In Marx's understanding, however, value is a social substance—abstract labor—that is separate from the visible exchange ratios to which it gives rise, and also from any directly ethical inquiries. Questions abound surrounding the nature of this substance, including the crucial matter of *why* commodities exchange for one another—"pull" one another—and how this "pull" is a masked or "fetishized" form of underlying social relations.

The debates surrounding these questions are difficult, seemingly no nearer to resolution than they were a century ago. (It is impossible to provide an adequate survey of this enormous literature. A masterful overall guide to the history of the value debate will be found in Howard and King 1989, 1992.) The "value" problematic has been hotly contested since it was first formulated. It has been consistently vilified by mainstream social theorists, who see (perhaps correctly?) dire consequences in the link between labor and value. But many thinkers in the Marxist tradition have also joined in this criticism, finding the entire set of value theory propositions to be metaphysical, a residue of nineteenth-century mysticism, and so forth; at a minimum, the prodigious effort required to defend value theory against a legion of critics has, in this view, diverted Marxists from the true task of researching and uncovering the nature and logic of capitalism (for a recent collection of views, Steedman, et al. 1981).

I share the view that the mystification of social relations—their conquest by and appearance as market relations—is a central element in capitalist reproduction. I therefore also find the value-theory enterprise to be still fruitful and significant, and am—in that sense—on the "orthodox" side of this debate. I also, however, have found that the value categories get in the way of my project in this book: attempts to summarize them using "conceptual geometry" tools such as the figures of chapters 1 and 2, without presenting the quantitative relationships explicitly, make the subject more, not less, difficult. I therefore leave that line of inquiry to other places (see, e.g., Laibman 2002a). In this chapter, I will instead try to answer the question, How does capitalism work?, in terms that deploy a conceptual geometry that at least gets at some of the questions for which the value enterprise was historically developed.

I. INGREDIENTS FOR A MODEL OF CAPITALIST EXPLOITATION

In the chain of antagonistic modes of production described by the PF–PR model, capitalism occupies the "highest" place. It is, as we have seen, the culmination of a process of dispossession of direct producers lasting centuries, fueled by the individual surpluses resulting from intensive PF development on the feudal manor. It results from a complex balance of insufficiencies: state power derived from archaic and embattled feudal surpluses, financial and mercantile power not yet soundly based on a system of exploitation in production. Our goal is to theorize that complexity: to explain how class power, the power-to-exploit, is enabled and reproduced in a society that has taken on the pure capitalist form. That form has this crucial characteristic: all social relations have been "marketized" (value theorists say: "valorized"), as the market moves from the social sidelines (long distance trade in luxury goods, for example), and takes over the heart of the PRs. Workers' labor, capitalists' capital, means of production and subsistence—all become commodities, goods produced for purpose of exchange; the physical goods and activities that define the labor process thus, for the first time, become subject to the principles that regulate all market exchange.

It is a main implication of the PF–PR conception that feudal PRs are significantly (qualitatively) more complex than slave PRs, in the simple sense of having more "moving parts," but also in the sense that they enable development of the PFs to higher levels. Similarly, capitalism achieves (because it requires) a still higher level of complexity, in relation to feudalism. To describe this complexity, at the level of the AST, I propose a model that interrelates three fundamental *principles*—the market, the state, and socialized production—with three social *sites*—the workplace, the sphere of ownership, and the social upper class. All of the principles and sites are, I argue, unique to capitalism. (I do not suggest that precapitalist societies do not have production or upper classes; only that specific forms of these entities that are peculiar to capitalism can be identified.)

We begin with the principles.

Principles for a Synthesis of Capitalist Surplus Extraction

A. THE MARKET. It is important to recognize, at the outset, that market relations have existed through all recorded history; there is no period of human evolution in which no forms of market exchange can be found in the anthropological-historical record. In a simple typology, we might speak of progression from the primitive market, to the simple market, and then to the capitalist market (our current object of attention). Primitive markets involve ritualized exchange, usually among cultural groups not individuals, that have extrinsic symbolic significance relating to status, religious worship, and so forth. They also include occasional exchange of useful goods at arbitrary ratios, as these are unique occurrences not subject to any regularizing tendency. Simple markets, in turn, develop among direct producers (peasants, artisans) who own and control their means of production. They are characterized by spontaneous formation of prices (exchange ratios), without being encumbered by preexisting symbolic meanings or restrictions; they also develop in the direction of widely repeated exchanges of similar goods by multiple individuals, so that the exchange ratios come to acquire sufficient uniformity and regularity for this to be observed and for the principles determining them to be sought. The important point for now is that, in the spirit of the PF–PR model, market relations, like other forms of social relations, evolve historically; markets are concrete social and institutional realities, not the embodiment of eternal principles.

The capitalist market is distinct from earlier forms because it implies a capitalist class structure. Its most significant feature, of course, is the famous "double freedom" of the worker: freedom from all forms of personal bondage or subjugation—to slaveowners, to feudal lords—and also freedom from ownership of means of production, that is, of direct access to the natural conditions for labor. Without such access, labor cannot be performed; this presupposes the development of production itself beyond some simple level at which access to nature could be effectuated spontaneously; a point to which we return below. Freedom from access to means of production is, in effect, a *coercive freedom*. The central questions of our inquiry are: How is that coercive freedom reproduced?, and: How does it result in surplus extraction? To answer these questions clearly, and in line with the methodology employed generally in this project, we study capitalist social relations in a pure form, absent any admixture with elements of direct physical coercion or subjugation, even though in actual social formations dominated by capitalism there are always significant or vestigial elements of precapitalist forms of exploitation.

The presence of a propertyless class that nevertheless participates in a market process—in its own special way—implies the existence of a propertied class whose property ownership extends beyond an amount of property—access to nature—necessary to set its own labor into motion. Since the propertyless class—the proletariat, in Marx's usage—must have a certain critical mass for the social relations involving it to be governing, the concentration of ownership of means of production in the hands of the propertied class must also have extension to the point at which that class' labor activity becomes a minor consideration, and allocation of the owned property for purposes of work by others—the nonowners—becomes the defining characteristic of the property in question. We are thus inquiring into the special relationship that exists between a vast majority class of nonowners, and a significant minority class of owners. It should go without saying that this relationship, whose core properties are our object of attention, is part of a wider social formation that contains all manner of intermediate strata, groups and classes formed from earlier or conjoined social formations, and so forth.

The market creates a new layer of reality involving goods—objects produced by labor for human consumption. The loaf of bread, which down through the ages is a collection of physical properties that satisfy a need, now also has a price: a socially determined characteristic of regularized command over, and by, other such goods, which appears to "reside" in the loaf of bread itself, or to be an objective fact of the bread's existence. Bread "costs" $1.29 per loaf because—it just does. Capitalist markets share and further develop a property found in simple markets: the social relations among producers and owners appear as characteristics of the goods themselves, as goods and markets assume fantastic forms and "act" in various ways. This "fetishism of commodities" (Marx 1967, vol. I: ch. 1, section 4) is a result of one feature of the markets that generate it: their spontaneity. By this I mean simply that market outcomes are the resultant of many individual actions occurring without prior coordination, indeed without anyone having the desire or ability to even try to visualize them. No single individual, or group of individuals, or social, or political body of any kind, experiences these outcomes in any relation to their conscious plans, intentions, perceptions. "The market" takes on a life of its own—even though it is nothing other than an embodiment of human consciousness and action within historically distinct sets of social relations. Since market forms have come to pervade life in capitalist societies, including not only labor, capital, and finance, but also areas of human life such as interpersonal relations, the family, and ideology, this emergence of market objectivity, replacing intentional human guidance and control, is a major feature of life after the capitalist transition, perhaps rivaling in importance the emergence of the superorganic and symbolic reference at the dawn of social evolution (see chap. 1).

This raises an additional question, of course: Is market objectification merely a form of a more general objectification, a necessary feature of any human evolution beyond some small scale at which each individual can be known to any other, and abstract categories are therefore required to define and regulate social relations? There is a certain "market logic" to the chance encounters with individuals not known to us in everyday life—events not under control by any individual will or consciousness. To this extent, it may be that there is a certain objectifying quality in all modern life, where "modern" means simply beyond the threshold at which social life becomes significantly regulated by processes, whether economic, political, or cultural, that appear as the resultant of uncoordinated individual wills, and therefore correspond to no identifiable intentional source. I will leave this larger issue to one side, for the moment, and concentrate on two specifically capitalist features of market objectification.

The crucial exchange that distinguishes the capitalist market from the simple form inherited from earlier times is that between the worker and the capitalist, in which the worker exchanges his capacity to work—subsequently activated by the capitalist in the labor process—for a wage, the means of subsistence. The objectification that characterizes all commodities occurs in the case of the worker's commodity—labor power—as well. The wage rate is a price, and, like all prices, it appears as an inherent feature of the commodity, or of the system involving exchange of that commodity. The "going" wage rate for a particular category of work is $15/hour, for example. For this objectification, or valorization, to occur, the exchange between worker and capitalist must not only *seem to be* one between autonomous, and freely interacting parties; it must *actually be* that sort of exchange. The social and political freedom of the worker, as party to the exchange that defines his life and life chances, his class position, is exactly what Marx called a "real illusion." Its reality, however, must be supported, and this is the role of the historically novel social site in which the worker's labor power is produced: the working-class *household*. Capital cannot appropriate this site, as it eventually does all other spheres of production; it is the one site that must remain autonomous, not under the control of capital, since one of the pillars of surplus extraction—valorized or successfully commodified labor power—would be undermined if the worker did not come forward as the independent possessor of a commodity, being brought to market to confront its equally independent purchaser, the employer.

Some readers may have observed the apparently one-sided use of the male pronoun, "his," in the paragraph directly above. This was not an accident, as we are talking here about a moment in the evolution of capitalist PRs in which the seller of labor power comes to be defined as male, and women are removed from the market and hidden away in the household. The "family wage" comes into existence in the "advanced" (post–Industrial Revolution) capitalist countries in the nineteenth century, and begins to disappear by mid-twentieth century. The reasons for the undermining of the family wage in a later stage of development pertain to the stadial nature of the capitalist MP, topic of chapter 5 of this study. Capitalist reproduction in its classical form, however, requires the autonomous household, from which the seller of labor power sallies forth, and this, in the technical conditions of the period of the Industrial Revolution, means that one (female) adult member of the working-class family must perform hidden labor in the household, labor that is indirectly sold to the capitalist and exploited, but concealed as part of the labor of the (male) worker. Capitalism initially therefore brings about the *second* "world-historic defeat of the female sex" (Engels 1964), the first having been the removal of women from an equal position in production and property ownership with the first emergence of private property, appropriation of wealth, and inheritance in antiquity.

(The literature on the household and the position of women within it is, like all of the other source literatures for a study like the present one, vast, and I make no attempt to summarize it or capture its scope. Some standard references are Vogel 1983, 1986; Barrett 1980; Fox 1980; Landes 1977–78; Smith 1978. A recent reference work is Peterson and Lewis 2003.)

The working-class household is a peculiar institution; it is not simply a mirror of the peasant household that is present in all historical periods, and in which labor and production are carried out by both sexes, with more or less equal recognition. By contrast, the working-class household in the capitalist MP is not—can not be—a site of independent production; it must rely on commodities purchased from the capitalist sector with the wage earned by the directly exploited (male) worker. It must, however, contain significant goods-processing activities—household labor—occurring within it. If it did not—if all homemaking activities, such as cooking, laundry, child care, were provided on a commercial basis to the household—the illusion of the household as the independent site at which labor power is produced would again be undermined.

The creation of the "housewife" is the work of history, but the role of the working-class woman in the capitalist reproduction process throws new light on many aspects of the early ("primitive") accumulation of capital. The fifteenth through eighteenth centuries in Europe were a period of intense repression, the disciplining of the dispossessed armies of the poor into a capitalist proletariat, but in this process women were singled out for especially serious and focused attack. Women in the Middle Ages were often able to work more independently than men, and were also carriers of local knowledges, cultural memory, and so forth, which served as sources of resistance to proletarianization. The witch hunts of the sixteenth and seventeenth centuries were designed not only to destroy these sites of resistance and to terrorize the population as a whole (see Federici 2004); but they also served, whether intentionally or inadvertently, to bring about the gender division of labor characteristic of the classical capitalist working-class household, even though that institution does not make its full appearance until the heyday of "liberal" capitalist accumulation, the nineteenth century.

I have devoted much space to the market principle because of its importance in the synthesis described below. Before turning to the production and state principles, one further aspect of market mystification needs to be mentioned. Capitalist property ownership always coexists with property in general, that is, with a wide variety of other forms of property, including many that are—unlike means of production—widely held: property in residential houses, household goods, heirlooms. There is also, of course, productive property held by intermediate strata, including artisans, small farmers, the urban small-business sector. All of these are targets for eventual capitalist predation and expropriation—capital countenances no form of private property other than itself—but in any given period these various forms coexist with capitalist property. Property ownership, therefore, becomes widely experienced and legitimized. Capitalist property, especially the *differential property ownership* that is relied on to a great extent in some accounts of capitalist exploitation (see below), acquires legitimacy and an aura of necessity by associating itself with property ownership in general. The market form of differentially owned property plays an especially important role. There is, after all, an element of luck in the distribution of statuses with regard to differential property, and this is embodied in popular folklore; we say, for example, "there but for the grace of God go I" (referring to the poor), and "anyone's ship might come in" (referring to the wealthy). The market, therefore, creates what I will call a "lottery effect": concentration of property ownership in a few hands is acceptable to the majority because the composition of those few was not predetermined, but rather a matter of chance, and any person could be among that select (lucky) group. This is another real illusion: while it is true that anyone can strike it rich (win the lottery), it is also true that the victory of one small group is premised on the exclusion of the rest. Nevertheless, market objectification is a major source of legitimation of differential property ownership, which would otherwise be called into question, especially in conditions of modern PFs and the associated levels of social knowledge.

B. PRODUCTION. In taking care not to fall into an overly mechanical conception of "productive forces primacy"—the idea that in the interaction between PFs and PRs the dominant causal link runs from the former to the latter—many writers in this area have neglected to give *any* account of that link. As we have seen in the preceding chapters, the PF–PR model does not require us to imagine that there is anything automatic, inevitable, or uniform in the role of the PFs shaping social evolution; Marx's "the hand mill gives you the feudal lord; the steam mill gives you the capitalist" should be taken as metaphoric, not literal. Nevertheless, the PFs do play *some* role in capitalist reproduction, and an account must be given of that role—unless we want to argue that *any* level/quality of production (PFs) can in principle be associated, in a stable manner, with *any* system of social relations (PRs).

Marx, we know, was fascinated by the Industrial Revolution—the transition from manufacture to machinofacture (see *Capital*, vol. I, part IV, especially chapter 15, "Machinery and Modern Industry")—and based his conception of the *real subsumption* of labor to capital on the massive transformations in production itself beginning in the late eighteenth century in England. Two features of this transition may be identified as perhaps central for present purposes: the division of labor within production, and the transfer of power to regulate work from the worker to the machine. The former establishes the irreversible and massive interdependence of industrial labor; it requires, and therefore legitimizes, hierarchical relations among shop-floor workers, foremen, and supervisors. The systems of authority that emerge in capitalist conditions would not be conceivable without production developed to a certain degree of complexity. Repressive hierarchy and the separation of creative and managerial functions from the workforce are, of course, not automatic or necessary features of PF development; in the spirit of the interactive approach developed in chapter 1, capitalist PRs shape those workplace relations in ways that are ultimately functional for capitalist reproduction. The point at present is only that certain degrees of PF development are a precondition for the formation of a managerial stratum—a power elite—within production, and this stratum, as we will see, plays a vital part in the reproduction and legitimization of the capitalist social upper class.

Transfer of control over the pace of work to the machine, or assembly line, or to the workstation programming function, and away from the worker, is also a feature of specifically capitalist PF development as shaped by capitalist PRs. Relations within the workplace are antagonistic, involving coercion: compelling activity against the will of the individuals performing it. The advent of machinofacture is ideal for this purpose; the engineering culture of a capitalist society will see that factory production evolves in a way that does not permit control over the quality of the labor process by workers, either individually or collectively—regardless of the impact of this restriction on productivity and productivity growth.

Capitalist PRs, especially the driving force of market incentives when labor activity is reduced to the status of consumption of a commodity sold by workers, are a powerful engine for *combined* extensive and intensive productive forces development (refer again to figure 1.2, chap. 1). In explaining how those PRs exist and are reproduced in their pure (AST) form, however, we will also need to invoke properties of the PFs that become defining for capitalism, with the transition from formal to real subsumption of labor in the industrial transformation of production.

c. THE STATE. As we will see in chapter 5, our present inquiry focuses on a particular stage of development within the capitalist era, in which the PRs finally emerge as spontaneously self-reproducing: the discipline that makes surplus extraction possible exists within production itself, without requiring external systems of domination (armies, police, etc.). This "liberal" stage is characterized by a passive state. As usual, this passivity can only be clearly observed at the level of the AST; uneven historical development, diffusion and cross-fertilization make it hard to observe this stage at a particular moment in the chronological record, as empirical historians will quickly point out. (The full stadial model of the capitalist era is presented in chapter 5.) Nevertheless, in the United States and Britain, the countries of the Anglo-Saxon model of capitalist accumulation (see Rosenthal 2000–01), the repressive functions of the state and its involvement in production and economic management are relatively attenuated in the classical liberal period of the nineteenth century and into the twentieth (until the Great Depression); this is the empirical ground for the theoretical conception of a liberal stage of capitalism in which the state plays an essentially passive and minimal role.

Even here, however, and apart from its constant presence in wars and in repression of trade unions, strikes, and other forms of resistance from below, the state has two crucial roles to play.

First, the legal process of contract regulation and enforcement gives the sanctity and legitimacy of state authority to the rights of ownership exercised over productive property, enhanced as always by the assimilation of productive property—property in means of production—to property in general. I won't say more about this function here; it will become significant when we consider the reproduction of differential property ownership, below.

The second role, however, requires more extended comment. This is the part played by state institutions in creating *national* identity and consciousness.

In the slave MP, ideology is more or less irrelevant; slaves are subject to direct and brutal physical confinement and coercion, and slaveowners care little about what they think. (This, of course, is less true of *upper-stratum* slaves; their relatively privileged position, however, rests on the viability of the bedrock slave PRs.) Feudal PRs, by contrast, require and therefore develop an ideological component, based (in England and northwestern Europe) on the Roman Catholic Church and the hold of religious authority over the minds of peasants and serfs, but also including moral rationalizations of feudal hierarchy, privilege, and obligations.

Capitalist PRs, as we must expect, require still more developed systems of ideological control, which play a much more central part in the overall reproduction of capitalist power. In particular, in the absence of the earlier direct or indirect forms of physical coercion, and given the market ideology propounding the abstract equality of individuals, sources of identification must be found that replace consciousness of social class in the thinking of the subordinate population. National identification and patriotism thus emerge as a system of social control, and the *political* power elite comes to embody this identification. The state and its representatives, then, serve as the symbolic basis both for deflection of class consciousness to national consciousness in the population in general, and for the projection of the national qualities onto upper-stratum individuals and lifestyles—the social upper class that, as we will see, is one of the sites performing a vital function for surplus extraction.

With this brief convocation of principles—the market, production, the state—in tow, we can now proceed to a similarly concentrated survey of the three sites—the workplace, property relations, the social upper class. The sites, in turn, will serve as the basis for a multidimensional theory of surplus extraction in the pure capitalist economy, liberal stage.

The Sites for the Capitalist Class Process

A. THE WORKPLACE. Not much needs to be said about the actual site at which the labor process unfolds, except to insist—against the powerful sensation of inevitability that accompanies a massive social reality—that it is not obvious why workers submit, day after day, year after year, to the despotism of workplace relations, and to the entire set of conditions enforcing hours of work, intensity of work, productivity, and the level of the real wage rate that result in surplus extraction. The image of the powerful foreman or capitalist supervisor, exuding authority and an intimidating presence, is compelling. We will, however, not want to take this for granted. What reasons prevent workers from individually or collectively resisting the force of that image, and challenging workplace authority? "The absence of alternatives" is a good way to begin, but that absence itself must be spelled out and explained.

B. DIFFERENTIAL PROPERTY OWNERSHIP. The concentration of ownership over productive assets in the hands of a minority is, of course, the central reality behind the transition to capitalism, and there is every reason to give this a central place in the theory. It must be remembered, however, that in capitalist conditions this is a matter of *property* relations, that is, a legal form. It is not a matter of, for example, minority monopolization of land by feudal lords, enforced by military might backed up by religious authority. In capitalist society differential *control* over means of production is established via ownership of legal titles to property, titles that are oblivious to any actual roles, capacities, or properties of the individuals who hold them. Titles to property are effective to the extent that the law underlying them is accepted by the subject population. We will want to know how that acceptance is guaranteed and made to persist over time.

The irony of capitalist PRs consists in the very proposition that *free* individuals—who, after all, by definition enter only into voluntary exchanges—can be exploited at all. The heart of Marx's *Capital* is, of course, the value-theoretic explanation for this "equal exchange that reproduces inequality" (Nicolaus 1967). In an attempt to give a rigorous explanation for this central feature of capitalism without incurring the liabilities associated with a substance of value, the Analytical Marxist school of recent years has taken differential property ownership as a datum, and argued that, on its basis, free (unrestrained) competition among rational individuals will result in transfer of labor (or products of labor) from those who own little or no property to those who own some or all (Roemer 1982, 1988; cf. Hahnel 2002). This is quite compelling: one can "derive" exploitation—the existence of antagonistic classes—using nothing other than the core assumptions of orthodox (neoclassical) economics: individuals, with fully formed rational (i.e., consistent) preferences, maximizing utility subject to natural and technical constraints, in an institutional framework that allows only voluntary, contractual interactions with other individuals. A Marxist conclusion is reached *from inside* a non-Marxist conceptual shell, and this constitutes an immanent critique of that shell. The problem with this—and it is a serious one—is that the conclusion—transfer of labor from workers to owners—is contained in the premise—differential ownership. It is precisely that differential, its stable legitimation, and reproduction of its real foundation in differential *control* over the labor process, that must be explained. Moreover, the coercive, alienating and dehumanizing quality of the labor transfer disappears in an account based solely on differential ownership among rational individuals who do not partake of any structural divisions into social classes other than the ownership relation itself. If workers are maximizing their utility by selling their labor-power to property owners (capitalists), why should they care if they are being exploited?

C. THE SOCIAL UPPER CLASS. The capitalist class, a defining component of capitalist PRs, has three essential moments, corresponding to the sites enumerated here. Management and ownership are the two of these already discussed; the third is the social upper class, which is a site of specialized consumption and social interaction, among households that are very different from the working-class households that effectuate the spontaneous reproduction of labor power. There is a large literature on the sociology of the social upper class (Baltzell 1964, 1989; Lundberg 1968; Mills 2000; Domhoff 1967; Bourdieu 2003) from which we may distill some key ingredients.

The social upper class is a site of differential consumption. It has the trappings of luxury entertainments, social occasions, expensive cultural activities, all encased in a series of institutions designed for the reproduction of its social exclusivity: debutante balls (to "corral the democratic inclinations of libidinal impulses"—Domhoff 1967), restricted-membership clubs, charitable organizations, and so forth. This carefully controlled social space serves several functions for class reproduction. First and (perhaps) foremost, it gives to members of the upper class a degree of identity and separateness, and of distance from the rest of society, which motivates and justifies the sense of mission to lead and control. Second, the social upper class' distinctive lifestyle and privilege serve as an incentive for members of what G. W. Domhoff, borrowing and reshaping a term from C. Wright Mills, calls the "power elite"—the actual operatives in leading positions within controlling institutions, both within the sphere of production and in wider political, educational, social, and religious spheres. Membership in the power elite is often achieved via promotion through the lower ranks of the class structure, usually of talented and ambitious individuals from the formally educated (professional) strata of the working or middle classes. This accomplishes two important regulating goals: it draws potential leadership up and away from the working class, depriving that class of a crucial ingredient for resistance and political independence; and it motivates the upwardly mobile individuals by inculcating in them values and aspirations consistent with capitalist rule.

A third function of the social upper class, perhaps less often noticed than the first two, lies in its relation to the national symbolic heritage. With disproportionate access to resources, the social upper class becomes the repository of the highest expressions of the nation in diverse areas: literature, art, music, patronage of science and scientific research, museums and the academic cultivation of the historical record—in a word, the many activities that embody knowledge and social leadership in their specific national form. This role of the capitalist upper class is of course in direct lineage to earlier ruling classes, which were, as noted in chapter 1, the site of the surplus-based leisure (in the narrow sense of liberation from productive labor) that alone can give rise to science, culture, art, mathematics, philosophy. This heritage, taking a national form in the capitalist era, is, as we know, a fundamental source of PF development. In the present context, we are more interested in its role in social legitimation. The social upper class acquires its legitimacy and acceptance by the broad population, because it appears as necessary for the production and maintenance of the very knowledges and practices that *define who we are*: determine the national identity that, in turn, deflects consciousness away from class, and therefore enables surplus extraction. In this role, as we have seen, the social upper class derives its power over the national by disproportionately contributing functionaries to the state, and by coming to share and wield patriotic symbols that are attached to state institutions. In effect, the state and the social upper class cooperate in establishing and maintaining national identity: its symbols, rituals, holidays, observances, and envidious distinctions vis-à-vis other nations and the rest of the world.

II. THE HOLOGRAPHIC DETERMINATION OF SURPLUS EXTRACTION

We now have three principles—the market, the developed form of capitalist production, and the state—and three sites—the workplace, the system of ownership, and the social upper class. With all of these ingredients in place, it is now possible to sketch out a view of exploitation, or surplus extraction, that draws upon the interaction of the principles and the sites, rather than reducing the process to any one of them in a one-sided, and to that extent superficial, way.

The story is told in figure 3.1, and as usual in our conceptual-geometric approach to theory, the reader is asked to consult this figure throughout the following discussion.

In section 1 above all of the foundations have been laid for this proposed synthesis. Everything interacts with everything else, of course, but if we can propose some priorities—some structuring of the relative proximities of various elements—we can get a better sense of that interaction.

The Inner Ring

It may be best to work from inside out. The figure suggests, as I have hinted above, that surplus extraction draws upon, and requires, all three of the entities I have called "sites": the workplace, differential or monopolized ownership, and the social upper class. These sites are, in an appealing metaphor, the three legs of a three-legged stool; the stability of the stool is undermined if any one of them is absent.

Differential ownership is fairly obvious, and is captured by the Analytical Marxist literature (Roemer 1982, 1988; Wright et al. 1992; cf. Hahnel 2002). It is the legal counterpart to the classic conception of dispossession of the means of production from one of the two defining classes of capitalist PRs, and their accumulation in the hands of the other. Widely legitimated differential ownership establishes the legal right of the employer to purchase labor power, and to exercise authority over that labor power in the performance of labor, once purchased. The lack of access to nature that drives members of the dispossessed class—the proletariat—to seek wages in exchange for labor capacity is embodied in this differential ownership, which must therefore be seen as one compelling moment of surplus extraction.

The capitalist also, however, has the authority to empower its managers and functionaries in the workplace to exercise discipline at that site. Once the wage bargain is struck, the worker enters into production and submits to the authority of managers who owe their allegiance to the firm's owners. Again, we need to hold onto the distinctiveness of capitalist PRs, and not succumb to the tendency to simply assume the obvious: people "work because they have to," and "it is too tiring to disobey authority." Accepting workplace discipline can be explained in this simple inertial manner for the short term, but in a more fundamental sense this sort of descriptive explanation degenerates into no explanation at all, or, rather, what Leslie White (1969) called "metaphysicial explanation"—"explaining" a reality by naming a cause that is nothing other than the reality itself, in other words. *Why* is it "too tiring" to challenge established authority? What prevents that authority from eroding over time and succumbing to, for example, a massive counter-challenge from a democratically constituted shop-floor structure of authority, one that accepts the principle of workplace organization and discipline, but seeks to change the priorities shaping them?

Clearly, the power of command in the workplace and the power of ownership interact and enable one another. Faced with challenges within the workplace, managers point to forces outside of their control: we, too, after all, are subject to hiring and firing by the firm's owners. Faced with challenges to their ownership, owners point to ownership in general: we are only exercising the same claim you do when you dispose of personal property in a manner chosen by yourself. Ownership and control at the point of production are mutually supporting bases for the antagonistic compulsion of labor to generate a surplus over subsistence.

The figure, however, suggests that this two-way interaction is not sufficient to guarantee this result. The third leg of the stool, the social upper class, plays an independent role in the process, regardless of the extent to which that class' existence and lifestyle are present in the consciousness of the society as a whole. The upper class is, as noted above, a crucial motivator and ideological controller for the power elite, including that part of the power elite represented by economic management. The authority of management rests on the sense that in implementing production in the forms designed for capitalist surplus extraction, it is merely carrying out the purpose of "the nation" in guaranteeing the life and development of "our society," "civilization," and so forth. Since these shared values are embodied in the practices and social image of the upper class, they acquire authority and help deflect any challenges that might arise from alternative hegemonies or legitimating systems.

To summarize regarding the inner mechanism of figure 3.1: Any of the three sites alone would be insufficient to explain surplus extraction. If, for example, one were to concentrate on workplace authority alone, in the absence of precapitalist forms of coercion, it would be difficult to explain the effectiveness of the authority of managers, at least over the longer term, especially in view of the level of the PFs associated with post–Industrial

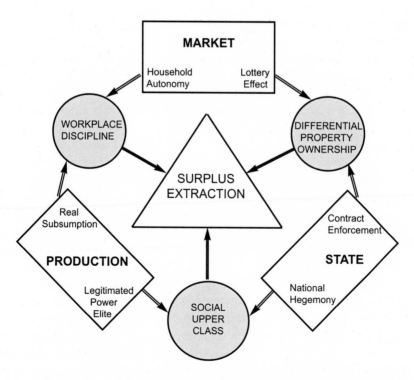

Figure 3.1. The Causal Multiplicity of Capitalist Exploitation

Revolution capitalism and the degree of devolution of control required to operate them effectively (see chap. 4 for more on this.) Workplace authority must rely on its instantiation within a wider social legitimacy, to which the social upper class makes a decisive contribution. It also relies on the accepted system of differential ownership, which makes capitalist power impersonal and hard to pin down.

One can, in fact, offer a parable, about a disgruntled worker who is seeking to locate and identify the source of her exploitation, approaching this problem, of course, in terms of perceived and perceptible social realities without benefit of the conceptual tools that will eventually—we may hope!— give her access to the deep-structural levels of the reality in which she lives. She first confronts the foreman, who is the immediate transmission belt for her troubles. The foreman tells her—truthfully!—that he is just another employee, and that if he fails to "motivate" the work teams under his jurisdiction, he will be replaced. He suggests she see the plant supervisor. She does so. The super tells her—again, truthfully!—that he is appointed by mid-level management, and is obliged to carry out management's wishes. One can see here, immediately, the role of the complex hierarchy associated with the capitalist production principle; see below, under the "outer ring" of figure 3.1. If our worker finally gets to talk to top management—no small achievement—she will then be told that even the CEO of the firm is ultimately hired by the stockholders, and here we make the transition from the workplace site to that of ownership. Stock ownership in private corporations is, of course, not a matter of public record, but we may assume our worker is able to get ahold of a list. She will discover that a typical shareholder in the firm is a mutual fund, which in turn holds the shares in the name of—people like herself! To make the story more poignant, assume that she picks a stockholder at random, and winds up with a poor widow, supporting herself and her children on the dividends from her shares, dividends that depend ultimately on the foreman's power to sweat the worker who has made this discovery. In this way, ownership-in-general serves as a mask for capitalist ownership.

But even if our worker persists, and finds her way to a *principal* stockholder, who exercises a controlling interest and therefore can be held responsible for policy, she will be deflected again, in two ways. First, the capitalist now in her company will insist—and, once again, truthfully!—that his firm is subject to the laws of the marketplace; this anticipates the outer-ring discussion, below. The firm's policies are dictated by the competitive struggle for survival and growth, and these are no one's responsibility; they exist independently, apparently, of all human will. This is the heart of Marx's dictum: "capital exists as many capitals." Second, the capitalist will tell our worker that the policies followed by the firm are in line with established social traditions that guarantee the maintenance of the finer aspects of our society, our nation, our civilization—as embodied in the institutions and practices of the social upper class. She will be confronted with the carefully cultivated and managed conception that the entire social "body" depends on the health of its "head"; that to remove the *social leadership* would be to plunge society into authoritarian ruin. (One thinks in this connection of Orwell's *Animal Farm.*)

The social upper class, of course, would also be a poor basis, in isolation, for surplus extraction. If it becomes too visible, its lifestyle becomes a source, not of personal envy, but of political opposition. (See the discussion of "legitimation crisis," chap. 4). The social upper class can, in capitalist conditions, only play its defining role when its wealth takes the form of differential market-based property ownership.

Differential ownership, as we have seen, is the most convincing candidate for a go-it-alone basis for surplus extraction. The logic is compelling, but by itself it reduces exploitation to an individual process that loses its interest, not to speak of its life-destroying qualities. Explanations based on differential ownership alone cannot adequate characterize exploitation, or explain why the ownership differential cannot be progressively eroded, as in some extant proposals for a "market socialism" (Roemer 1994), what in fact used to be called "people's capitalism." In the inner ring of figure 3.1, differential ownership, workplace discipline, and the ideological-cultural-political power of the social upper class all work together to enable surplus extraction, in a pure capitalist MP, that is, absent all forms of precapitalist coercion. The outer ring, in turn, will go beyond this point, to explain the permanence and effectiveness of the inner-ring sites.

The Outer Ring

Again, the elements have all been put into place, in section 1. Starting from the workplace, we ask, again, *how* capitalism's representatives there make their authority credible and effective, and continue to do so over a historical time period of stable capitalist evolution. The answer suggested in the figure is that it rests on contributions from two of the "principles": the market, and production.

The market is the great abstractor of social relations. It is how the interviewer in the firm's hiring hall is able to tell a worker (when he is first hired): "You will get the going wage rate, and be expected to perform in the same way as everywhere else"; that is, we are not imposing the terms and conditions of work upon you, the "market" is doing that. The labor market thus instantiates an aura of social irresponsibility, which renders the power of capital impersonal, and to that extent unaddressable. The worker is forced to submit to the discipline of a particular workplace, because he has no prior right to a connection to that workplace, or to any workplace in general. The "great transformation" (Polanyi 1957) removed any social responsibility for his very existence, and this imposes a continuing coercive force that is *defined by* his freedom: he can walk away from any wage-employment bargain, and can therefore enter into any bargain only of his own free will.

Figure 3.1 suggests also that the market form of capitalist social relations works upon the workplace in a special way through the household autonomy feature. When the worker leaves the workplace after a work shift, he "returns home," where home is a physically and socially separate space. The social ideology maintains that "at home, the worker is king." This royal authority, indeed, has often been exercised by male workers in an oppressive manner over other members of the household, but especially over its other principal adult member, the housewife. The oppression of women within the household—a central feature of classical capitalist accumulation that is progressively eroded at a later stage, a story that we will not pursue here—plays, then, two roles. First, it serves as an ideological deflector of the potential rage of the (male) worker at his employer, and therefore as an enabler of workplace discipline, one of the three legs of the surplus extraction stool. The worker's wife serves as a scapegoat. Second, the labor of the housewife is fundamental to the processing of goods obtained by the household from the capitalist consumer-goods sector. Without that labor, the capacity to work would not be adequately reproduced, and the system whereby the worker brings "his" commodity to market, to participate in the wage-employment negotiation on a formally equal basis, would lose its foundation. One need only think of what the wage rate would have to be if the worker had to pay for the cooking, childrearing, and cleaning services of the homemaker, if contracted for on the market. The existence of the housewife within the household, then, makes the market-basing of workplace discipline possible. Without going into the implications of this for current developments in which the family wage has been progressively eroded and working-class women have massively entered the labor force, we can see that the switch from indirect to direct exploitation of female labor is simultaneously a partial liberation of women from an oppressive status—only partial until working-class culture can irreversibly conquer the redistribution of housework on an equal basis—and a cannibalization of the household, with significant implications both for the quality of working-class life (especially with regard to the environment for raising children) and for the continued reproduction of the *real illusion* of the independence and autonomy of the labor-power commodity.

The production principle also contributes to the reproduction of workplace discipline, in that the level of complexity, division of labor and need for hierarchical coordination typical of the advanced PFs generated by the capitalist transition require and legitimate the real subsumption of labor to capital: surrendering of control over, and understanding of, the production process, whose pace, intensity and impact on the work experience are now governed by higher authorities within the workplace and transmitted to the worker through machinery and other means of production, surveillance and control.

Moving counterclockwise around the outer circle of figure 3.1, we note the role of the production principle also in supporting the social upper class. The social upper class in most periods of its existence cannot produce, from within its own ranks. all of the individuals needed to staff the directive positions in the power-elite institutions; it must draw from the lower ranks of society for this purpose. Indeed, according to Marx (as quoted by Baltzell), "the more the upper class is able to assimilate into its ranks the most talented members of the lower strata of society, the more stable and dangerous its rule." The transmission belt for this crucial continuing process of upward assimilation is the power elite, the core of which is attached to the production process; for the present purpose, we can think of that process broadly, to include many aspects of social production—education, state-directed social support functions, and the like. The stability of the social upper class, in terms of both its membership and its ideological power and acceptance within the society overall, depends crucially on its relation to the power elite, which in turn rests on the valid role of that specialized skilled managerial and creative stratum determined within modern production conditions.

The social upper class also draws upon its connection with the state in its role as embodiment of the symbols, institutions, and rituals of national identification. It achieves its hegemonic role, in the classical Gramscian sense of successfully establishing its values as those spontaneously held within the wider population, partly but significantly through its connection to state authority, which enables it to speak for "the nation," or "the people." This is the role of the state principle in supporting the social upper class as one of the three interacting sites enabling surplus extraction.

The state is also the repository of the legal system: a structure of civil law regarding contracts and other business practices, as well as both civil and criminal avenues of redress for wrongs committed in the course of management of property relations. The importance of this for the maintenance of property ownership in general, and differential ownership, in particular, should be clear. As usual, in capitalist conditions, the crucial differential aspects are upheld by these being part of a wider realm of noncapitalist relations. The authority of ownership over workplaces that determine the lives of tens of thousands, ultimately millions of workers is established and enforced through the same legal machinery as authority over personal property, and the latter legitimates and enables the former.

Continuing in counterclockwise movement, we return—rightly—to the market as a major enabler of differential ownership. Again, and in contrast to the Analytical Marxist position, the analysis here refuses to regard differential ownership as the ultimate datum, the preexisting fact, for a theory of capitalist exploitation. It must itself be explained. In addition to the necessary role of the state in contract enforcement, the market works in various ways to support the continued existence and efficacy of differential ownership of the core social productive assets—not least by mystifying it, as noted above, and assimilating it to ownership in general, of both personal property and of small-scale productive property. Differential ownership, in effect, can only exist in the absence of precapitalist coercive systems, because it takes on a market form, and its exercise is therefore transmitted to those affected by that exercise in the form of impersonal, spontaneous market "reality"—"elemental," like the weather, outside of human control and responsibility. When any social relations put on the mask of market relations, the result is fetishism and mystification of underlying social reality. When a social process of antagonistic surplus extraction—exploitation— is embodied in differential ownership in the market, the result is a concentrated expression of the more general fetishism and mystification. This concentration involves nothing less than a magnification of the power-to-exploit, and consequent intensification of the results of that exploitation. The market form of capitalist social relations makes possible a quality and degree of surplus extraction power that would be inaccessible to the most charismatic warlord or demagogue, the most authoritarian political leader, the cleverest thinker, or the monarch or religious ruler most endowed with power associated with popular superstition. Nothing but the magnifying effect of capitalist market relations can ultimately explain the unprecedented reach of the power of a handful of transnational financial giants in the world of today's neoliberal global aggression, which is creating a world polarization of income and wealth and transforming the social landscape, with dire consequences for ecological and human survival, over entire continents. The multiple millions of people affected by this onslaught would never accept it, would rise against it in a (historical) minute, if it did not take on the form of an "inevitable" event not under the control of any responsible party, against which no opposition is possible ("there is no alternative").

This is the most general point that can be made in the development of a political-economic view of "the market"—the "embedded" market, as a social and therefore evolving form, rather than an abstract expression of interactions among rational individuals. This market, as it has evolved to specifically capitalist forms, concentrates economic power. The contrary claim of neoclassical economics, most forcefully expressed in the classic work by Milton Friedman (1962, 2002), to the effect that "the competitive market" disperses political power, because it disperses economic power, rests on a symptomatically superficial view of all three terms (market, economic, and political power).

Aside from the general efficacy of the valorization of social relations—the central point of the PF–PR model regarding the necessity and effectiveness of capitalist PRs at a given stage of PF evolution—we may conclude by noting the specific role of the "lottery effect" in supporting differential ownership. Any attack on a capitalist's "right" to dispose of my labor power as it pleases appears simultaneously to be an attack on *my* right to dispose of my personal property as I please. I am tempted to think that there is an outside, if small, chance that I, or my children, might win a lottery—literally or figuratively—and get to dispose of vast quantities of wealth. (Most working people, in my experience—mainly with working-class students—have no conception of this wealth as a repository of abstract power, and think only in terms of upper-class levels of luxury consumption.) I therefore make a Rawlsian deal: I accept a long upper tail on the income distribution, in exchange for a minute chance that I or my family might some day occupy that tail.

III. SUMMARIZING AND CONCLUDING

Figure 3.1 is, like all of the conceptual geometry proposals in this study, an evolving conception. It is an attempt to make persuasive my belief that capitalist exploitation, as the most highly evolved in a long chain of successively more complex antagonistic PRs, is not in any way obvious. In the conception traced out here, it is based on the interaction of three sites—workplace, ownership, upper class—and in a sense is like a holographic projection, in which the sites are the beams of light, none of which alone can produce the image; only the interaction of all together can do that. The sites, in turn, require explanation; their reproduction draws on the three larger principles—the rectangles in the figure. These are not necessarily equal in their effectivity. The market may be first among equals among the principles, but it is the *capitalist* market (not "the" market, let alone that horrendous abuse of language, the "free market"); it is also the product of social evolution, and it does not act alone. Confined within market logic, the essence of capitalist exploitation gets lost.

The laudable effort of the Analytical Marxist authors to place the theory of exploitation and class on a secure foundation ultimately fails to convince, because it confines its attention to rational actors who have lost all social character, and reduces all relevant processes to those involving optimal choice among such actors. While this strategy truly enables John Roemer, and others, to get under the skin of their mainstream economics counterparts—and anything that accomplishes this is worthwhile at some level—it is ultimately too high a price to pay. The conception developed in this chapter suggests that, in addition to the logic of optimal choice in the interaction between those with property and those without, there are other systematic tendencies at work—such as the formation of uniform expectations concerning the terms of the wage bargain, the nature and extent of the authority of workplace managers, and the consensus supporting leadership by the social upper class and its representatives and hegemonic adoption of their overall project—that also play essential roles in the reproduction of exploitation and class. In fact, the differential ownership that gives rise to surplus extraction cannot itself be explained outside of this wider framework.

The wider framework also explains, at least potentially, why exploitation cannot be reduced simply to the transfer of labor, or the product of labor, from one class to another. Even exploitation in general, that is, across all antagonistic MPs, has a richer content than this: the extraction of surplus is coercive, and therefore inherently conflictual, and destructive to the subordinate (laboring) class in the absence of resistance and struggle from below. Capitalist exploitation begins as part of this general picture, but the conflictual and destructive aspects, as well as the purely extractive ones, now acquire additional historically specific features, associated with the precise institutional and structural qualities stemming from the historically unprecedented level and pace of PF development. These features stem from reification and alienation, as these terms progress from being characterizations of the valorization of the core social relations—amply discussed above—to becoming part of the psychological and social reality of life in capitalist society: the sense of estrangement from one's own labor activity, from other people, from social purpose. Characterization of capitalist exploitation thus involves *rich abstraction*; we need to think about capitalism in general in richly complex terms, even though we are still talking only about an abstract foundation for the analysis of actual capitalist social formations, with unique cultures, histories, and interactions with varieties of precapitalist formations. The goal is to hold onto the general within the specific, without reducing the general to still more general features of social reality as such, or identifying "capitalism" with existential conditions of human life, such as "scarcity" or "desire for betterment" (Adam Smith), or, indeed, some transhistorical notion of "complexity" or the "modern." Finally, we need to find and study this complex abstraction, the core of capitalism, without eclectic juxtapositions involving perceptions of particular institutions and structures, as in the various hyphenated "capitalisms" partially enumerated at the beginning of this chapter. Like the task of theorizing socialism, addressed in Part III and mentioned in the Preface, truly a tall order.

This chapter has offered an initial presentation toward an adequate picture of what the late Robert Heilbroner called the "nature" of capitalism (see Heilbroner 1985)—its inner reality considered statically, not in a large sense involving timeless, ahistorical abstractions (that would be contrary to the entire spirit of this study), but only in the sense that the effort here is to grasp *what* capitalist PRs are, before attempting to see how they evolve. The latter study involves the "logic" of capitalism (Heilbroner's terminology again), and is the topic of the next chapter, on the path of development of capitalism and the development of crisis within it. There we build upon the elements summarized in figure 3.1, but place them into a more dynamic framework. The focus, however, is still on a classical liberal stage of development, in which the core properties of capitalist accumulation emerge most clearly. Chapter 5 then represents a synthesis of the "nature" and the "logic," returning to the stadial approach of chapters 1 and 2 in an attempt to sketch out a model of theoretical stages for the capitalist era as a whole.

Chapter 4

THE LOGIC OF CAPITALISM

Growth and Crisis

I n the last chapter, we got a sense of the enormous complexity of capitalist PRs. To describe the core exploitation process defining them means to grapple with valorization of social relations: the commodity form enables and perpetuates differential ownership of and access to means of production, and the latter enables surplus extraction in the most general case of "pure" competition and unhindered access to markets. Leaving to one side, for the moment, the difficulties of transition to capitalism and the original formation of the conditions for its stable reproduction, we now have the elements in place to understand the core capitalist process. The dependence of workers on capitalists for employment, and the power of capitalists to extract surplus, in value form, on the basis of ownership, involve all of the moments of the capitalist class process. These include: the formal, political equality of the worker as abstract citizen; the autonomy of the working-class household sector (where labor power is produced as a commodity), and of public space (where the workers' citizenship is established and validated); the elemental, "natural" quality of "the market"; the pervasive presence of property relations at all levels of society, which legitimizes the specifically capitalist instances of those relations; the valorization of labor power and of capital (the stock market); the transmission of power from ownership to management; and the reproduction of managerial authority in the workplace. This singularly complex system of incentive, control, and coercion now makes possible a *combination* of extensive and intensive principles in the growth of the PFs (the reader may now refer, once again, to figure 1.2 of chap. 1, the segment referring to "capitalism" in the stadial progression of MPs). The bringing together of scale and productivity is the "colossal" development of the forces of production (Marx and Engels 1998) that surpasses everything accomplished in the precapitalist epochs, resulting in the industrial and electronic revolutions that secure the reproduction of capitalist PRs (see Schorsch 1980–81).

In contrast to the theory of the slave and feudal MPs, the theory of capitalist development requires, as we will see in detail in chapter 5, a second stadial conception, nested within the "macro" stadiality of the PF–PR model. I will not address the details of that conception here, except to note that much of the work done in the general political economy of capitalism in effect refers to a particular stage of development—the one that immediately transcends the prehistory of "primitive" or "mercantile" accumulation of capital. For present purposes, it is enough to state that the diffusion of market relations and the differentiation of the population of peasant producers into propertied and propertyless classes has progressed to a point at which the social and territorial homogeneity of the social space now permits spontaneous surplus extraction and accumulation to occur. In other words, a flash point—culmination of centuries of commercialization, expropriation, colonization, and plunder—is reached, at which the power-to-exploit need not be imported as a supplement to the production relations within the labor process itself, but rather has come to coincide with those relations. Capitalism *is* the stage of antagonistic class development in which the market form "takes over" the core surplus extraction process and "enters" the PRs; once its manifest superiority to the preexisting forms becomes evident those forms, as embodied in communal organizations, guilds, but especially in the precapitalist state and its military apparatus, wither away rather quickly. This is the classic stage of capitalist development, in which state power has atrophied and become passive, and capital has become self-regulating and self-reproducing.

Attention in this chapter will be focused on this classical stage (to be defined more precisely in the next chapter). We now turn, however, from the conditions of existence and perpetuation of capitalist exploitation to the analysis of its dynamic of development—the "logic," as opposed to the "nature," of capitalism, in Robert Heilbroner's apt formulation. In short, this chapter will try to assemble elements for analysis, in the terms of the PF–PR model, of the "contradictions" of the capitalist MP.

I. CAPITALISM AND CRISIS: THE PROBLEM STATED

The Marxist tradition of thought about capitalist accumulation and crisis contains many interdefining elements. The classical texts, especially Marx's *Capital*, are a rich source for ideas concerning the roots of cyclical instability, as well as the processes that define capitalism's line of march—its maturation, general crisis, and eventual transcendence.

In the early twenty-first century, we see signs that capitalism is struggling toward its immanent universal quality, as globalization lurches forward and both production and class power become increasingly transnationalized (see Burbach and Robinson 1999; Robinson and Harris 2000). The mediated forms of accumulation resulting from strong and independent nation-states, as well as from the existence of spheres of influence and systems of domination-subordination in world production and markets—not to speak of revolutionary states proclaiming post-capitalist paths of development—appear to be giving way to more direct patterns, as the classical "laws" of accumulation come into their own.

Against this backdrop, we find a bewildering array of positions among Marxist political economists. Some have retreated to an implicitly agnostic view concerning the postulate of *general crisis*: not finding any of the existing models of long-term crisis convincing, they preoccupy themselves instead with labor-process studies, poverty, or other micro phenomena; document the social realities and effects of exploitation, uneven development and polarization; or elaborate on the elements of cyclical—periodic—instability in labor, commodity, and financial markets. The literatures on the workplace and the labor process draw upon much of contemporary social science, going well outside work done under the Marxist label. The interdisciplinary field of labor studies has developed in a wide-ranging manner, under both Marxist and non-Marxist umbrellas (Braverman 1974; Lembcke 1995). Post-Keynesian economics has also explored sources and sites of crisis in capitalist economies, with particular attention to the financial sphere (Davidson 1994; Minsky 1982). All of this work provides valuable material for synthesis. Whether in Marxist or other theoretical frames, however, it does not envision that synthesis or contribute directly to it.

Under the rubric of "crisis theory" we find a range of positions, from "weak" to "strong." At the "weak" end some theorists seek to show that capitalism, organized through spontaneous market competition and irresponsible private accumulation, always contains the *possibility* of periodic instability and disorganization, which result in social loss and suffering. In this view, it is enough to note that the anarchy of capitalist production always makes possible the instability and associated human suffering that have come to be accepted realities of life in capitalist societies. Addressing instability and suffering then becomes a matter for ameliorative policy only, and social reform is not driven by any underlying pressure coming from the PRs; it is simply a matter of finding the will to do better.

Moving along the spectrum a bit, we find a claim that the outcome of periodic crisis, statistically possible, actually becomes *inevitable*. This is in part due to a sort of statistical Murphy's Law—what can happen will happen. But it also comes closer to the historical materialist conception developed in this book: it sees the capitalist process as class-antagonistic, yielding a stronger sense of the inevitability of crisis. Cyclical crises *must* occur, in this scenario, due to the unavoidable need for periodic restructuring of accumulation and class relations. This, in turn, has two basic elements. First, in order to function without systemic crisis, capitalism needs to periodically rediscipline the working class and reproduce the proletarian dependency on which the extraction of surplus value rests. Second, it needs to shake out weak units of capital and consolidate capitalist power in a form suitable for continuing accumulation (Clarke 1990–91; Weeks 1981; Sherman 1972).

However, even the most persuasive depiction of the *inevitability* of *periodic* crisis does not establish the historically delimited character of capitalism in general. It describes capitalism as a system with inbuilt and unfortunate properties (unfortunate from the standpoint of human well being), but one that can, in principle, go on forever. From the standpoint of the general AST model, this conception has its own inadequacy—its "defect," as Marx might say—that points further along the spectrum of crisis theory. The problem is that cyclically recurring crisis, no matter how intense its effects, can eventually be foreseen, and its critical impacts subjected to institutional offset or containment. An analogy with drug addiction is apparent: there is a progressive aspect, in which given doses of a drug (or of cyclical crisis) become increasingly ineffective, making stronger doses necessary. This, of course, follows Marx's insight that what appears politically as the "crisis" is actually the *resolution* of the actual, underlying crisis: the emergence of structural contradiction on the path of accumulation. Crises that are resolved, or contained, or even significantly foreseen, do not do the work they are "designed" to accomplish (the quotation marks around "designed" warn, as usual, against a teleological reading of this term; no actual intention is implied). There is a need for crises of *increasing* severity, and, indeed, novelty, for the simple reason that any given degree of severity or novelty, once experienced, necessarily gives rise to class resistance and institutional responses, which then nullify its "creative-destructive" role. This is the core reason for capitalism's inherently "wild" character, and for its long-perceived resistance to regulation. It also constitutes the core of truth in the free-market ideological claim that policy to regulate capitalism, in the classical Keynesian mode, cannot ultimately be effective. Capitalists—not, or course, "rational individuals"—do anticipate and offset policy designed to influence their actions, and increasingly so as internationalization of production and finance place the decision-making units farther and farther beyond the reach of national governments (we look at this much more closely in the next chapter).

We have arrived at the final move along the spectrum of crisis theory to the most ambitious position: cyclical crises must not only necessarily recur; they must become progressively more severe, suggesting a *long-term* path of *intensifying* crisis.

This position corresponds most fully to the basic claim of Marxism, which sees capitalism as a historically delimited social form. Capitalism only comes into being when conditions for it are ripe. It plays a unique role in developing the productive forces and in the political and social maturation of the working class, but it then reveals its own immanent limits as a vehicle for human development, in the form of *increasingly severe* periodic instability and dislocation. The transcendence of capitalism and its replacement by social-ism/communism, then, are not a matter of mere contingency and desirability. Neither are they inevitable; they are, however, necessary for continued human development, a necessity that is revealed with ever-greater urgency, especially to the social classes that are at the receiving end of the chaos, relative deprivation, and social deterioration associated with recurring and chronic crisis.

The difficulty with attempts to stake a claim at this most ambitious end of the crisis-theory spectrum, however, is that the strong position at-tained there has not seemed to rest on secure theoretical foundations. There has always been a minority within Marxist political economy that upholds what is essentially an orthodox view, usually based on an inevitably falling rate of profit (e.g., Weeks 1981; Freeman and Carchedi 1996). However, both the quality of the theory and the occasional perversity of the evidence make this approach appear suspect in the eyes of many observers, who therefore refuse to place much weight on it. Indeed, even some of those who have upheld the falling-profit-rate approach to long-term crisis have hedged their bets by invoking the Kondratieff long cycle, suggesting that the fall-ing trend revealed in current data may in fact be followed by a fifty-year upward cycle; in this way, a cyclical theory and retreat toward the weak end of the spectrum is concealed within an apparent preoccupation with long-term trends (e.g., Shaikh, 1978).

Orthodox falling-profit-rate theory aside, other aspects of capitalist crisis that have come under study, and been emphasized by other schools within the Marxist tradition, do not bear the weight of the ambitious, increasing-severity position. Thus, a tendency to stagnation in mature capi-talism, based on insufficient aggregate demand, has been analyzed by Marx-ists influenced by John Maynard Keynes. Similarly, sources of instability located in the financial system have come under scrutiny. The "Monthly Review school" emphasizes the role of demand limitation and stagnation in the "monopoly capitalist" stage of mature capitalist evolution (see Steindl 1952; Baran and Sweezy 1966; Foster and Szlajfer 1984). Paul A. Baran and Paul M. Sweezy built their "monopoly capital" conception in opposition to some aspects of the "state monopoly capitalism" approach that was central to political economic thinking in the world Communist movement (see, e.g., Pevzner 1984). The question of stadiality *within* the capitalist MP is of great importance, and will occupy our attention in the next chapter. It cannot, however, serve as a substitute for the theory of the core contradictions in the accumulation process as such—that is, as this occurs within the "classical," or "liberal," stage of capitalist development. The studies of the labor process and workplace relations, referred to above, have indeed revealed areas of tension and inefficiency, but have never been related systematically to longer views of capitalist evolution. Similarly, the critiques of the vast inequalities in income and wealth that increasingly characterize capitalist societies—their compelling moral force aside—do not carry the required analytical weight.

Against this backdrop, and in the continuing "meta" spirit of the AST (PF–PR) approach, I will try in this chapter to build up the elements of a model of long-period, intensifying crisis of the capitalist MP—one that can stand comparison with the stadial conceptions of contradiction and crisis in the much simpler slave and feudal MPs. However, in view of the singular complexity of the capitalist case, it appears that this will require drawing together the major strands of thinking about capitalist crisis, to seek out common or complementary ingredients that might tie them into a more unified explanatory framework (for background, see Laibman 1992, ch. 12, 1997, ch. 11).

II. A TAXONOMIC OVERVIEW OF CAPITALIST CRISIS

Tendencies, Barriers, Sites: Definitions

My proposal for a framework to bring the several Marxist investigations onto common ground involves three conceptual building blocks. These are: *immanent critical tendencies*, *target variables*, and *barriers*. These elements appear in several distinct *sites* of crisis; the elaboration of these sites, and their interrelationship, forms the heart of the approach I am suggesting. I explain each of the building blocks in turn.

Any directed process in capitalist accumulation may be an "immanent critical tendency," or simply *critical tendency*, if it results in increasing tension that can only be resolved by institutional transformation, either within capitalist PRs or (eventually) beyond them. Critical tendencies affect the target variables; in fact, each critical tendency will "chase" a *pair* of target variables, forcing one or the other of these, or both, to change in determinate directions. (Note that the direction of the change is not uniform; it will vary from case to case.) The target variables, in turn, are forced into confrontations with the barriers, one for each target variable. The barriers are levels of the target variables, in the direction toward which they are being pushed, that, when reached, signal the onset of a particular form of crisis. The critical tendency, therefore, has a dilemma-like aspect: it drives a *pair* of variables into an increasingly problematic position, by, for example, requiring a choice between an increase in one variable and an increase in the other; between an increase in one variable and a decrease in the other; or between rise or fall in a target variable and its approach to a pair of strategic limits. The critical tendency thus imposes an increasingly severe tradeoff between two trends, each of which must eventually attain a strategically critical level. When a target variable reaches its barrier, this does not mechanically result in social breakdown or transformation; it does, however, make the crisis phenomena associated with the barrier value of the variable chronic and permanently present. Cyclical crisis associated with these phenomena in turn becomes "nonreproductive" (my source for this term is Gordon, et al. 1983), in the sense that the crisis phenomena cannot be transcended or the critical tension alleviated without structural change.

In this way, the model combines some of the directed or determinate quality of "immanent crisis" theory with a desirable degree of contingency in the actual path of evolution: the critical tendency places the system (at a given site; see below) on the horns of a dilemma, but does not predetermine which horn will be taken—that is, the actual path along which confrontation with the barriers will proceed. And that confrontation, in turn, does not result in any mechanically or deterministically programmed outcome. Crisis potential becomes transformation potential, but no rigid notion of "breakdown" is implied. (The dilemma-crisis model in this chapter owes much to Martin Bronfenbrenner, 1965, which applied a related conception to the process I describe at the "technical change site"; see below. See also Laibman 1983.)

Figure 4.1 is a visual aid, along the "conceptual geometry" lines guiding the presentation of many arguments in this book, that may help the reader to understand the basic elements of the process, before detailed illustrations are given. In the figure, the critical tendency is a change in the variable called A (ΔA). The downward arrow from ΔA to the target variables, B and C, is based on the structural relation among the three variables; it is not arbitrary (as we will see in the cases analyzed below). The change in A (in the given direction, not specified at this stage) requires a determinate change in B (either up or down) or a determinate change in C (or some combination of the two); these changes are represented by the double arrows showing B moving to the left, and C moving to the right. The vertical bars are the barriers. The change in A, then, forces *at least* one of the target

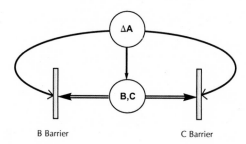

Figure 4.1. Critical Tendency and Barriers

variables toward its barrier. The situation is even more dynamically critical than the eventual confrontation between one or another target variable and a barrier, however, and this is represented by the curved arrows from ΔA to the barriers themselves. The critical tendency forces the barriers inward; that is, progressively narrows the space within which B and C are able to maneuver without confronting the barriers. Homer's famous Greek sailor, Odysseus, was forced to travel between twin evils: Scylla, a seven-headed monster who would eat seven of his men if he sailed in that direction, and Charybdis, a whirlpool that would destroy the entire ship. Odysseus, according to legend, chose Scylla—the lesser evil. Capitalism. however, faces a more dire situation—in each critical site; see below—in which Scylla and Charybdis move progressively closer together as accumulation proceeds.

Figure 4.1 captures the critical tendency/target variable/barrier process as fully as may be possible, without mathematical formalization. In preparation for figure 4.3, the main heuristic tool of this chapter, however, the relation between changes in the critical tendency, A, and its twin target variables, B and C, can be depicted more simply; this is done in figure 4.2. There, the barriers, pressure on the barriers from the critical tendency, and the oppositional movement of the target variables are not shown; all we see is that A causes, alternatively or jointly, change in B and C, as shown by the causal arrows running from ΔA to ΔB and ΔC. Figure 4.3 constructs an overlapping and interlocking network of these relations among the three variables—in effect, a system of relationships, each as depicted in figure 4.2.

A final preliminary point may be made here. The force of the theory obviously requires substantiation not only of the critical tendency—the necessity that the critical-tendency variable will evolve in the stated direction—but also of the position and efficacy of the barriers. How far, for example, must the target variable B move, in the required direction, in order for the crisis phenomena associated with B to become nonreproductive? As we will see below, barriers at one site may define a strategic level of the critical-tendency variable,

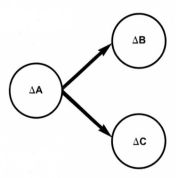

Fig 4.2. Critical Tendency and Alternative Critical Paths

A, which then operates as a barrier at another site. A barrier at one site, therefore, is defined by the critical process at work at another. There must, of course, be some "ultimate" barriers at certain sites, in the sense that they are not defined by critical processes occurring elsewhere.

The Sites: A Guided Tour

The following survey of the terrain will be conducted in entirely intuitive terms, as throughout this book; readers desiring a more formal treatment should consult Laibman (2000, appendix). The number, naming, and juxtaposition of sites is an evolving conception, and no claim is made that the version outlined here is final or complete in any sense. The purpose of the exercise is to show how we might proceed to bring the studies of the various parts of the capitalist political economy together, and how the critical quality of capitalist accumulation is revealed most fully through an interactive and comprehensive conception.

The tour that follows refers to a single comprehensive diagram of crisis sites and their associated tendency/barriers dynamics, presented here as figure 4.3, to which the reader, as always, is invited to turn continuously throughout the discussion in this section.

THE CENTRAL SITE. We begin with a process that is arguably the root of capitalist dynamics, but has not usually been regarded as a *critical* tendency: the secular rise in the productivity of labor. This is the intensive aspect of PF growth, and its substantiation goes all the way back to the emergence of symbolic reference and human labor, with its inherent tendency to transformation of the environment. The empirical reality of a rising trend in productivity is not generally in doubt, except of course for specu-

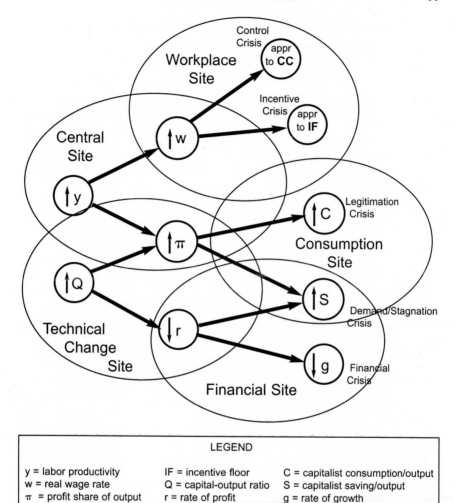

Figure 4.3. Taxonomy of Crisis Sites

lation concerning the worsening ecological crisis—the "second contradiction" of capitalism (O'Connor 1994). Leaving deep ecology to one side for the present, we may view rising output per unit of labor as a central weapon of capitalists against workers: it is the basis for increase in profit per unit of labor if workers' living standards can be held to slower rates of growth—Marx's "increasing relative surplus value." It is also a crucial weapon in intercapitalist competition: differential advantage in productivity growth enables individual capitalists to increase market share at the expense of their rivals and to win in the struggle to centralize control over units of capital, again at the expense of competitors. The existence of an immanent tendency for productivity to rise should not be in serious dispute.

In what way is rising productivity a *critical* tendency, however? At the *central site* (refer to figure 4.3), the figure 4.1 process shown asserts that a rise in productivity must have a determinate effect on the two target variables, the real wage rate and the profit *share* of income produced in the labor process. It must, specifically eventuate in either a rise in the real wage rate, or a rise in the profit share, or both. This trade-off should be intuitively obvious (for an algebraic statement, see the appendix to Laibman 2000; Laibman 1997, ch. 11). Rising productivity means that output is rising faster than labor employed. With the real wage rate constant, total wages, rising in step with the labor force, grow more slowly than output. The difference between output and wages, profit, is therefore growing more rapidly than output, and the profit share is rising. The tendency/barriers logic places a barrier in the path of each of the derivative trends, rising real wage rate and rising profit share.

One crucial assertion, therefore, is that *rising* real wage rates are ultimately problematic for capitalism, as expressed in the confrontation of this trend with a barrier—the *maximum* real wage rate. This may seem strange to those accustomed to thinking about crisis and revolutionary potential in capitalism as being associated with *falling* wages and living standards, not rising ones; both scenarios may of course be studied, but the logic of the upper-limit barrier to the real wage rate is of crucial importance. It will be explored in connection with the workplace site, below.

The critical nature of a rising profit share—which is, after all, equivalent to a rising rate of exploitation, or "relative immiseration of labor"—may seem more plausible at first. We will explore the approach of the profit share to a barrier—its upper limit, the maximum profit share—in connection with the technical change site, immediately below.

THE TECHNICAL CHANGE SITE. Here the critical tendency is the rising "organic composition of capital." This site depicts the famous—and controversial—hypothesis put forward by Marx in *Capital*, vol. 1, ch. 25, and vol. III, part III, concerning the tendency of the rate of profit to fall as a result of composition-increasing technical change. Sidestepping for the moment a huge discussion of the appropriate measures for the relevant variables (see Laibman 1992a, part 2, 1997, 1998a), we may define the composition of capital as the ratio of the labor value of the stock of nonhuman physical inputs in production to the current flow of living labor; this is equivalent, in terms of quantities of physical goods, to the stock of physical capital divided by the flow of *net* output. It should not be hard to see that the *rate of profit* is the ratio of the profit share to the composition of capital (thus defined). Since the profit rate is profit/capital, simply divide both numerator and denominator by net output; the numerator is now profit/net output, or the profit share, and the denominator is capital/net output, or the "capital-output ratio." Finally, if we think of this latter ratio in terms of embodied labor, or labor equivalents, then it is seen to be equivalent to the labor embodied in the physical capital stock divided by the current labor input. Finally, from profit rate = profit share divided by capital composition, we can find the tendency/barriers dynamic shown at the technical change site in figure 4.3: the rising composition of capital must eventuate in either a rise in the share of profit, or a fall in the rate of profit, or both.

Capitalist accumulation, assuming it takes this form, imposes a dilemma of major importance: either it must lead to a long-term, tendential fall in the rate of profit, or to a long-term tendential rise in the profit share. The former is a measure of the ability of the capitalist economy to grow, since the rate at which capitalists can accumulate capital will depend directly on the relation between extracted profit, that can be used for accumulation, and total capital in place. A fall in the rate of profit, therefore, is a significant weakening of capitalism from the standpoint of the defining motivation implanted in its key actors, the individual capitalists: growth-for-survival. The profit share, in turn, is a measure of the rate of exploitation—the relation between surplus extracted from labor and the total product produced by labor. Its rise represents increase in the inherent antagonism between capital and labor, an increase that presumably has consequences, and limits. We can thus identify barriers, in the form of the *maximum* profit share (the same barrier as identified at the central site), and the *minimum* rate of profit. The underlying tendency of the capital composition to rise imposes an increasingly severe trade-off between the two things capitalism must do well: exploit, and grow.

Unlike the rise in productivity, however, the rise in the composition of capital is far more difficult to confirm, both in theory and in evidence for most capitalist countries. It clearly requires that capitalists choose techniques that increase the degree of mechanization, or capital per worker, faster than the associated increase in productivity. The conditions in which this will be the case have been the subject of studies by the present writer going back some twenty-five years. I will try to give a summary description of where this research, which is still ongoing (see Laibman 1992a, part 2, 1997, 1998a), has led. The key finding is that certain aspects of the historically specific capitalist environment shape the path of technical change so as to create a likelihood—*not* an inevitability—that when capitalists rationally choose technical changes that yield the highest possible *momentary* profit rate—to the innovator of the new technique, in the brief moment before imitators rush in and spoil the fun—these choices will indeed involve composition-increasing technical changes. The likelihood of this happening is greater, the more the following conditions hold: intense, atomistic competition among firms; a strong balance of class power in favor of the working class, as that class increases in strength, both numerically and in organizational, political, and ideological maturity; diminishing returns to mechanization (each new degree of mechanization brings progressively smaller increases in productivity); high overall returns to mechanization in the short run, owing to an engineering culture that searches for and rewards *short-run* gains in productivity and profit; relatively low *autonomous* rates of increase in productivity, owing to comparative neglect of basic research in favor of applied research (a short time horizon); a significant degree of vertical integration enabling capitalists to anticipate productivity increases in the production of inputs under their control; and a significant level of time-impatience—failure to wait for innovations to be confirmed and substantiated in the laboratory before installation in production—which results in loss of potential productivity increases inherent in them.

Given the contingent but likely increase in the composition of capital, the critical tendency at the technical change site is operative, and imposes the dilemma: rising profit share vs. falling profit rate. Each of these then becomes a critical tendency at other sites; the resulting critical processes will be described below in connection with those sites.

The site at which increasing severity of the trade-off between the profit rate and profit share is identified may, in fact, well be reidentified as one that encompasses more than technical change in the narrow sense. Technical change, in the form of the rising composition of capital or capital-output ratio, is the classic process driving the fall in the profit rate (given the profit share), or the rise in the profit share (given the profit rate), in the approach that has come down to us from *Capital*. The change in the capital-output ratio due to "technical change" is clearly a function of capitalist PRs, as we would expect. The reasons for optimal choice of technical changes by competitive capitalists that increases this ratio are quite specific to capitalist PRs, as the paragraph directly above makes clear. The question is, can the capital-output ratio be more broadly conceived, so that additional aspects of the social evolution of capitalism help to determine it?

Total net output is in fact divided into portions, one of which is the output that is potentially serviceable for accumulation and reproduction, the other not. I will use the term "serviceable output" to refer to output that is available for working-class consumption, capitalist luxury consumption, or accumulation (investment). The latter portion, by contrast, is used up in various forms of wasteful activity: bureaucratic, supervisory, advertising, ecological destruction. If the total to serviceable output ratio rises over time, then the capital to serviceable output ratio will also rise, independently of any rise in the capital to total output ratio. This identifies one more long-term trend in the capital to output ratio defined using a *relevant* concept of output—in this case, serviceable output.

To this we may add an additional factor that becomes increasingly important once capitalist evolution moves beyond its "classical" phase and the state is no longer passive with respect to the accumulation process (see chapter 5). Taking "output" now to mean "serviceable output" in the above sense (potentially serviceable for accumulation or social reproduction through consumption), that output is further divided into a portion that is commandeered by government, through the power to tax, and the portion remaining after taxes are paid. If the ratio of (serviceable) output to nontaxed output rises, owing to increasing weight of public-sector activity in the late capitalist economy, this constitutes one more reason why the ratio of capital to *relevant* output (relevant: nonwasted, nontaxed) will rise, independently of rises due to the previous two factors (rising capital to total output; rising total to serviceable output). In sum, the ratio that embodies the immanent critical tendency at the technical change site—the ratio of capital to serviceable, nontaxed output—has *three* reasons to rise, and therefore three bases for the critical tendency: composition-increasing technical change; secular increase in output that is wasted by the increase in bureaucratic, coercive, and manipulative activity; and secular increase in the share of state-sector taxing and spending. Any combination of these that produces a net increase in the capital to (finally) relevant output ratio will increase the wedge between the rate of profit and the profit share; the critical tendency at the technical change site is therefore operative. Of course, in this broadened scenario the role of the state, financed by taxation, in managing crisis and mitigating crisis potentials must also be explored. Moreover, the role of the waste factor should not be obscured by the fact that certain capitalists profit from waste management, by supplying the requisite services. Nevertheless, there is reason to think that the line of analysis beginning from the rising composition of capital and leading to downward pressure on the profit rate remains relevant, especially when reconceived to include a broad range of social forces operating on it.

Once the critical tendency at the technical change site is in place, however, there remains, as always, the problem of substantiating the barriers at that site. What sets a maximum to the profit share, and a minimum to the profit rate? We will return to these questions, but part of the answer must lie in the dynamics at the adjacent sites, to which we now turn.

THE WORKPLACE SITE. The capitalist "point of production" has been the object of intense scrutiny in Marxist and wider circles (e.g., Braverman 1974; Gordon, et al. 1982; Edwards 1979; Schor 1991). In my "dilemma" presentation—the workplace site, in figure 4.3—we find a *rising* real wage rate as a critical tendency, as we have seen, and this requires some explanation.

A crucial strategic problem for capital in the workplace is to choose a degree of *devolution* of managerial and scientific functions—the extent to which these functions are shared among the lower strata of the hierarchy of authority in the workplace—in a sense, the degree to which the creative aspects of control over production and innovation have become democratized. (For present purposes we treat the two aspects of creativity—managerial and scientific—as one, although clearly this issue should be revisited later.) The question is: to what extent should the creative aspects of the labor process be segregated out and allotted to managerial/creative strata placed above the general workforce, and to what extent should they be devolved, i.e., distributed democratically so that large sections of the workforce have significant experience of creative participation in management, research and development of new products and processes? We can think of a *devolution ratio*: some sort of quantitative measure, however provisional, of the degree of devolution. How high or low, then, should the devolution index be? This is one of the strategic questions any capitalist firm must answer. The answer is by no means obvious.

Start with a given value of the real wage rate—a historically determined level of the workers' standard of living. We can then imagine setting the devolution index fairly low, so that the labor process is very routine and subject to a great deal of authoritarian control from above. Capitalist production, however, is not slave production; here the concept of evolutionary levels of sophistication and control, appropriate for different MPs on the AST ladder, kicks in. Capitalism requires high levels of skill, autonomous workers who can credibly function as sellers of labor power, and as "masters of their own house" in the household sector when they are away from the production site. All of this provides a barrier to unlimited fall in the devolution index. At some critically low point, should that be attempted by capitalists in a particular historical situation, the morale-sapping effects of the highly alienated working environment create what I will call an "incentive crisis." This might even become a full-blown *devalorization crisis*, if the deprivation of autonomy and creativity were to reach a stage that calls into question the juridical and social independence—the *citizenship*—of workers, ripping away the veil that the "market" imposes over the fact of domination and exploitation. Crisis along this dimension may result in high accident, absentee, sabotage and turnover rates (cf. the analysis in BGW 1983); it may provoke intensified resistance, organizing drives, and political independence on the part of workers; it may also have negative implications for productivity (a feedback loop to the central site that I do not explore further here). It definitely has the quality of a critical barrier: it is a lower limit to the devolution index, at or below which a chronic incentive or morale crisis is in effect.

Now consider the opposite strategy: raising the devolution index. This is consistent with a certain degree of autonomy and creative possibility for the workforce, and is therefore congenial to high levels of productive development, presumably characteristic of capitalism. (Modern economic theories of "efficiency wages," wages sufficiently high to provide desired levels of incentive and morale, are of course closely related to this conception.) The capitalist workplace, however, is inherently antagonistic, and if the devolution index rises to some critical level, the knowledge and power conferred on the ranks of the workers may result in loss of discipline and effective control—a weakening of the power of capital. That power, of course, is crucial to the extraction of surplus value; the sale of labor power being complete, the extraction of labor from that labor power is never a foregone conclusion, but always "up for grabs." There is, accordingly, a certain high level of the devolution index at which a *control crisis* may set in, with implications for productivity, social control, and political legitimation. The general strategic problem for capital, therefore, is to find a level of the devolution index that falls between the *incentive floor* and the *control ceiling*. At some given historical moment, we may imagine that there is sufficient room to maneuver between these twin barriers, so that a range of choices of more or less devolved workplace strategies coexist, all of them consistent with reproduction of worker discipline along with the required levels of productivity and productivity growth.

As the wage rate rises, however, and the working class is thus increasingly empowered, the control ceiling *falls*, and the incentive floor *rises*. This is the barriers moving inward, crowding out the living space of the target variables, in the imagery of figure 4.1. At this site, the devolution ratio is both B and C; it can be raised and lowered, but only within ever narrower limits. (Remember the dynamic, converging Scylla and Charybdis.) In this scenario, there will be a certain (high) level of the wage rate, the maximum rate, at which the incentive floor and the control ceiling actually meet; at that rate, there is no workplace organization strategy at which incentive and control crises can be avoided; in fact, staying at (not below) the floor and at (not above) the ceiling, both barriers must be encountered simultaneously. This identifies the high level of the wage rate at which, given the overall antagonistic character of the workplace, the entire system of capitalist control at the site of production is called into question.

In this perspective, then, capitalism cannot deliver ever-increasing standards of living—something that it will never do in any case, of course, unless it is forced to do so by working-class pressure—without placing itself in jeopardy. While falling wage rates clearly represent a critical process, for both obvious and subtle reasons, the real Achilles Heel of capitalism (if the reader will pardon yet another image from Greek mythology) is its tendency to raise productivity and therefore *make possible* steady increase in the real wage rate. A rising standard of living is then revealed as the main critical tendency in the workplace site; its encounter with the barriers—the incentive floor and the control ceiling—determines the maximum wage rate, which in turn is one of the barriers at the central site. This, after all, expresses a defining feature of capitalism's historical finitude: increasing productivity and living standards are ultimately problematic for a system based on anarchic, irresponsible control over accumulation by private centers of power and wealth. We will return to the crucial relationship between productivity and empowerment in connection with the socialist-communist MP, in chapter 7.

THE CONSUMPTION SITE. The alternative to rising wages and living standards, of course, is a rising profit share. From its role as a target variable at both the central and technical change sites, this variable now reappears as the critical tendency at the consumption site. It engenders the dilemma of either a rise in the ratio of capitalists' consumption to output, or a rise in the ratio of capitalist saving to output. Since profit must be partitioned into those two components, the trade-off here should be obvious without explicit algebraic statement. If the sum of two components increases, either or both of the components must increase.

Exploring the two branches of this dilemma, one at a time, we first consider a rise in the capitalist consumption share of output. The lifestyles of the social upper class have been subjected to investigation in a long-standing literature; high points include Thorstein Veblen (1975); Jürgen Habermas (1975); G. W. Domhoff (1967); Ferdinand Lundberg (1968). The dilemma model, as we will see, makes possible an analytical approach to this aspect of social reality.

In different historical periods, the capitalist upper class has either flaunted its consumption, or concealed it from society at large. In the United States, the decades just before and after the turn of the twentieth century are often referred to as the "robber-baron" era; members of "society" (the wealthy social upper class) were given to lavish and conspicuous display of their wealth. This sort of display, when it occurs, is not merely incidental to accumulation. It plays a significant role in establishing incentives for upward mobility to the middle and professional classes, and indeed to the most talented individuals from the working class as well. This enforces ideological control over the upper- and middle-managerial strata. Ruling classes are rarely in a position to staff all positions of power in the varied institutions of society from among their own members (see Domhoff 1967), and therefore need mechanisms to assimilate "new blood" into their ranks, as well as to establish their ideological dominance and deprive the subaltern classes of potential leadership. Conspicuous consumption also establishes hegemony: it displays power, and signals to the dominated and exploited classes their own powerlessness, and consequently reinforces the sense of inferiority and inability at those levels. In short, upper-class levels of consumption play a major role in the reproduction of class power and the conditions for continuing accumulation.

In the middle of the twentieth century, given the massive shift in the balance of class forces brought about by the Great Depression, and also by the fact of the Soviet challenge on the world scene, ruling classes in the capitalist countries retracted their conspicuous consumption to a large degree. From ostentatious urban palaces and highly visible restricted residential communities such as Grosse Point, Michigan (where the Detroit automobile elite resided), they withdrew into exurban and offshore locations not widely known or accessible to the population at large. This may also have resulted from the high rates of taxation on the upper levels of income instituted during the Franklin D. Roosevelt presidencies, which may have bit more deeply into upper-class consumption than into other uses of profit income.

With the reversal of the balance of forces in favor of the ruling strata in the late twentieth century, and continuing into the twenty-first, and spurred by the retreat of progressive taxation and rising rates of exploitation and profit, capitalist consumption has increasingly come back into its own. This, however, raises the specter of what I will call, borrowing and redefining a term from Jürgen Habermas (1975), "legitimation crisis": the political fallout from the outrage experienced by workers at the sight of stretch limos, multimillion dollar duplex and triplex apartments, executive "salaries" many hundreds of times the wages of working people, and so forth. When levels of upper-class consumption greatly exceed what is functional for ideological hegemony and recruitment, that excess becomes dangerous for continued reproduction of capitalist domination, and invites the possibility of political insurrection. This then sets a maximum to the "consumption share" (the ratio of capitalist consumption to total net income), and defines one barrier to the critical tendency for the profit share to rise.

Legitimation crisis can be avoided, of course—here the contingent quality of the dilemma formulation, according to which no actual path need be laid down in advance, is again revealed—by moving along the other horn of the dilemma at the consumption site: rise in the capitalist saving/output ratio. This links the consumption site to the financial site, and will be considered in that connection.

THE FINANCIAL SITE. The rise in the profit share imposes the dilemma traced above, at the consumption site, between legitimation crisis resulting from a rise in relative capitalist consumption, and a rise in the capitalist saving ratio. If the rise in the profit share is sufficiently large, it will offset the downward pressure on the profit rate resulting from the rising capital to output ratio. If the rise in the profit share is *not* large, then this offset will not be occurring. In that case, we can turn our attention to the fall in the profit rate as the critical tendency at the financial site. While my discussion of this site will focus on the major variables such as the profit rate, and will not address more finely tuned institutional matters, there is a large literature on finance and financial crisis that complements the analysis presented here (see, e.g., Minsky 1982; Davidson 1972; de Brunhoff 1978; Foley 1986).

For a given ratio of saving to income, the fall in the profit rate will produce a fall in the *rate of growth* of capital (essentially, the rate of accumulation). This is true, strictly speaking, only if the saving ratio is defined as the share of saving in profit, rather than the share of saving in income. With a constant profit share, a falling profit rate imposes a necessary tradeoff between a rising saving/investment share of income and a falling rate of growth. This trade-off, however, is also revealed as an expression of the ultimate source of critical movement in this site: the rising composition of capital.

We have, then, given the profit share and the saving ratio, a direct line from a falling profit rate to a falling growth rate. The barrier in this case is a minimum level of the growth rate. This, in turn, like every other aspect of the terrain sketched in this chapter, requires further analysis.

The following story may be outlined. Accumulation normally takes place under conditions of continuing technical change. This, however, requires capitalists to accumulate capital goods (machines) of varying age and productivity. Different "vintages" of capital stocks thus come to exist side by side (Laibman 1992a, ch. 8). The reason is simple: capital is increasingly fixed capital, equipment that lasts for significant numbers of years; capitalists cannot scrap their entire capital stocks each time the latest, highest-productivity vintage emerges. They are, in fact, on the horns of yet another dilemma: if they scrap aggressively, and ahead of physical depreciation schedules, the average age of their capital stocks will be low and productivity high, but the scale of production will be restricted. Small firms, no matter how productive, are juicy targets for takeover by larger capitals. (This danger may be especially acute since these "lean" firms must shoulder the burden of the continuing financial obligations associated with the scrapped vintages, and be able to absorb the losses of the original investments.)

If, on the other hand, firms maximize scale and market power by clinging to old vintages, average productivity will be low—yet another source of vulnerability.

When growth rates are high, capitalists can address the drag on profit rates created by retention of old low-productivity equipment. They do this by aggressive scrapping, absorbing the losses of sunk investments by acquiring the extra profits accruing from new, high-productivity equipment. The old debts associated with the cost of outdated equipment can be rolled over or paid down—financed—by virtue of the firm's demonstrable competitiveness, a process that might be termed "dynamic collateralization." High growth rates enable normal depreciation to occur rapidly, and the capital stock to turn over fairly quickly. The higher the growth rate, then, the lower the average age of the capital stock, and therefore the greater the room for creative refinancing.

This then is, I believe, the source of the minimum growth rate barrier. When the rate of growth falls to a critical level at which even the aggressive, front-runner firms cannot count on financing to retire obsolescing capital stocks, they experience significant liquidity problems. *Financial crisis* sets in at this barrier, and for this reason. There can be all sorts of contingent reasons for liquidity crunches in particular firms or sectors, especially inventory overhang resulting from bad product assortment decisions. The key barrier to financing, however, is the rollover problem when growth is slow and the natural turnover of capital stocks becomes problematic.

Theories of the falling rate of profit—in addition to the burden of demonstrating that the rate of profit must fall, to a significant degree, and in significantly finite time—must address the issue: why does a falling profit rate matter? Why would capitalists care if the profit rate falls, so long as it is accompanied by a rise in the amount of profit or in the profit share? The interrelation between the technical change site and the financial site, sketched above, provides a line of answer to this question. The fall in growth brought about by falling profit rates forces encounter with the minimum-growth-rate barrier, which takes the form of chronic financial crisis. It should also be noted that in this portrayal the crisis-enhancing role of the historical cost of obsolescing capital goods takes shape as a *result* of the fall in the rate of profit; it cannot be used as an *explanation* for that fall (cf. Kliman 1996).

The fall in the profit rate, then, is a critical tendency in the direction of a falling rate of growth, *unless* that fall can be averted, again with resort to the dilemma formulation, by a rise in the capitalist saving ratio. This rise is then a critical tendency emerging from the combined action of the financial and consumption sites, and must now be considered.

Quite simply, the rise in the saving ratio is the triggering mechanism for the classic problem of underconsumption, going back to the work of T. R. Malthus, but with any number of more recent expressions (Keynes 1961; Kalecki 1968; Robinson 1962; Kaldor 1960; Garegnani 1991). This is a complex and well-known story. What the present account adds is context: it situates the problems of limited aggregate demand and stagnation in a wider framework of crisis sites and processes. The problem is essentially one of time horizon. With rising quantities of unconsumed surplus value, capitalists are in effect asked to invest—accumulate capital stocks—in anticipation of markets farther and farther removed from the present. As an issue arising at the financial site, this again places increasing strain on the collateralization aspect of the financial system, even without falling growth rates. Firms must justify to holders of both their debt and their equity commitment of resources to expansion of production capacity, to service markets that are situated ever farther in the future, and therefore conditioned by events and circumstances that increasingly cannot be fathomed. In the absence of widespread public assumption of this risk—something that might be considered appropriate for production capacities with wide linkages to social goals and concerns—individual capitals cannot invest beyond a certain point without endangering their autonomy and survival. This, then, is the stagnation barrier associated with the maximum level of the capitalist saving ratio, at which crisis associated with insufficient demand becomes chronic (see Laibman 1992, ch. 12, for more detail).

The crisis sites and their elements are brought together, for summary purposes, in table 4.1. In that table, the columns represent the five sites: central, technical change, workplace, consumption, and financial. The first row is the critical tendency (ΔA), and the second and third rows are the two target variables. The critical tendencies are all increases—in productivity, the capital composition, the wage rate, and the profit share—except for the profit rate, which falls. Each critical tendency necessarily gives rise to the changes in B and C (either, or both), in the stated direction. Note that at the workplace site

Table 4.1. A Summary of Crisis Potentials

	SITE				
	Central	Tech. Change	Workplace	Consumption	Financial
ΔA (Critical tendency)	Rise in productivity	Rise in capital composition	Rise in wage rate	Rise in profit share	Fall in profit rate
ΔB (Target variable)	Profit share *rises*	Profit share *rises*	Devolution ratio *rises*	Cap. Consumption ratio *rises*	Growth rate *falls*
ΔC (Target variable)	Wage rate *rises*	Profit rate *falls*	Devolution ratio *falls*	Cap. saving ratio *rises*	Cap. saving ratio *rises*

the "two" target variables are the same: the devolution ratio. It is the movement of that ratio in one direction or another that encounters the relevant barrier and triggers the associated crisis (incentive; control). The ultimate barriers—those that are not derived from critical tendencies at other sites—are the maximum capitalist consumption ratio, the maximum capitalist saving ratio, the minimum growth rate, and (in a sense) the maximum wage rate (although this depends on the position of the incentive floor and control ceiling, and their behavior as the wage rate rises). Note the interaction among elements in the table. The rise in the profit share (ΔB at the central and technical change sites) becomes the critical tendency (ΔA) at the consumption site. The rise in the target variable, the wage rate (central; ΔC) is the critical tendency at the workplace site. Finally, the fall in the target variable, the rate of profit (technical change; ΔC) is the critical tendency at the financial site. As always, a model of this kind is provisional, not exhaustive; there is no presumption that every possible linkage has been explored in it. One hopes that at least some of the major interactions among sites of crisis in capitalist accumulation are nevertheless highlighted by this construction.

Interaction Among the Sites

Figure 4.3 in fact invites us to think about ways in which the critical pressures at work in the several sites shown there may interact with one another. There is a certain tension between alternativity and complementarity: to the extent that the processes at work at the several sites combine to establish the necessity of worsening crisis in general, somewhere, that helps to keep the central question of the transcendence of capitalism in focus. On the other hand, to the extent that development at one site may relieve pressure at another, the various forms of crisis appear as alternatives. This offers a way of describing the distinctiveness of different paths of development, revealing the multi-textured varieties of capitalist accumulation. It also, however, opens up the possibility that creative displacement of crisis pressure may continue indefinitely, and postpone any sort of ultimate convergence to general crisis.

Working from the bottom to the top of figure 4.3, the various types of crisis initially appear as alternatives. Begin with the financial site. Financial crisis associated with a fall in the rate of growth can be mitigated only by means of a rise in the capitalist saving ratio, which raises the specter of limited aggregate demand and stagnation. Alternatively, the profit rate must be protected against erosion due to a rising composition of capital; this necessarily requires a rise in the profit share, which—again assuming the accumulation path steers clear of the shoals of stagnation—imposes an increase in the capitalists' consumption share, with its associated dangers of fallout from widespread revulsion against the immoral parasitism of the wealthy (consider the travesty of George W. Bush proclaiming allegiance to his "social base," the "haves" and the "have mores"). Financial and stagnation crisis are thus both averted—in, say, some particular period or "regime" of accumulation—but at a cost in terms of legitimation crisis (in the limited sense that I have attached to this term).

The link to the workplace site is more indirect. Even with a non-increasing composition of capital—and the model outlined here makes possible the construction of long-term crisis theory even without this controversial postulate, should that be considered desirable—the presumably unfailing pressure from rising productivity suggests that legitimation crisis can be postponed only if wages rise sufficiently to keep the profit share within reasonably low bounds. The rise in wages, as argued above, is perhaps the most fundamental contradiction of capitalism: rising material standards of life afford, actually or potentially, a level of freedom for the working-class majority that is simply incompatible with the unprincipled and antagonistic systems of control associated with private ownership of capital. (If, however, productivity indeed falls, or stagnates, that may be seen to invoke a legitimation crisis of an even higher order. It suggests that the PFs are so distorted and confined by archaic productive relations, so "fettered," to use the classical metaphor, that the capacity of capitalist society to carry forward productive development is increasingly called into question.)

The incentive and control crisis at the workplace site, stemming from rising real wages, may be seen by some to be the most questionable aspect of the model, viewed from widely held Marxist perspectives. This is, however, a bit of rethinking whose pursuit I seriously advocate. From its classical origins, Marxist thought has always insisted on studying the connection between experience, ideology, consciousness, and motivation in terms of concrete social structures and relations. It is, for example, the fact of being *exploited* in a capitalist form—rather than being generally oppressed, dominated, or starved—that gives the working class its place of importance in the analysis of social agency (a fact that has nothing whatsoever to do with "privileging" any group; but that is a story for another time). All manner of privations have been forced upon subordinate classes and strata from time immemorial; it is the particular manner of capitalist exploitation in relation to the way in which capitalism develops objective and subjective possibilities for resistance and, ultimately, counteroffensive that establishes the agential uniqueness of the modern working class.

In a similar manner, the analysis of crisis and revolutionary possibility must keep the focus on specifically capitalist workplace relations. Insofar as the real wage rate falls, for example, and "absolute immiseration" occurs, workers may rebel, as all people in all times, pressed up against the material limits of subsistence or at least faced with significant deterioration in their living standards, have eventually done. But when their rebellion is based on the range of possibilities opened up by *rising* wages—never, of course, automatic, but always a result of organization, ideological perspective, and struggle—it takes on, at least potentially, socially transformative forms. In fact, we may even see capitalism's abiding need to keep proletarian status intact by holding living standards down as the driving force that sets the range of other crisis potentials in motion: the low real wage rate implies a rising profit share (given rising productivity), which then enforces the dilemma-like choice between legitimation crisis and stagnation crisis, or (given falling profitability) the choice between the latter and financial crisis.

As a final remark, I should reiterate that none of the crises associated with confrontation between critical tendency and barriers at any site is thought to be inevitable or automatic in its impact. Nothing about either breakdown or social transformation is implied. The incentive/control and legitimation crises perhaps reveal this most clearly: these depend in obvious ways upon the ability of the working class to perceive alternatives, and therefore to organize realistically and politically to achieve radical social goals. In an ideological atmosphere of TINA ("there is no alternative"), no amount of arbitrary workplace despotism or manipulation, and no degree of outrageous and parasitic luxury consumption, necessarily emerge as truly *critical*. It comes down, ultimately, to the question of how much the working class will tolerate. The same is true for the proximate results of crisis at the more objective financial site: stagnation and financial crisis result in unemployment, poverty, social insecurity (failing medical and pension institutions), housing crisis, etc., and the critical impact of all this again depends on the extent to which the subaltern social classes have the capacity to respond, politically and effectively.

III. SUMMARY AND CONCLUSION

Following this very brief tour of figure 4.3, it remains to pull the entire picture together and draw some overall lessons.

Does this exercise "prove," once and for all, that capitalism must die of its internal contradictions, and soon? Fairly obviously, the answer to this question is "no." What then does it accomplish?

First, it establishes a research agenda, and one that is clearly too big for any one school of thought, let alone any single individual. Every one of the ultimate barriers—the control ceiling, the incentive floor, maximum capitalist consumption, maximum saving ratio, minimum growth rate—must be substantiated: its rationale further explored and levels estimated. Many linkages, some of which were hinted at above, exist among the various barriers and processes, linkages that are not described in figure 4.3. The danger is that the entire construction will collapse once again into total reciprocity and indeterminacy, but the danger must be faced.

Nevertheless, I believe the tendencies/dilemmas/sites construction shows very clearly the fruitfulness of a synthetic approach to crisis theory, one in which the endeavors at the various sites of the capitalist process are valued and efforts are made to bring them into interaction with one another. The tentative conclusion is that a sense of the ultimate determinacy of capitalist contradiction is reinforced by considering each crisis site in connection with the others. The variety of possible pathways lends itself to study of individual country experiences and concrete temporal or regional histories. I will not propose any links of particular paths or outcomes to particular countries; that would be schematic and unproductive at this stage. But the model does seem to provide for a combination of variety and contingency in actual accumulation experiences with the systematicity and determinacy of the general process of accumulation. Capitalism is both one and many.

Some observers may note the absence of state theory and dependency theory, or of any reference to imperialism, in my account. These are features of capitalist reality that require development and integration into crisis theory, and some aspects of these dimensions of capitalist reality will be addressed in the stadial model of the ACS, in the next chapter. Work at the level of capitalism in general—the "liberal" stage II of the model of chapter 5, but possibly also reflective of a fully globalized capitalism, not yet achieved in reality—does not address aspects of accumulation that derive from uneven development of and hierarchical relations among capitalist nations and regions, and from the role of the nation-state. I must also mention briefly the role of racial and national oppression, and the associated racist and chauvinist ideologies, in dividing the working class and structuring surplus extraction, in many historical capitalist formations. There is the further issue of monopoly power, and I would not want to ignore the contributions of the several traditions (monopoly capital, state monopoly capitalism) that have considered this power to be an essential feature of mature capitalism. This is further considered in the stadial theory of chapter 5.

But even with these indications of absence and of work remaining to be done, the model of crisis sites, each with its tendency/barriers constellation, helps us to integrate the work of Marxist and other researchers in the various areas—the workplace, the financial system, research institutions, the goods markets, the social upper class, the political system—and bring that work together into a comprehensive framework.

As this work and cross-fertilization go forward, the model of the inter-relationships will undoubtedly evolve. Some version of it seems essential, however, if we are to progress to a fruitful vision of capitalism that discerns its essential properties, and contradictions, at work in diverse and evolving sites of accumulation and struggle.

Chapter 5

A STADIAL MODEL OF THE CAPITALIST ERA

To this point, I have presented a stadial theory of social evolution on the large scale of history: the entire sweep of development out of human prehistory up to the present, and the (unknown) future. I have also outlined (in chapter 3) the nature of the capitalist MP—how its class-antagonistic structure is maintained and reproduced in conjunction with intensive and extensive growth of the PFs—and (in chapter 4) the logic of capitalist accumulation—the contradictions on the growth path and the forms of crisis that reveal those contradictions. The implicit basis for this analysis of "capitalism in general" has been the earliest stage of capitalist development in which systemic reproduction occurs internally and spontaneously, relying on its core defining feature: valorization, or the merging of market relations and production relations.

The path of capitalist maturation could be analyzed using the accumulation/crisis model outlined above, for that given "early" stage of development. The complexity of capitalism, however, in relation to the earlier antagonistic MPs, impels us to consider whether capitalism has its own internal stadial path of evolution, which is nested within the larger stadiality—the PF–PR model of chapters 1 and 2. If it does, then this structure of stages of the abstract capitalist society (ACS) will necessarily figure in any attempt to determine where we are at present, and to grasp the current situation in the world. This chapter will propose a theory of stages of the ACS. Along with the theory of accumulation and crisis at the level of capitalism in general, a stadial framework seems essential if we are to grasp the present moment; I will argue, as throughout this book, that this requires getting outside of that moment and grounding it in a more general, historical and abstract conception of the underlying social reality behind the press of current events.

The next section will collect some of the ingredients for this project. The following section will outline a new stadial—stage-theoretic—analysis, drawing on historical materialism and political economy in what I propose are novel ways. The goal is a sounder approach to the questions: How mature is capitalism at present? How does today's world reflect the degree of development of the dominant—capitalist—mode of production and of the potential and actual forces for its transcendence?

I. INGREDIENTS FOR A STADIAL ANALYSIS OF THE PRESENT

Thinking about the Marxist tradition from the standpoint of the present reveals significant weaknesses. In the Soviet Union and its allied states, Marxist social science had the resources of state power and official status at its disposal; this made possible a mature academic practice and a highly articulated "normal science," which produced a large amount of data, empirical research, and significant scholarly output (including definitive editions and annotations of the classical Marxist texts). The downside, as is well known, was the authoritarian politicization of academic and scholarly life and a failure to distinguish between popular and scientific levels of discourse which, together with deeply entrenched bureaucratism, generated dogmatic and "scriptural" approaches to Marxist theory.

In capitalist countries outside of the Communist political environment, Marxism faced a different set of challenges. Principal among these, perhaps, has been a tendency to succumb to a certain impatience and foreshortening of time projections that understandably arises from lack of practical experience with political leadership and social construction on a large scale. In addition, "Western" Marxism, owing to its increasing confinement to the academy, has made inordinate concessions to the disciplinary boundaries and specializations that have evolved in the universities since the mid-nineteenth century.

Against this background, I identify four essential problem areas for the revitalization project: re-envisioning of time, the role of theory; transcending arbitrary separations and specializations, and, finally, reconceptualizing stages, and the stadial principle, in thinking about social evolution and the place of the present in that evolution.

Time: Foreshortening, Condensation

For "official" reasons in the East and "utopian" ones in the West, Marxists have repeatedly compressed the time line for social change. If we are to pose in a newly rigorous way the question, How mature is world capitalism today?, this problem must be faced. It began in the late 1840s, when the young Marx and Engels saw the democratic uprisings throughout Europe as heralding imminent proletarian revolution. It continued into the twentieth century, with Lenin's "highest and last stage" formulation, and persists in the sting carried by the standard critique from mainstream liberal circles— "where *is* this revolutionary working-class movement that Marx projected?" The Frankfurt School took shape in an attempt to "explain" the "absence" of proletarian revolution in the West; the complexity of the requirements for revolutionary class agency in advanced capitalist countries is also a central axis of Antonio Gramsci's thought (Jay 1973; Gramsci 1992; Cammett 1967). Georg Lukács scandalized the Hungarian officialdom of the 1950s by saying: "It took six centuries to get from feudalism to capitalism; so it will take six decades to get from capitalism to socialism." All of this reveals an important shared assumption: transcendence of capitalism will (or will not) take place in a greatly foreshortened time span—perhaps even within "our" lifetime (or so Marx predicted and so his theory presumably requires).

But we must be clear about this. There is simply no reason to assume *any* preordained time frame for social change. The drive to accumulate and innovate under the pressure of competition produces a sense of an increased rate of change under capitalism, as compared with precapitalist social formations; thus Marx' and Engels' praise for the bourgeoisie, which "during its rule of scarce one hundred years, has created more massive and more colossal productive forces than have all preceding generations together" (Marx and Engels 1998, 10); thus also Lukács' quip. On the other hand, socialist revolution is not just replacement of one form of class exploitation with another but transcendence of class exploitation as such. This most complex of all social transitions therefore pursues political power on a society-wide scale *prior to* decisive transformation of the production relations (Aptheker 1960). Capitalist market relations have a "totalizing" quality, like a gas expanding to fill the entire social space they inhabit; they therefore require a revolutionary political movement that is capable of *envisioning* alternative social relations. It might be noted, parenthetically, that in its opposition to "totalizing" narratives postmodernism deprives us (in its own peculiar "totalizing" manner) of the opportunity to confront the *spontaneous, implicit and structural* totality of capitalist social relations and power (see González 2004). The point is that capitalism creates an *implicit* and *structural* metanarrative, against which the socialist political movement must create a conscious alternative. (On the socialism envisioning issue, see the special issue of *Science & Society* on "Building Socialism Theoretically: Alternatives to Capitalism and the Invisible Hand," Spring 2002.) Opposition to *explicit* metanarratives is thus inherently biased.

The complexity and historically unprecedented nature of the socialist task explains why socialism (to use the term that has come into common use) has had any number of failed or protracted embodiments, beginning with the Paris Commune, and continuing with the Russian and Chinese revolutions, the associated transformations in Eastern Europe and Asia, the Cuban Revolution, various forms of "noncapitalist" development in Africa, and even such cooperative movements as Mondragon in the Basque provinces of Spain. These historical moments should not be regarded as "failures" (this term handily conveys the sense of one-time, apocalyptic transition that has bedeviled much socialist thinking), but rather as episodes in which experience is harvested, lessons learned, foundations laid. Perspective on this can be derived from the insight that capitalism, in turn, had "failures" going back thousands of years into the ancient world: the vast systems of trade and finance in several Mediterranean civilizations and references to wage labor ("service for hire") in Aristotle, plus the existence of enclaves of early bourgeois systems of production within many feudal societies, especially on overland trade routes and waterways.

The point is *not* to replace the mechanical assumption of an accelerating pace of change with its opposite. It is not that the time for decisive transformation is long; it is, rather, incalculable. Once we have a firm grasp on the prerequisites for socialism—technical, institutional, cultural, and ideological—we can explore the pathways through which those prerequisites mature, without any prior commitment to a time frame derived from a rigid set of evolutionary categories. In particular, there is a process of *condensation* (the Bolshevik theoreticians spoke of "combined development") through which a given maturational step, resting on a long prior history, may be accomplished relatively quickly (in historical time). We need not repeat the errors of some Second International thinking, which used the then-new Marxist concept of social evolution to envision a *postponed* revolution; but neither should we use the critique of that mechanistic approach to reject the social-evolution problematic as such.

The Role of Theory

It should be clear by now that an appropriate sense of time can be established only by means of a *theoretical* understanding. While theory has come under attack in recent years, we need to rebuild the theoretical habit—given suitable caution learned from our long confrontation with non-Marxist thinking and heightened demands for epistemological sophistication. This habit is a simple affirmation: the deep structure of reality is not immediately apparent, and continual bombardment by sense-data and "information" will not suffice to reveal that structure's essential properties.

Is this "theoreticism"? The postmodern impulse, now slightly tarnished but still very much present, warns against hyperextension of the theoretical. The problem is undoubtedly real, and we should certainly avoid "theory for its own sake." Theoreticism, however, is hardly the most pressing problem for the left, in the United States and elsewhere. (One remembers Marx's comment about the French public, "always impatient to come to a conclusion" [Marx 1967, 21].) The much more prevalent tendencies are toward empiricism, and *sensualism*: the overwhelming of thought by the impress of current events and moods. Especially in turbulent times, we need to hone the theoretical faculty, which enables us to "take a step back" and look at the present in a framework that offers systematic perspective.

Synthesis: Transcending the Disciplinary Boundaries

A partial list of components crying out for synthesis includes: political economy; the theory of precapitalist formations (and the historical materialist concept set in general) (Hobsbawm 1964); state theory (Holloway and Picciotto 1978; Jessop 1990; Das 1996); and "nation theory" (study of the territorial/cultural/ linguistic unities loosely called nations, or nationalities) (Luxemburg 1976; Lenin 1967). The disciplinary boundaries of academia have not helped here, but the problem runs deeper. Thus, Marxist "economists" work on the theory of the capitalist "economy" (itself an abstraction with consequences). Along the spectrum running from theory to policy, those who work at the former end often never "get around to" the latter, and have no distinctive opinions on policy issues. Current or topical writers, in turn, reveal, in their failure to use political economy in their work, a more or less conscious assumption that the latter has little of use to offer. We experience different "comfort levels" working at different levels of abstraction. It is not the existence of this divide that is troublesome; it is, rather, the fact that the divide is often accepted unquestioningly, with little effort to overcome it.

Our prime case in point is study of the present-day global economy. Many writers in this area draw upon the imperialism and dependency literature without thoroughly confronting it. They also tend to ignore political economy, implicitly asserting, for example, that Marx's *Capital* is at best only marginally relevant to their interests. State theorists often (not invariably) ignore political economy, focusing instead on a different "problematic"—the nature and extent of the relative autonomy of state managers. Others debate the existence or nonexistence of a transnational capitalist class, various fractions of that class, and similar issues, without (again, not invariably) realizing that the inter*national* and trans*national* cannot acquire precise meaning until and unless we have a clear concept of a *nation* as such. What makes the "nations" of the capitalist era distinctive, in relation to similar territorial-cultural unities from earlier periods? Enough has been said here to establish the main point: the various streams of inquiry must be brought together and to bear on each other, if we are to address the insufficiencies arising in each of them separately.

Stages and the Stadial Principle

This is, of course, a central theme of this book, but it may be useful to bring some of the elements together here. Stadial thinking is central to the Marxist tradition; consider, for example, Marx's enumeration of "the Asiatic, the ancient, the feudal, and the modern bourgeois" epochs in world history in the preface to the *Contribution to the Critique of Political Economy* (Marx 1913, 13), or the absolute-relative surplus value distinction and the concept of Primitive Accumulation in *Capital*. Still, it has often been met with suspicion in "Western" circles; *any* talk of stages smacks of determinism—of a mechanistic presumption that all social formations must pass through them in linear succession, or that the very positing of stages invalidates the role of consciousness and agency in social change. The concept must therefore be developed with great care, especially since the conclusions reached will have major implications for our view of the deep structure of the present.

The Marxist tradition offers a rich variety of approaches. The Bauer/Lenin/Hilferding/Kautsky/Bukharin generation proposed a "late" stage of capitalism, variously called "imperialism," "finance capital," "monopoly capital." Ernest Mandel (Mandel 1975) later popularized the term "late capitalism," which has the advantage of not foreclosing on the principle underlying the early-late distinction, but might also be seen as an end run around the need to nail down that principle. In fact, the notion that the *current* stage is "late," if not the "highest"—not to mention the other term in common use, *"advanced* capitalism"—already contains a conclusion that is not warranted by an underlying theory. (For a useful survey of early-twentieth-century periodization theory, see McDonough 1995.) None of these early/late or lower/higher approaches, however, establishes a basis for the definitions of stages, or for transitions between them. Capital accumulation evidently reaches a point at which the nature of capital shifts from, in some sense, competitive to monopolistic, and its behavior changes from parametric (responding passively to external price signals) to strategic. Lenin (1933) speaks of the fusion of banking capital with industrial capital to form finance capital—although it is unclear why that fusion could not have taken place decades earlier, what prior conditions made it possible, or why it results in the qualitatively new epoch in world capitalist behavior that he so well describes.

"State-monopoly capitalism"—the central concept for the Communist parties in the twentieth century and therefore generally ignored or vilified by non-Communist Marxists—observes, in relation to the earlier liberal or competitive era, a decisively enhanced role for the state, and a tighter interpenetration between state executives and the representatives of monopoly capital (Kuusinen 1960; Pevzner 1984). Contrary to the usual Western Marxist view of the state-monopoly position, there is a variety of precise formulations concerning the relation between state and monopoly within this framework; a crude instrumentalism is not an inherent element in it. The state-monopoly theorists, however, use the same essentially descriptive methodology employed by the first post-Marx generation: new qualities are announced as they appear on the horizon, and at some point, for reasons not explicitly formulated, are deemed worthy of adumbration as a new stage, or phase within a stage. The emphasis on the state, of course, suggests a different periodization from that of the imperialism generation: state-monopoly capitalism comes into its own only in the 1930s, as a result of the Great Depression.

The "Monthly Review" or "monopoly capital" school has its source in Paul Baran and Paul Sweezy's *Monopoly Capital* (1966; see also Foster 1986), which drops the "state" qualifier (in an explicit move to differentiate itself from "state monopoly capitalism"). The monopoly stage in this conception is based on the demand constraint and aligns with the stagnationist view: maturing capitalism becomes increasingly prone to stagnation and depression, due to restricted demand (Steindl 1952; Minsky 1982). Also in the Western Marxist camp we find Regulation Theory (Aglietta 1979; Lipietz 1987) and the Social Structures of Accumulation model (Bowles, Gordon & Weisskopf 1983). These schools propose a succession of regimes of accumulation, or social contracts; Fordism/post-Fordism is a core concept for them (for a useful survey, see Kotz, 1990). Finally, in a brief summary the position of the Uno School must be mentioned. Uno theorists take their inspiration from the Japanese Marxist Kozo Uno (see Uno 1980; Itoh 1980; Sekine 1975). They posit three separate levels of inquiry: Principles of the purely capitalist economy; Stage theory; and Historical analysis. The overriding theoretical commitment is to keep these levels separate, whereas Marx, and many others subsequently, tend to slide among them without complete methodological awareness. In this way, the theory of stages is kept separate from the "pure" theory of accumulation, as a matter of principle. The stages—

mercantilism, liberalism, and imperialism in most formulations—are thus programmatically deprived of a foundation in theory in the sense that I intend, and remain, therefore, essentially arbitrary and untheorized (see Albritton, et al., 2001, for a compendium of periodization theories). Other stadial conceptions involve the predominance in one period or another of particular use-values. Thus, railroads, automobiles, the assembly line, electronics, the "information age" (e.g., Carnoy, et al. 1993), may each represent a stage of capitalist accumulation. The problem here, of course, is that "stages" of this sort have no clear relation one to the other, and provide no basis for anticipation of the number and character of stages that might succeed. Once again, explanation is forsaken in favor of historical description, and this gets us no farther forward in our attempt to define the present in stadial terms.

Theoretical Periodization

The next section presents a preliminary model of stadiality for the capitalist epoch. The model draws upon three elements, explained briefly in this subsection: (*a*) theoretical stages, and theorized transitions between them; (*b*) layered abstractions, and in particular three levels of abstraction that can usefully be distinguished; and, finally, (*c*) capitalist diffusion. This latter was undertheorized by Marx; it should be placed at the same level of abstraction as the much more clearly grasped capitalist accumulation.

(A) THE THEORETICAL STAGE AND THEORIZED TRANSITION. This concept has already been developed, in connection with the general PF–PR model of chapter 1. *Theoretical stages* are distinguished from *descriptive stages*, which are distilled from empirical observation and practice and are an essential step toward identification of theoretical stages. What distinguishes the latter, however, are the necessities that link the stages into a chain, in which each stage requires specific prerequisites from the one preceding; accomplishes specific developmental tasks unique to itself; and lays precise foundations that determine essential characteristics of the succeeding stage.

The term "teleology" often surfaces when people are confronted with the concept of theoretical stages; a word may therefore be in order. Teleology is the "fact or character attributed to nature or natural processes of being directed toward an end or shaped by a purpose" (*Webster's New Collegiate Dictionary*), as in the animistic beliefs found in many preindustrial cultures, or in (some interpretations of) Hegel's notion of a drive present in partial and inadequate reality toward fulfillment in the Absolute Idea. Nothing of the kind, of course, is invoked in the proposition that objective processes in history contain stadial properties. Stadial evolution is, to use a phrase from Althusser, a "process without a subject."

Theoretical stages are stages in the development of a *theoretical object*, which stands in the usual complex relation to the actual historical process. The paradigmatic case for this distinction is the general theory of the AST, with its sequence of interlinked stages. This sequence, as usual, exists *nowhere* in real history, which is a complex and contingent embodiment of the evolutionary principles revealed by the abstract model.

Whether or not a compelling account of the capitalist epoch in terms of theoretical stages can be constructed, the existing periodization literature (see Albritton, et al. 2001) does not meet this criterion. Descriptively rich accounts of economic life in given time periods—Fordist industrial production, the Age of the Internet—clearly do not derive their meaning from any stadial concept set with the "chain-linked" property. Their contribution depends on the possibility of their incorporation within a more rigorous theoretical structure.

As in the general PF–PR model of the AST, identification of two juxtaposed theoretical stages is the basis for determination of the *theorized transition* between them. This point should be fairly obvious, and will be elaborated only later in connection with the model of section II. A theorized transition is an explained transition, and this explanation precedes in order of importance the matter of dating—identifying in chronological time the transitions in concrete history that correspond to the theorized transition under investigation. The point for the present is that the core necessities of the preceding stage provide the answer to the "why" of the transition to the succeeding one.

(B) LAYERED ABSTRACTIONS AND SUCCESSIVE CONCRETIZATION. The distinction between the AST, on the one hand, and concrete history, on the other, calls for elaboration. There are not just two useful levels of abstraction, for example, but several; this gives rise to the concepts of "layered abstractions" and "successive concretization" (Sweezy 1956; dos Santos 1970; Mavroudeas 2004). Periodization at the abstract level, for example, is complicated ("overdetermined") by a second periodization at the level of (relatively) concrete capitalist social formations. This rests on the variety imposed by differentiated geographical, climatic, and resource contexts for capitalist evolution, giving rise to uneven development, diffusion, conquest, and expansion. Uneven development is a major reason why theoretical stages are hard to "find" in the data, giving rise to interminable (and often unnecessary) debates about the "dating" of transitions between stages. The dates are inherently uncertain, because the transitions are in fact "blurred" by different stages of development of capitalist societies that are nevertheless shaping one another through trade, colonization, foreign investment, and general cultural interchange. Theoretically well-defined transitions between stages are only rarely found at precise locations in chronological time.

For present purposes a three-level model will be deployed. This is not a general commitment; additional levels may become useful later and in other connections (for a three-level approach to analysis of social classes, see dos Santos 1970).

The first level, of course, is the AST, in which the social formation and mode of production coincide. To derive theoretical stages at this level, we must in effect imagine—to recall an image from chapter 1 of this study— that capitalist evolution is taking place on a planet with only one continent; with a uniform natural environment in terms of temperature, rainfall, flora, fauna, and soil; no internal waterways, narrow isthmuses, mountain ranges, or any other barriers that might create localized and isolated paths of development. We, in short, abstract from uneven development and all that that implies. The central organizing concept of Jared Diamond's monumental work, *Guns, Germs and Steel* (Diamond 1997), geographical determinism, is thus relegated here to a secondary order of invocation, corresponding to a lower level of abstraction than that of the abstract social totality. (To the extent that Diamond is concerned with the tens of thousands of years of *pre*-history, however, geographical differentiation is indeed the proper focus.)

With this abstraction in place, short of full historical contingency (including the role of individual personalities) another level can be identified. Experience is absorbed into consciousness and embodied in institutions and cultures so as to generate agency on a significant scale, only over time, and sometimes over considerable stretches of time (Lembcke 1991–92). Marx wrestled with this problem in the *18th Brumaire* (Marx 1928). In the first half of the nineteenth century, the underlying mode of production and class structure in France were not undergoing significant change. A political dynamic—the restoration of the monarchy—was nevertheless unfolding, and this produced the almost eery drive of the absolutist ghost to inhabit every republican form, leading to *retrogressive* stages in which restorationist forces took on various republican guises. On top of the stadiality of the underlying mode of production, therefore, lies an additional dynamic stemming from a *long cycle of advance and retreat*—of the bourgeoisie in relation to the nobility and monarchy in nineteenth-century France, or—an obvious extension—of the working class in relation to capitalist power in the twentieth century and up to the present.

This long cycle is essential to our understanding of the early twenty-first century. In the model of the next section, in fact, the second level—

uneven development—will be compressed, with attention centered on theoretical stadiality at the top and the advance/retreat cycle at the bottom.

(C) CAPITALIST DIFFUSION. Capitalism spreads outward to areas where precapitalist relations prevail. This cannot be taken for granted. How capitalism emerges within, and eventually replaces, precapitalist relations is the heart of the theory of feudal to capitalist transition (*Science & Society* 1977), and that inquiry is the starting point for a *theory of capitalist diffusion* in general. Diffusion is the penetration of capitalism into previously noncapitalist (usually precapitalist) space. It must be distinguished from capitalist *accumulation*: the self-propelling and self-reproducing system of sale/purchase of labor power and appropriation of surplus value, in a space where capitalist class relations have already been established. Marxism has made much more progress with accumulation than with diffusion; this may be partly because Marx himself approached the former as a matter of theoretical interest in *Capital* while the latter was confined mainly to historical description. Placing diffusion squarely in the realm of theory will help in establishing a sufficiently rigorous stadial framework.

II. ACCUMULATION, DIFFUSION, THE NATION AND THE STATE: A SYNTHESIS OF CAPITALIST PERIODIZATION

The stadial model can best be developed in connection with a diagram (figure 5.1), which is a logical summary of the argument—another application of the conceptual geometry methodology. The reader is, as usual, invited to refer regularly to this figure while reading this section.

The organizing principle of figure 5.1 is a pair of crosscutting distinctions: between capitalist diffusion and capitalist accumulation (along the vertical), and between internal and external fields of operation (along the horizontal). The internal/external distinction itself depends upon the evolutionary path; it only comes into existence during transition I. In the upper left box of the diagram, therefore, "internal" essentially coincides with "total."

Stage I and Transition I

The story begins in the upper left box, which combines "diffusion" with "internal." While not synonymous with the common labels "mercantilism" or "primitive accumulation," Stage I does draw upon those labels for content. "Internal" refers to the formation of home markets in countries experiencing transition to capitalism. External colonization, the looting of the Americas, the gold inflow, and enslavement of African and American populations of course play a highly

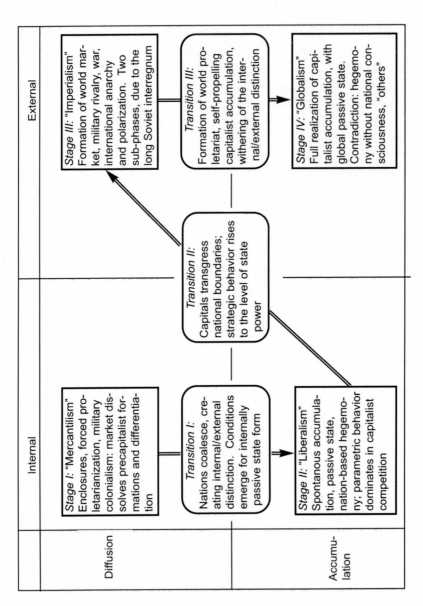

Figure 5.1. Stages in Capitalist Development

visible role in this period. The crucial dynamic, however, has to do with internal transformation, which determines the efficacy of external empire building and international trade; thus, the "internal" label. Only after nation building is complete does the external come into focus.

The precondition for the market to assume a dynamic, developmental quality—as distinct from its ever-present passive externality in much of recorded history—is the specific form of productive forces development in feudalism: the emergence of the *individual surplus*—a surplus over subsistence needs in *individual* production—as contrasted with the *collective surplus* of earlier epochs that grounded the original formation of exploiting classes (see chapter 1 for a detailed exposition). This surplus emerges, for necessary reasons, only within feudal (manorial) production, which combines small-scale class exploitation (the capture of the surplus) with relative autonomy for the direct producers and the associated incentive to innovate. This system, never embracing more than a minority of the population in the countries of feudal western and northern Europe (including, of course, Britain), was nevertheless the basis for intensive development of the productive forces, and therefore the "hothouse" or incubator of the individual surplus. This surplus makes possible the expansion of trade in the late Middle Ages (Pirenne 1939; Sweezy 1977); trade thus loses the deus ex machina quality that it acquires in all manner of descriptive accounts (cf., on this, Wood 1999).

The transition to capitalism (Transition I) is both problematic and protracted. It requires accumulation of means of production in the hands of a minority ruling class whose wealth exists in valorized form, and the dispossession of the majority, transferring control over production away from the direct producers. The surplus available to finance coercive institutions (for colonization, enclosure, dispossession) is generated within archaic precapitalist relations, while the dynamic element, production for the market, generates an unstable and unreliable surplus (the core capitalist coercion mechanism, of course, has not yet been established). Merchants enforce relations of unequal exchange with direct producers through the putting-out system and through control over channels of trade. They also, however, confront a reduced but fortified feudal nobility (and promote absolute monarchies, which they come to control financially, for this purpose). In many parts of Europe, an equilibrium trap thus emerges, which, along with plagues and famine, goes a long way toward explaining the centuries-long time frame for this transition.

The emergence of capitalism, or capitalism-like features, in Stage I is a matter of *diffusion*—of the slow spread of both commodity markets and wage labor into an external environment of feudal and simple-market (peasant) production (admixed, perhaps, with still other precapitalist forms: despotic tribute, monastic landholdings, residual slavery, etc.). In this process, markets act as a solvent, dissolving long-existing cultural, linguistic, and local-economy differentiations and gradually creating a wider social space within which people come to share a common identity. The practical need for uniform roads and waterway systems for transport, common weights and measures, shared practices regarding tolls, fines, taxes, and a generally accepted currency, imposes progressive homogenization of social life. The original cultural entities, akin to tribes with small populations of people generally known to each other, are gradually merged into larger unities, and social identification shifts to these. In Britain, to take a case in point, the many warring cultural groups—Angles, Saxons, Welsh, Celts—slowly coalesce into Britons; the Norman invasion facilitates this unification process, and eventually there emerges the "English," who face the French, Germans, Dutch, and so on. The question for theory is: Why does this process stop short of world unification? Why do *nations*—the unities that take shape in the period of capitalist ascendancy as a result of Transition I—solidify into permanent entities that continue to characterize global society in the twenty-first century?

The nations as we know them did not always exist. At the time of the French Revolution only about 10 percent of the population of the territory we today call "France" spoke a language recognizably close to the one we call "French"; this was the population surrounding the Paris region, and it would be reading history backwards indeed to simply assume that that language had to eventually dominate the entire region, in which scores of languages were spoken. Spain was not "Spain"; it was "las Españas," a loose amalgam of Basques, Catalans, Moors, and others. The question arises: What is it that arrests diffusion, resulting in definite territories each with a common language and culture? A water barrier, the English Channel, helps explain the formation of England and France; but all such formations cannot be explained in this way. In the homogeneous environment of the abstract social totality, what would explain the break in the diffusion-unification process and the formation of the modern nations? An answer to this question will tell us something about the nature of capitalism itself.

For capitalist exploitation to become stably self-reproducing, the *social space* over which it occurs must be large enough for the newly forming proletariat to consist of abstract and interchangeable individuals, who must see themselves as such. Small-scale markets do not support this degree of abstraction. Capitalist protorelations in small towns—think of "company towns" in the United States in the nineteenth century—where everyone is known to everyone else and where the workers form an identifiable concrete group in relation to the employer, represent an early and insufficient form of capitalism. The conditions for valorization of labor power, as analyzed by Marx in *Capital* I, include creation of a socially uniform space sufficiently large so that the worker confronts capital entirely as an interchangeable and dispensable individual, and moreover confronts capital in general—not just the capitalist owner of a particular production process or a particular sector of production. The worker is a worker-in-general, over the entire potential range of commodities; this is the historical formation of *abstract labor*.

Stage II begins at the point where immanent coercion based on abstract proletarianization becomes *possible* as the central mechanism for production and appropriation of surplus value. When this happens, and the process of capital *accumulation* filters into the experience of capitalists and workers alike, the old "extra-economic" coercive machineries that propelled the diffusion process in Stage I become insufficient and problematized. The state retreats from being an active player in accumulation and an active coercive force (both internally and externally) and adopts its classical, "liberal" form. Accumulation is capital spontaneously annexing surplus value and expanding, by taking on market (valorized) forms, without having to rely on the coercive power of the state financed by taxation or borrowing. This is when—and why—the state ceases to act as the motor of continued diffusion and cultural unification, and the nations "harden" into the form with which we are familiar.

Two observations are relevant here. First, a connection has been proposed between the classical, passive state and the modern nation; thus, the nation-state. The condition of sufficient scale for the abstraction of both labor and capital is the qualitative basis for the distinction between the nation, in this sense, and similar entities in earlier periods (e.g., the city-states of Mediterranean antiquity). Second, we now have a prime example of a theorized transition between a pair of theoretical stages, in which one clearly requires the other as prior foundation. Empirical historians provide the rich factual basis on which theoretical stages can eventually be perceived. The factual record, however, is, as we know, massively "overdetermined" by variations in geography and accidental circumstance, so that stadially generated elements overlap in time, obscuring the underlying determinations. It is, then, broadly true that the raw data do not reveal these qualities; that the English state was *never* "passive," that national sentiment long predated the system of wage labor, and so forth. The proof of the theoretical pudding is in the eating, which in this case must mean the ultimate fruitfulness of the stadial conceptual armory in giving meaning to the disorganized complexity of raw history, and suggesting new lines of research.

Stage II and Transition II

Once the transition to spontaneous coercion within production and the associated hardening of the modern nations is complete, accumulation replaces diffusion as the central dynamic. Accumulation takes place within nation-states, and the national/international, or internal/external, distinction becomes significant. This is Stage II, located in the accumulation-internal box of figure 5.1, lower left. It is the experience from which Marx distilled the core concepts of his theory of capitalism, as summarized and reinterpreted in chapters 3 and 4.

Just as the feudal manors served as incubator of the intensive surplus, so the nation-states provide protected domains within which capitalism can grow in its classical form. The nation-state becomes the locus of personal and cultural identification; this, together with the market fetishization of capitalist social relations, forms the hegemonic ideology that binds the working class to the system of its exploitation. The nation inhibits consciousness of class, which only emerges in times of crisis. "The market" is an elemental reality ("elemental": like the weather), operating on all social actors with the force of natural law. This, of course, is the key to the high degree of sophistication of capitalist exploitation, compared with its precapitalist counterparts.

Establishment of a social field sufficiently large so that valorization and abstraction of class can be accomplished is the basis for the predominance of spontaneous market relations as the principle guiding social reproduction, and the associated passivity of the state. In Stage II the behavior of the capitalist units of control (capitals, or firms) is most clearly *parametric*: capitals experience prices, including the price of labor power, as competition-determined parameters, outside of their direct control. The textbook economics concept of "perfect competition" is a pallid abstraction from this reality. The parametric quality, however, is always relative: capitalists in every period act strategically within a local framework, in competition with other capitals for growth and market share, and in conflict with workers at the point of production over the terms and conditions of purchase/sale of labor power and extraction of labor from it. Parametric domination appears as a continual override of individual capitalists' strategic choices by processes, such as price formation and the growth imperative, that appear as external compulsions corresponding to no one's conscious choice. This is the kernel of truth in the commonplace capitalist assertion, often made during negotiations with labor, that "we are all bound by the laws of the market"—a *real illusion* that is part of the intricate machinery ensuring the reproduction of capitalist class structure and the accumulation process.

The immanent contradiction at the core of this regime is the subject of an enormous body of work going back to *Capital* I. To recapitulate: the conditions for *existence* of capitalist exploitation—an adequate rate of exploitation but one sufficiently low to enable realization (sale) of goods—and the conditions for *expansion* of capitals—an adequate rate of profit—come into conflict. This contradiction, which incorporates the shaping of technology by capitalist imperatives but is by no means limited to that factor, intensifies as the system matures through Stage II. One aspect of this process is growth in the size of capitalist units of control—the "concentration and centralization of capital." This growth undercuts the parametric valorization basis of Stage II, and paves the way for Transition II, in which internal accumulation is replaced by external diffusion (the upper right box of figure 5.1).

Transition II captures the essential elements of the state-monopoly conception. Strategic behavior was always admixed with parametric behavior; the sharp dichotomy between these two modes of functioning must, I think, be rejected. However, the *relative* submersion of the strategic aspect comes to an end when and as capitals grow to the point where a significant proportion of their activity has transcended national boundaries. A system of what can be called (for the first time) "international trade" emerges within Stage II. This signals that units of capital have grown to the point where they are able to influence and manipulate state power, and therefore to form strategic perspectives that incorporate the making of national political policy. The structural role of the state in ensuring conditions for capital accumulation, regardless of the degree of autonomy of state managers, is now supplemented, and therefore transformed, by the competition of capitalist class fractions for control over state policy and use of the state machinery, including its military component, to further the various fractions' domestic and international interests. This is, perhaps, the core observation of the "state-monopoly" school.

Stage III and Transition III

Growth in the scale of production fosters the emergence of a world market. This market faces an immanent barrier: the hardened nation-states from Transition I and Stage II, which prevent further extension of state power in correspondence with the growing scale of economic relations. The outcome is Stage III: an epoch characterized by a growing contradiction between the transnational field of operation of capitals—first trade, then investment, then finance—and the limited and conflictual terrain on which state power is exercised. This international anarchy finds its expression in colonization, imperialism (Lenin's "highest and last stage"), military rivalry and war. The general correspondence between Stage III and the twentieth century should be clear.

With Transition II, the focus shifts back again from accumulation (always taking place, of course) to diffusion, now, however, centered on the external aspect: the spread of capitalist power, and then capitalist relations of production, to the as yet noncapitalist areas of the world.

As noted above (in Section I), capitalist *diffusion* has not been theorized in a manner comparable to the existing body of work on capitalist *accumulation*. This gap cannot be overcome in any single study; following are some preliminary observations.

First, it is reasonable to expect that the *regime of diffusion* in Stage III is internally contradictory, just as is the *regime of accumulation* in Stage II. Working out the theory of this contradiction is a task of central importance. The trajectory of this stage is clearly the formation of a *world* proletariat and self-propelling accumulation on a world, or transnational, scale; this is the substance of Transition III. Comparison of Stage I and Stage III is instructive. In Stage I, state military and financial power are used to conquer the internal social spaces for capitalist production relations. This, however, occurs long prior to the formation of large-scale strategically oriented units of capital, whose own imperative for survival/growth/predominance requires them to extract surplus from the subordinate populations at the highest possible rate. Put another way, in Stage I the size of the units of control of capital is still limited compared to the extent of the market, and this makes the market incentive available for transformation of the underlying production relations. The market, in effect, is able to act in its role of solvent of precapitalist relations, *because* the productive forces are (relatively) underdeveloped and the existing capitalist units of control do not dominate. The opposite, however, is true in Stage III, which relies on the extensive productive forces and state-level units of control (the transnational corporations) developed within Stage II. The contradiction of Stage III, then, is the inconsistency between the large scale of the capital that is attempting to penetrate, and the small scale and powerlessness of the actors in the precapitalist environment being penetrated. Stage III, therefore, reveals a *crisis of capitalist diffusion*, or *diffusion crisis*: a persistent failure to establish capitalist relations "on the ground" in most parts of the "third world" (which now includes major sections of the former "second world"). This is a point of considerable importance, and I will return to it in the next section.

Second, as our exploration of the model approaches more closely to the present, the layering of abstractions (explained in the previous section) must be introduced. As promised there, we will pass over the second level, involving geographic differentiation and uneven development, and move directly to the third level: the balance-of-forces cycle. In this regard, the twentieth century represents not only a protracted, drawn out implementation of Stage III due to the diffusion crisis; it also reflects what may be called the "Soviet interregnum": the period of Soviet power between 1917 and 1989–91. The Russian Revolution and its aftermath—including especially the Chinese Revolution of 1945–48—were a forward movement for the working class on a world scale, despite the underdeveloped conditions of that class and its conditions of existence in most of the places where the surge took place. This working-class offensive was compounded by the popular mobilization in the more advanced capitalist countries during the Great Depression, and all of this constituted the upphase (from the working-class viewpoint) in the balance-of-forces cycle. The consolidation of capitalist power after World War II and the emergence of deepening contradictions within the socialist-bloc countries signal the turn of the cycle in a downward direction, a phase that is still unfolding.

The upshot is that Stage III, generally characterized by international anarchy and protracted efforts at diffusion, can best be understood as divided into two phases: before and after the Soviet interregnum. Prior to 1917 we witness Stage III in its classic incarnation, as the rivalry of nation-states that have been captured by the strategic interests of the capitalist centers within them and launched into the struggle for spheres of influence and empire that culminates in World War I. The interregnum is a qualitative shift, in which existence of a Second World outside of capitalist control causes a period of strategic alliance among the warring capitalist powers (the cold war), and (ironically) serves to enhance the diffusion of capitalist relations in the Third World. With the Soviet collapse, the second phase of Stage III appears: this is the contemporary "globalization" phenomenon, and it brings into full light the inherent contradiction of this stage: the vast size and financial power of the units of control, combined with their extension beyond the reach of the nation-states, which alone have the capacity to transmit the influence of subaltern populations and of the more farsighted elements in the ruling capitalist regimes. The result: unprecedented polarization, and stalling of the diffusion process. Transition III is thus a troubled and protracted one.

Stage IV

If Transition III can be accomplished, it will mean the emergence of capitalist accumulation on a world scale—the junction of "accumulation" and "external" in figure 5.1, lower right box—which is, as will by now be clear, much more than a set of simultaneous national accumulation processes (a sort of Stage II without an external precapitalist environment). Stage IV would involve a global, passive state, an end to diffusion (which has essentially been completed), and an accumulation based, once again, on the inherent coercive force of valorized production under capitalist control. (It also essentially abolishes the internal/external distinction that was brought into existence by Transition I.) The possibility of Stage IV turns on whether a world state can ground a form of nonclass identity—in the absence of "others," the external alien element that motivates the "we" of national identity—sufficient to maintain capitalist ideological hegemony. The role of valorization in fetishizing social relations and reproducing hegemony becomes more central in the absence of national division. While some form of the classic contradictions of capitalist accumulation, originally identified in Stage II, will persist, the role of "free-market" ideology becomes crucial. To the extent that national identity cannot be completely replaced, the existing crisis-potentials within accumulation are supplemented by a "hegemony crisis." This tendency of Stage IV to generate inadequate national-ideological cover for capitalist exploitation—a hole in the hegemony layer, so to speak—is a major inherent contradiction. Within this conception, "Transition IV" (not shown in figure 5.1) would be socialist revolution: at this point, capitalism indeed has nowhere else to go.

In closing this discussion, I return to the methodological theme: the requirements of a genuinely (theoretical) stadial model. The chain-linked property of the stages should be clear: at the level of the abstract totality of the capitalist epoch being described, each stage requires the previous one as foundation, and each bequeaths to the following one some essential condition for that stage to emerge. Stage IV, for example, requires the global state that transnational capitalist class theorists observe as immanent in the emerging world institutions (World Bank, IMF, etc.) (see, e.g., Robinson 1996; Robinson and Harris 2000). That state cannot develop except on the basis of more or less universal capitalist relations on the ground—the diffusion accomplished in Stage III. Stage III, in turn, requires the trans-statal capitals that can only result from the accumulation made possible by the passive state of Stage II. Putting to one side the intermingling of elements among capitalist social formations at different stages of development, we have a *determinate* stadial conception of capitalist evolution at the level of the abstract totality. This has been extracted from the complex history of social existence and transformation throughout the centuries of capitalist predominance, and is the organizing tool for serious thinking about the inner reality of that history—including its appearance in our ultimate object of attention, the present moment.

IMPLICATIONS FOR NOW: APPLYING THE STADIAL MODEL TO THE CURRENT CONJUNCTURE

Some commentators, as noted above, regard all stadial thinking as inherently conservative. I (obviously!) do not accept that view. Nevertheless, working out the stadial inner logic of the capitalist world economy is a clear invitation to ask about the *objective requirements* for transcending capitalism. It is an affirmation that the agents of social change in any period of history do not operate in a vacuum; do not "make their history just as they please," to refer once more to the famous phrase (Marx 1963, 15). Nothing in the stadial approach denies the role of agency, organization, and consciousness, or suggests that our *will* to move toward a society worthy of human potential must be thwarted by some sort of mysterious *telos* of history. Nevertheless, there are limits to what can be accomplished in any period, which point not to ultimate limitations on human progress but rather to the *path* that can be effective in moving each step forward. This problematic simply must be faced, unless we are to argue (not in the name of the Marxist tradition, surely?) that will to achieve is all, and anything is possible.

That said, and with reference to the model of the last section, I believe we are, at present, deeply embedded within a highly troubled Stage III. This means, concretely, that the capitalist conquest of the globe is highly incomplete. Capitalism has parts of Stage III, and all of Transition III and Stage IV still ahead of it; to that extent, and however compressed this evolution may turn out to be, terms like "moribund" and "obsolescent" applied to the world capitalist system are premature (for an important example of a contrary argument, Amin 2004).

What does this imply for socialist transition? A principled democracy that can (eventually) replace the spontaneous market and overcome the alienation of social existence requires the historical development of a thoroughly abstract proletariat—one that is, *in its own core experience*, the bearer of the most general human concerns. A worldwide working-class community will have transcended national, religious, ethnic, and other primal divisions, even as these traditions contribute texture and variety to a *shared* world culture. Capitalism produces this proletariat, its true gravedigger, only in Stage IV. Indeed, what it produces spontaneously is an alienated abstract proletariat; transcendence of alienation and the emergence of a principled, cooperative culture require the fullest development within capitalism of conscious struggle from the side of the working class (see Lebowitz 2003, for a full statement). From this perspective, the failure of the Soviet experience was not an inherent weakness in the planning and management systems in place, nor even a result of the authoritarian deformation as such. Rather, the basis for that deformation is the absence of a prior historical experience of civil society and universal identity, at the level of Stage IV rather than Stage II. Without that prior development, it is very difficult—although *not impossible*—to replace the market with advanced forms of democracy, in such a way that these do not revert to an authoritarian bureaucratism and concentration of power that is essentially a reprise of precapitalist conditions. From this perspective, the standard capitalist ideological claim of a link between the market and personal freedom (Friedman 1962) is valid, *within the limited horizon of capitalist development, pre-Stage IV*. It becomes precisely invalid with the development of a universal proletariat that suffers from the most abstract exploitation possible, and therefore carries within it the principled universality of general human aspiration.

To evaluate these claims, we have the advantage of a deepening understanding of exactly what capitalism is, as a result of the stadial model, especially Transition I and Stage II. This is where *political economy* is essential to the project of grasping the present. To recapitulate: capitalist accumulation—the successful internal motion of capital, as a sophisticated means of exploitation and class reproduction adequate to a relatively high level of PFs development—requires a social field large enough to sustain the *abstract* class identities that enable full valorization of labor power: complete and reliable fetishization and obscuring of class. This, in turn, permits the powerful coercive force of exploitation to work without external (state) support.

From this standpoint, full-fledged capitalism has been much more rare on the world stage than we customarily believe. Just as feudalism took root in one small region of the world (or perhaps two), and its key component, the manor, involved a minority of the population even in those regions, so has capitalism emerged *on the ground* in only a few parts of the world, and has had difficulty spreading (the Stage III diffusion crisis). To see this, we must not confuse diffusion of capitalist production relations with the global dominance of the transnational corporations (which is not being denied). The capitalist centers of course control world trade, and their products and images have penetrated everywhere; the famous T-shirt with the Coca Cola logo in Arabic is the best possible symbol of this. But "Coca Cola-nization" is not synonymous with capitalism. Nor is the existence of capitalist enclaves in the Middle East, China, the rest of South and Southeast Asia, and elsewhere. Workers in the Chinese industrial zones (which cause the capitalist centers in the West so much concern) are not a capitalist proletariat; they are overwhelmingly based in rural, quasi-communal villages that still house the majority of China's population, and still have property, family, and wider kinship ties to those villages, undercutting the valorization of their labor power. The capitalist *social space* defining abstract individuals and abstract classes is not present. Similarly, oil workers in the Middle East—historically the foundation for left-secular progressive politics in that region and the best available counterweight to monarchical despotism, on one side, and religious fanaticism, on the other—are not abstract workers in a classical capitalist labor power market. They are identified in relation to a particular industry—oil—and not in relation to capitalist industry as such.

Even in Latin America, capitalist labor markets are often confined to the large enclaves represented by major cities such as Buenos Aires and Santiago. The surrounding countryside contains ambiguous social relations, with a large component of peasant agriculture. And in the former Soviet bloc, the emergent social formation is topped by a criminal oligarchy (Mafia), whose wealth comes largely from theft of property built up in the Soviet years (see Kotz 2001, 2002; Laibman 2002). It is not based on the exploitation of "free" wage labor—let alone the wage labor *system* required for spontaneous valorization.

As noted above, the failure of capitalist diffusion in Stage III results from the combination of concentrated and centralized capital built up in Stage II with an exterior ("third") world in which the specific prerequisites for spontaneous spread of market relations—the individual surplus stemming from intensive productive forces development—are largely absent. To put this point in a nutshell: in large parts of today's Third World, capitalism must be *imported*; it cannot be *ignited*. This, together with the demise of the Soviet counterweight, is the source of the extreme and unprecedented polarization of income and wealth, both across countries and within them. This polarization has now become a threat to basic survival in the poorer areas of the world, especially in the Islamic regions of the Middle East, Central and South Asia and North Africa. (Sub-Saharan Africa is a different, and distinctively tragic, case.)

The material base is thus identified for the current upsurge of Islamic fundamentalism, in its destructive and destabilizing form. It can be argued that Islam, in ironic contrast to the older religions, Judaism and Christianity, is in effect a *precapitalist* religion: it has never adapted to the existence of civil society or accommodated itself to the concept of general citizenship in a state that is separate from religious institutions and power. (To be sure, the rise and damaging potential of right wing fundamentalist Christianity, however, may make it necessary to qualify this distinction.) The upsurge of Islamic fundamentalism is the expression of the world social polarization associated with the diffusion crisis, increasingly revealed following the Soviet demise. Combine it with modern technology and the legacy of U. S. imperialist instigation of religious fanaticism as a weapon against the Soviet Union, and the road leading to September 11, 2001 is clear.

A further implication for the present flows from the perspective sketched out here. The United States Imperium, however powerful it may seem at the moment, is in fact an anachronistic holdover from the Soviet interregnum. The bipolar cold war required that the capitalist world produce an executive leader, and given the current phase in the cyclical rise and fall of centers of temporary dominance within the hierarchies of capitalist economic and political power, that role fell to the United States. Even before the demise of the USSR, many observers noted a contradiction between the economic decline of the United States relative to Europe and Japan, and its political-military predominance (and role as reserve currency provider). Now, with the bipolar world a thing of the past, this contradiction is strengthening. U. S. dominance is subject to constant erosion, from the emergence of new centers of economic power, including those in East Asia, and from the growth of transnational capitalist power and interests, both private and political.

Turning to implications for the working-class and progressive movements around the globe, the main message is sobering. We used to say that the choice facing the world is "socialism vs. barbarism"; in an ultimate sense, that is still true. Nevertheless, at the present moment, the choice may well be between "*capitalism* and barbarism." We simple must recognize that today's capitalist class, unlike the bourgeoisie praised by Marx and Engels for "nestling everywhere, settling everywhere" one hundred fifty years ago, is having difficulty shaping the world after its own image. We are in a crisis of *capitalist* expansion, not a crisis associated with the challenge of socialism. Capitalism is increasingly finding it difficult to do what it does best: spread outward. The consequences are increasingly dangerous, from the standpoint of basic social reproduction in many parts of the world: looming ecological deterioration and increasing attacks on positions in social provisioning long held by the working classes and allied strata in many countries.

This boils down to a conclusion concerning political strategy. The progressive and revolutionary working-class movements have an interest in *alliances* with other social class forces to promote secular development, even when those alliances are led by capitalist interests and promote—for the present—development along capitalist lines. Broadly based secular development—urbanization, basic medical provision, education, sanitation, housing support—is exactly what, with incessant prodding by class struggle from below, capitalism classically was able to achieve (Stage II), but increasing is not able to provide in many parts of the world. When working-class and popular forces support *capitalist* secularization—because that is what is possible in the given political circumstances—while simultaneously protecting and advancing their own interests and power within that process, they help determine the nature of capitalist development and build the positive side of abstraction toward a universal humanity—a major instance of "combined development." It must be stressed that the stadial understanding does not posit a static or linear conception in which we must *first* accept the alienating universality of commodity status and only challenge that status *after* it has been established worldwide. This would be like the error of transferring the stadial determinacy found at the abstract totality level to the concrete terrain of socioeconomic formations. Rather, understanding the complexity and scale of the tasks still faced by capitalist world expansion provides the firmest foundation for moving beyond capitalist hegemony and priorities to posing the possibility of socialist transformation.

This may seem a distant hope in the present climate, but we should remember that the balance-of-forces cycle always turns, and will turn again in favor of the working class, largely as a result of what we do in the present. Understanding the complexity and stadiality of the present, and accepting objective limitations on what can immediately be done, do not amount to giving up on long-term goals or mechanically relegating them to some distant future. To the contrary: they are a matter of acting realistically in the world as it is, so as to bring it to the point where new advances in social evolution are objectively possible—sooner, rather than later.

The capacity to challenge the long-emerging capitalist world order has a material base: the organizational and practical capacities of the world's working class, its ability to overcome obstacles to unity and coordinated action, its skills, knowledge, political consciousness—in a word, its capacity to assume, irreversibly, the leadership of society. An important element in this *material* base is the extent to which, from its experience of struggle, both inside and outside of state power, it is able to construct and maintain, in the face of the massive ideological hegemony of capitalism, a countervision or *consciousness* of an alternative to the present. Socialist theory is an academic practice, but it is also (actually or potentially) a practical force, when it is effective within the large-scale secular movements that are (whether self-consciously or not) the embodiment of working-class agency. Socialist theory is not utopian as such; it is the way in which alternatives to the present capitalist world order can be grasped systematically, rather than randomly and sporadically, and their elements brought together into an organic vision that can pierce through the hegemony of the capitalist present. Laboring in the vineyards of socialist theory, then, is not a diversion from the practical tasks of resistance and countermobilization; to the contrary, it is crucial to making popular forces effective in the pursuit of those tasks.

So it is to the theory of the mode of production transcending and replacing capitalism, identified in a massive literature going back two centuries by the terms "socialism" and "communism," to which we now turn.

III.
BEYOND CAPITALISM:
AN ENVISIONED FUTURE

Chapter 6

SOCIALISM

Beyond Capital, Beyond Class

The model of the abstract social totality, and the theories of crisis and stadiality in capitalism, all lead up to the question: can this conceptual toolkit illuminate what lies beyond the fourth Great Transformation (or the second, depending on your point of view)? In this transformation, a non–class-antagonistic mode of production replaces, simultaneously, capitalism and the entire historical epoch of antagonistic MPs. Bowing to the existing lack of consensus on terminology, I will call this the "communist MP," or "communism," with "socialism" as the lower of two stages in its development, following the classical definitions in Marx, 1933. Since the lower stage has, in most conceptions, a protracted existence relegating the higher stage to a separate study, I will often use socialism to identify the MP transcending capitalism, and communism to refer to the higher stage alone.

Socialism, of course, must be studied on an entirely different plane than the other MPs in the stadial model whose development is the central concern of this book, for the obvious reason that it cannot be grounded on a long-standing historical record. Unlike primitive communism, for which we have the contemporary ethnographic record and whatever archeological clues may exist, and unlike the class-antagonistic MPs, for which the materials of recorded history can be drawn upon, in the case of socialism we are at the threshold of experience, and must therefore rely much more on deduction and extrapolation from the regularities and potentials revealed in the PF–PR analysis of the antagonistic MPs. I argue below that the historical experience of twentieth-century postcapitalist construction must not be ignored or belittled; it contains much that can be used in redeveloping socialist theory, including both positive and negative lessons. Still, in the spirit of the PF–PR model and of the stadial conception of the capitalist

144

epoch, I would insist that the time line is long, and our conception of the communist/socialist MP must reflect our grasp of that fact. I will try to use all of the relevant experiences, both within capitalism and beyond it, without tying the model of the abstract socialist totality too closely to any one historical situation. A good place to begin is with the legacy of socialist theory in the Marxist tradition.

Marxist thought came into existence in the nineteenth century as a reaction against the ahistorical utopian schemes of the then-existing socialisms. Instead of writing "recipes for the cookbooks of the future," the left sought to comprehend the actual movement of class formation and struggle, and to draw only the most general implications for the postrevolutionary future from the tendencies and contradictions of the present, as revealed by science and by practice.

In the short twentieth century (1917–1991), an additional element emerged—most significantly for those on the left who embraced the Soviet Union as the embodiment of the revolutionary overthrow of capitalism: it was said that there could *now* be a political economy of socialism, because socialism had actually come into existence and was available for study on a scientific basis. The Soviet experience (and, later, those of eastern Europe, China, Cuba, etc.) provided the material foundation on which socialist society could be theorized, in a nonutopian manner.

All of this, however, fails to face up to a crucial tension within the Marxist enterprise. As Marx and Engels knew from quite early on, the transition to postcapitalist society is unlike any previous revolutionary transformations: it requires its agents to build the new social relations consciously—to implement a political program based on a body of theory, or vision. This follows from a central fact about capitalism: unlike earlier ruling entities, the capitalist class maintains its domination through a spontaneous process that invades all sectors of social and economic life. The pervasiveness of the market form of capitalist relations means that socialism cannot be established piecemeal. It cannot grow spontaneously in small units, only later to be acknowledged and sanctioned by political change. "The proletarians . . . have nothing of their own to secure and to fortify. . . . their ends can be attained only by the forcible overthrow of all existing social conditions" (Marx and Engels 1998, 22, 62). If this is true, then the question of what the proletarians' "ends" are must be faced squarely.

In several recent papers (Laibman 1992, 1995, 1999a, 1999b), I have tried to contribute to the reconceptualization of socialism, in the wake of the demise of the Soviet and eastern European socialist regimes. I have argued that those experiences—the Soviet one in particular—contain important elements for the positive reconstruction of socialist theory, elements that are often overlooked in Western Marxist circles (see Khudokormov 1967; Ellman 1973, 1979; Lange 1956, 1962; Zauberman 1967). Precisely because there is no longer (or should no longer be) a compulsion on the left to establish adversarial stakeholdings on the "nature" of Soviet society, it should now be possible to draw both positive and negative lessons from that set of experiences, and this is one way to distinguish Marxist from utopian modes of projecting a socialist future at the beginning of the twenty-first century. The entire movement of capitalist society is one material ground for socialist theory; the experience of twentieth-century postcapitalist social construction is another.

As a final preliminary, I believe we should now strive to avoid the error of splintering socialist theory into discrete and warring "models." The desire for product differentiation should not prevail over the very real task of developing a complex and nuanced vision, which will undoubtedly incorporate many elements from the various positions currently being put forward. No single model is likely to be adequate to this task, and we must recognize that we are at an early point on a long road of discovery. This road leads to a theory and an understanding that will progressively incorporate new qualities as it draws upon (what will hopefully be) a growing left and working-class movement worldwide.

In the next section, I will briefly enumerate some elements of what I see as the necessary core of a socialist vision. The key concern of the PF–PR model with the production relations of incentive and control in class-antagonistic MPs suggests that, in overcoming the class principle of social organization new patterns of incentive and motivation will be of central importance. This follows also from the premise that the socialist vision under development is intended to be relevant for a modern society, with complex problems of coordination, management, and information processing, as well as a highly educated and diverse population with critical and dynamic expectations. The specter of "millions of equations," thrown at socialism from the libertarian right, and more recently from the camp of "market socialism," must be confronted head on.

This leads to a reconsideration of economic coordination—commonly but misleadingly called "planning"—as a central element in the socialist economy. The problem of building a common social project *in conjunction with* autonomy and self-fulfillment of individuals and collectives suggests a change in the role of central bodies, away from the traditional conception of that role. This too will be explained in the next section, which leads up to one core idea in the model of the socialist MP developed in this chapter: the role of *parametric forms* in supporting the structures of direct democracy. The concept of parametric forms draws upon the new microeconomic field of incentive design (a field that had its origin, in fact, in the Soviet economic reforms of the 1960s and 1970s). Parametric forms are related to the problems of price formation and incentives (income distribution), and these are discussed within the framework of multilevel coordination, the central embodiment of socialist democracy in a maturing socialist economy. The chapter ends with a few specific institutional suggestions toward the implementation of economic democracy—which, as a political concept, requires transcendence of spontaneous market relations.

"Maturing socialism" raises the question: maturing toward what? In the next chapter, I will address some aspects of Marx's higher stage conception of full communism—a topic that has been widely neglected in socialist theory but that needs to be brought into focus to complete the overall project of this book.

BUILDING BLOCKS: COMPREHENSIVE DEMOCRATIC COORDINATION

Market Socialism, Hurrah Socialism, and New Socialism

The new visions of socialism have emerged against a backdrop of "market socialism," on the one hand; and the classical Marxist texts and formulations inspired by them, on the other. Market socialism (viz., Roemer 1994; Wright 1996; Schweickart 1992, 1996; Roosevelt and Belkin 1994; cf. Ollman, et al. 1998) performs the service of reminding us that capitalist PRs are not synonymous with market relations (remember the distinction between simple and capitalist market forms, developed in chapter 2); conflation of capitalism with "the market," or the "free" market, is in fact the stock-in-trade of orthodox economics. The market socialists fail, however, to see that, if capitalism and markets are not the same thing, they are nevertheless deeply intertwined and mutually defining in the period of advanced capitalism in which socialism comes forward. Market relations have profound legitimating and system-reproducing functions within capitalism, which I have tried to capture with the concept of *valorization*. Spontaneous markets assure that the social whole functions without the benefit of intelligence and conscious guidance; outcomes are known only after the fact, and take on lives of their own independent of human will. The idea that alienation, cyclical instability, crisis and polarization can be removed from "the market" by simple legislative or administrative expedients—laws against private ownership, or "clamshell" schemes to separate trading in shares of ownership from trading in commodities—is the hallmark illusion of market socialism.

It is, however, insufficient to answer this illusion with semantic generalities drawn from the classical Marxist tradition. In an earlier period, it might have sufficed to use inspirational phrases—"the commonwealth of toil," or "freely associated producers"—or to make grand references to the "abolition of the law of value" (see, e.g., H. Ticktin, in Ollman, et al. 1998; cf. Lebowitz 2003). Today, I propose, this sort of wooly semantic socialism is no longer viable. The hard, operational questions must be faced squarely, if socialism is to become a significant political force once again (cf. Nove 1983).

Some recent initiatives help greatly in this effort. Models of participatory planning have been put forward (Devine 1988; Albert and Hahnel 1991a, 1991b, 1992) in which collectives of workers, organized as producers and as consumers, negotiate patterns of production and distribution of goods. The model proposed by Michael Albert and Robin Hahnel, in particular, is designed to eliminate all forms of market relations from economic life, and also to avoid hierarchical principles of organization. This derives from their fear of state power, which occupies a position equal to class power as a source of oppression. For this reason, they project a socialism without any central bodies or structures of authority, which could be corrupted and turned against democratic principles by an incipient bureaucratic caste. An Iteration Facilitation Board, without power to affect outcomes, mediates among producer and consumer collectives, passing proposals back and forth, in a system of horizontal coordination, until consistent proposals and agreement are reached.

An opposite approach is taken by W. Paul Cockshott and Allin F. Cottrell (1993, 1997), who tackle the "millions of equations" problem head on. Taking their cue from modern computational methods and capacities, they argue that central coordination is possible after all. They propose a novel approach to matrix inversion (the core mathematical procedure in the solution of simultaneous linear equations) that reduces the time required for calculation from a matter of years to a matter of seconds. State enterprises submit their production parameters to the center—electronically, of course. Demands for goods are either registered directly and aggregated electronically, or monitored from inventory changes. The coordination problem is then compiled and solved centrally, as often as necessary. Decision problems, such as choice of technique, are also solved using computed (nonmarket-generated) labor-value prices. Detailed but viable plans are then conveyed to enterprises, which carry them out. There are, in principle, no obstacles to

Lenin's "One Big Factory" conception, despite the enormous and increasing variety and complexity of production, coordination, and distribution.

Each of these conceptions, in my view, contains useful elements for a renewed socialism; each, however, also misses an important part of the problem and by itself leads to insufficient outcomes. The horizontal planning idea captures well the potential of democratic participation. However, in their zeal to avoid any possible abuse of authority, Albert and Hahnel in fact—and despite their clearly expressed intention—reproduce much of the alienation associated with spontaneous markets. There is nothing in their model that encourages or facilitates development of social consensus concerning the outcome of the iterations; the Iteration Facilitation Board is constrained to play a completely passive role. So once again, global outcomes are known only after the fact, and it is not clear that oversteering, cycles, and other elemental phenomena would not reemerge. Despite their programmatic abhorrence of markets, the iterations must result in the formation of swap ratios—prices. As these are not planned or subject to political control or criteria, they in fact replicate the "equilibrium" prices of neoclassical theory—as Albert and Hahnel themselves indicate in their discussion of the similarities between their model and Walrasian general equilibrium. Finally, the constant meetings and negotiations among participating producers and consumers raise the specter of overorganization and endless talk, aptly characterized by Nancy Folbre in her well-known quip about this conception as resembling "one long University of Massachusetts Student Government meeting." This observation brings to the fore an important question: do socialists want participatory democracy? How much? Is participation in decision making an ultimate end? Is it something to be maximized, or optimized?

The modern electronic central coordination model, on the other hand, goes too far in the other direction. The Austrian questions immediately arise (Hayek 1935, 1945). To what extent is the information relevant to production activity not only locally specific, but locally specific in forms that do not permit of transmission and aggregation? Local traditions and customs, for example, result in products with distinctive properties. The Apple Butter Festival that takes place every October in Burton, Ohio is part of a culture in which buying and consuming apple butter is a sharing of the life of the Amish farm community; besides, the apple butter you find there simply tastes unique! Putting this apple butter into a central production-distribution matrix, along with the products of other food producers, simply misses the point—not to mention the flavor.

Moreover, the idea that central solutions to the coordination problem are *possible* misses the point in another, and perhaps crucial, respect: are such solutions even *desirable*? The participation of producer collectives (and in some cases, referring to what are commonly called "public goods," consumer collectives) in the economic planning process is not only itself desirable, but may even be a signal advantage of socialism. Coordination in both capitalist and socialist contexts may in fact not be the main aim of the respective *primary* coordination mechanisms of each mode of production (market and plan, respectively); the primary goals of these mechanisms are valorization (in capitalist societies) and *consensualization* (in socialist ones) (see Laibman 1995). The purpose of participatory planning is, first and foremost, the progressive creation of consensus and shared vision: a sense of intentionality and control over the social process. The central-planning conception, even in its most modern electronic guise, does not appear to address this level of the socialist problematic at all.

Multilevel Democratic Coordination

I think we can take a cue from the historical evolution of what I have called "comprehensive planning," mainly in the Soviet Union but also of course in a number of other countries. Beginning in the mid-1960s, the Soviet literature presented a conception of multilevel planning, including both central planning and planning at the level of intermediate regional or industrial bodies, individual enterprises, or even brigades or teams within enterprises. A simple model of this conception can work with two levels, which I will call "central" and "decentral."

We pause briefly to note a terminological problem. "Planning" is actually a misnomer; this term should be reserved for the process of shaping the future course of development, including forms of urban settlement, siting of production facilities, transportation, land use, and so forth. (I address these issues later in this chapter.) "Coordination" is a better term for the ongoing process of directing economic activity and facilitating the flows of goods and information. However, in the context of the capitalism-socialism comparison, I have needed "coordination" to refer to the general economic problem, to be solved by "planning" or by "markets" (separately or in combination). We are, apparently, stuck with "planning" as the term for *socialist* coordination.

The governing insight of the central-decentral conception is that neither level can function successfully without the other: central planning requires "good numbers" (i.e., solidly grounded, "correct" information) and these can only be produced "on the ground" at the local level, where people have the particular knowledge (and the incentive; see below) to derive a set of real possibilities. Decentral planning, on the other hand, requires the framework of stability and the grasp of relationship to larger patterns that can only be provided by the central planning function. Opposed to the usual textbook notion of conflict between central and "market" decision making, then, the comprehensive conception sees the central and decentral planning sites as complementary, not competitive, and the maturing of socialism as consisting in the strengthening of both levels and of their interaction.

The concerns of the proponents of horizontal iteration, however, about possible abuse of power in a formally hierarchical system, are certainly legitimate. Democratic controls are necessary at both the central and the decentral levels; the point is to transcend the common category error of counterposing democracy to *central* planning. On the one hand, there is nothing automatically democratic about decentralization; local tyrants abound in history. On the other, the central planning bodies in a viable socialist society would necessarily be subject to a forcefully promulgated and frequently renewed popular mandate, and also to constant public scrutiny and critical debate. I need hardly belabor the fact that these vital elements were largely absent in the Soviet experience. It is also worth observing that, despite the massive attack against central planning in the scholarly and popular literature on "existing socialism" over at least six decades, neither central nor comprehensive planning regimes have yet had a historical opportunity to function and to prove themselves in an environment of unfettered public discussion.

The question now arises: in the iterative process of coordination between central and decentral bodies, how much latitude can be accorded to the decentral level in setting product assortment, finding suppliers and customers, etc.? Again, the Soviet experience appears to have been mainly of a rigid process: at first simply top-down, later involving down-up-down iterations, but never sanctioning direct ties among enterprises (despite the existence of unofficial practices along these lines). The idea remained essentially undeveloped, a fact that may have been important in limiting the success of economic reform.

I have tried to envision the development of horizontal search and contracting, in the context of multilevel or comprehensive socialist coordination. A key requirement is visibility: to avoid the alienating and disinforming effects of spontaneous activity and competitive secrecy, the horizontal process must be subject to immediate and full disclosure. The rule is that enterprises inform the center (and everyone else) of contacts and contracts as they happen. The center, for its part, does not intervene, except in instances in which its mandate allows and requires it to do so. This would be true in situations where the activities of enterprises have significant external effects: on transportation or warehousing, on the environment, on water or power supplies, on residential communities and education. These interests may be brought to bear on decisions through the central body, although in some situations there may be direct participatory processes as well. The goal is to find a good (we need not require an "optimal") combination of concentration of criteria through the central authorities—where those authorities are subject to democratic control—and participatory mechanisms. These, one hopes, may bring popular interests forward in cases where central intervention has insufficient democratic guidance or where the mandate is unclear—without, one may hope, allowing these mechanisms to degenerate into an endless, well, student government meeting.

The Socialist Price Mechanism

Horizontal contracting implies some price flexibility. Before this issue can be addressed, however, the general problem of price formation in the socialist context must be posed (for background, see Abouchar 1977).

It is useful to distinguish between a core socialist sector, in which a set of basic producer goods and centrally distributed consumer goods are produced and traded; and an informal sector, containing local products, many personal services, and so forth.

In the core sector, and to a degree which I think has not been well understood, the essential impact of central planning is on prices rather than on quantities. At the central level, coordination/planning is first and foremost a matter of prices; price formation is the main task of the central coordination body. By contrast, except perhaps in cases of certain strategic materials, there is no need to preplan exact output levels, which can be settled by the enterprises *en route* as demand indicators change. Inventories are held as buffer stocks, to make coordination of goods flows possible while output levels vary within normal tolerances. It should be clear that the *basic* assortment of output is subject to political control, as the central bodies renew the mandates of existing enterprises, and commission new ones. This belongs to the study of planning proper—the projection of the future course of economic development. Planning the detailed output composition—its "fine tuning"—belongs to the decentral level.

Planned price lists, then, are in effect in the core sector. Enterprise incomes are formed on the basis of the official prices, and evaluation of alternative products and techniques is done in terms of those prices as well. Horizontal contracts are about quantities, except insofar as deviations of goods from custom specifications require some adjustment of prices, in accordance with cost-based formulas. Note that, since horizontal latitude implies some degree of competition among enterprises, this competition must be based on quality and service, not on price. Price competition implies the possibility of choosing to compete by restricting (someone's) income. The link between price and income in general is crucial to the quality of workers' lives, and this is precisely why competition in the price form is prevented.

All of this is in contrast to the informal sector. With the general shape of income distribution and overall economic stability determined in the core sector, the lack of price planning in the informal sector need not have adverse consequences, and the flexibility of pricing there can be useful for ex post coordination. Of course, certain fundamental principles such as basic wage rates, labor and environmental regulations and progressive income taxation apply to the informal sector, so that it cannot become a base for retrograde social development.

The rationale for comprehensive price planning in the core sector is complex and multiform, and can only be summarized here. I have developed a concept of *social reproduction prices* (Laibman 1978, 1992a, ch. 14; cf. Brody 1970). These are benchmark prices that allocate to goods a proportion of the social stocks of productive resources, held typically in the form of housing, education, medical, and other social provisions in the public trust generally and not by individual enterprises. These stocks would not shape a spontaneously formed competitive rate of profit, and the social reproduction price vector therefore differs in principle from the long-period normal prices of the classical–Sraffian literature (see Sraffa 1960; Pasinetti 1977), which I take to be essentially the same as the Marxian *production prices* (Marx 1967, vol. III). Insofar as all stocks, including the usual means of production held by enterprises, are progressively regarded as directly or indirectly labor-reproducing, and therefore assimilated to the rest of the social reproduction stocks, the social reproduction prices converge upon direct-plus-indirect labor-embodied prices—the "labor values" of Marxist theory. The fact that they do not do this immediately or completely has two profound implications. First, the simple labor values emerging from flow input-output data are not optimal from a socialist standpoint, except at a late stage of development in which social consciousness has matured to a point at which enterprises can be trusted to ignore (not to be accountable for) locally "owned" stocks of productive resources. Second, and of greatest importance for the "debate among socialists" (Ollman et al. 1998) it is clear that spontaneous competition—

"market socialism"—must fail to generate good prices for socialist coordination. This is a major element in the theoretical critique of the market-socialism position.

Having said that, however, it is clear that, once we leave behind the free-market ideology, in which the term "market" is abstracted from the social context in which concrete forms of market relations are embedded, actual market institutions may play a role in a comprehensive socialist society, a role that has nothing to do with "the" market as spontaneous regulator of production and distribution (cf. Elson 1991). Markets within the informal sector, surrounded by the commanding heights of the core sector, are one example. Another is the role of locally initiated horizontal relations among producer and/or consumer collectives in the core sector: these clearly involve contractual exchanges—markets—in some sense. Given that these relations (*a*) are subject to an overall structure of planned prices; (*b*) take place in conditions of complete visibility; and (*c*) are subject to the key socialist process of evaluation in determining rewards (on which much more below), they may be called "intentional markets," or "socially controlled markets." We have the prospect that the social content of exchange, or market, activity changes and deepens as socialism matures.

This reference, incidentally, underscores an important element in socialist theory: the dynamism, and stadiality, of socialist development, in this case with reference to the changing nature of market relations. In much recent post–market-socialist literature, socialism is still seen in nonhistorical terms, that is, as a thing rather than a process. The notion of socialism as an emerging reality, which passes through stages of development, is a holdover from Soviet-era thinking, in this case a welcome one. The alternative is the failure to distinguish between the lower and higher stages of communist society (Marx, 1933b); we will return to this distinction, and to the theory of the higher stage, in ch. 7.

In maturing socialism, then, market relations, originally existing as residues of prior social systems and necessary during long periods of early development—especially in countries where technical and social prerequisites are poorly developed—now take on new roles, as advanced forms of horizontal ties within comprehensive planning. In the same way, planning, originally appearing as top-down command coordination, becomes increasingly interactive, with significant elements devolved to the local or decentral levels. With both "plan" and "market" evolving, the gap between them also becomes less sharp, and socialist thought does well to evolve away from the rigid "plan vs. market" dichotomy.

II. INCENTIVES, PARAMETRIC FORMS, INCOME DISTRIBUTION

We are moving progressively closer to the heart of the matter.

Consciousness, Incentives, Motivation

A central historical materialist claim—indeed the core organizing concept of this book—underlies the necessity of socialism: development of the productive forces within capitalism progressively undermines capitalism-constricted, unprincipled, forms of motivation and control. More advanced levels of consciousness and incentives to productive activity are *necessary* if further social and economic development are to take place (Laibman 1999a, 1999b).

The (neo)liberal critique of socialism has always rested on a postulated conflict between the advanced incentives presumed to be required for socialism to function, on the one hand; and the limitations imposed by biologically or theologically defined human nature, on the other. The Marxist answer to this is the entire research program based on the *Critique of the Gotha Programme* (Marx 1933b), which envisioned stages in the development of incentives with corresponding stages in the development of postcapitalist society. Thus, socialism does not require preexisting "good" human beings, as the building blocks of new social institutions; rather, these institutions will develop on the basis of human beings as they emerge out of (are "stamped with the birthmarks of") the old society. The construction of socialism is a long, slow dialectic of transforming circumstances and transforming human consciousness.

To propose a materialist approach to the problem of incentives and income distribution, we will need two distinctions in the nature of incentives: that between *material* and *moral* incentives, and that between *individual* and *collective* incentives (for background in the Soviet experience, see Kirsch 1972; Ellman 1973). These are crosscutting distinctions, resulting in four cases, which can be represented schematically as follows:

Table 6.1. A Taxonomy of Incentives

Incentives	Material	Moral
Individual	piece wage	individual honor
Collective	group bonus	group honor

Now the central proposition of materialist incentive theory may be stated: at any given stage in the development of social consciousness, material and individual incentives *exist*. At early stages dominated by the recent capitalist past, they are prominent. At any given stage of development, therefore, it is simply not a matter of "choosing" whether emphasis on individual and material incentives or on collective and moral incentives is preferable. Choice between them is not a proper policy objective. Both sorts of incentives *will be operating*, irrespective of income distribution policy. The problem is therefore not whether or not to "use" individual/material incentives, but how best to combine them with collective/moral ones, to achieve the most rapid advance of both production and consciousness, in the given conditions.

A major implication follows: ignoring the existing balance among types of incentives will place obstacles in the path of development of consciousness. Thus, for example, a socialist regime, by choosing for ideological reasons to stress collective/moral incentives against (rather than in combination with) individual/material ones, may cause the more advanced and skilled workers to resent their less advanced and skilled compatriots. Resentment may emerge, especially against those who do not shoulder the same burdens as their coworkers ("carry their weight"), but receive the same pay nevertheless. This resentment breeds cynicism and evasive action, and the result may be less rather than more socialist consciousness—the opposite of the intention behind the policy. Levels of consciousness and corresponding need for a certain degree of individual and material reward are real; they cannot be ignored, any more than can the real differences in skill, accomplishment, and motivation among workers, and among different grades of workers (unskilled, semi-skilled, skilled, professional).

The crosscutting distinctions in Table 6.1 suggest that a nuanced policy might be possible. For example, would the general movement from "northwest" to "southeast" in the table be promoted by a combination of *collective material* (southwest cell) with *individual moral* (northeast) incentives? If material differentiation is required, place it on a firm basis of collective accomplishment; to the extent that individual reward is needed, stress forms of recognition by one's colleagues rather than monetary reward. This may certainly be possible to some extent, but the possibility should not be overstated. For example, without at least some pay differentiation, advanced workers may become cynical and disrespectful of sincerely intended gestures of personal recognition. Moral rewards may also ring hollow to those who do not receive them, if the associated pay differentials are perceived as being too large. No amount of subtlety in the formation of the incentive package can change the central reality of confrontation of income distribution possibilities with objective conditions.

The removal of the capitalist property-based principle of income distribution (surplus value) wipes out, at a stroke, the vast bulk of the income and wealth inequality of capitalist society: gone—hopefully forever, but we know that historical materialism does not rule out reversion to earlier forms—are the billionaires and multimillionaires. In this sense, socialism is fundamentally and massively equalizing, from its inception. Further equalization, however, is development-dependent: it relies on the evolution of equality in education, skill, responsibility, and creativity in work, and corresponding advance of consciousness. It would be harmful to try to accelerate this evolution artificially, just as it would be to retard it unnecessarily.

The Problem of Enterprise Incentive and Planning

Comprehensive planning requires that the agents at the decentral level—enterprises, in the two-level model—assume responsibility for both creating and executing their own plans, in each relevant plan period. This has given rise to an enormous literature on the problem of how enterprise income is to be formed, so as to reward both ambitious but realistic planning, and competent and energetic plan execution.

The working hypothesis is this: in the rather long period in which a developing socialist society experiences a trade-off between extensive participatory or authoritarian structures, on the one hand, and loss of control to spontaneous market processes, on the other, the use of parametric forms (formulas) can be of decisive importance. "Parametric" here means that an enterprise knows the weights that will be attached to different aspects of its activity, and is thus encouraged to act in a certain way. Social evaluation criteria are embodied in the weights (parameters) according to which enterprise income above a secure minimum level—often, but possibly misleadingly, called "bonuses"—will accrue. Parametric procedures are, in effect, an admission: we are not, as a society, yet ready to go "directly political" with the most difficult decisions, and yet we insist on making these decisions democratically, on the basis of consciously promulgated socialist principles.

This is the classical problem in the theory of incentive design (an accessible introduction is Campbell 1995; a classic text is Tirole 1988; for the Soviet background, Ellman 1979). Can a system of central-decentral planning be devised, in which the ground-level production collectives can be entrusted with formulating their own plans? If they can be expected to plan ambitiously—to form "taut" plans, in Soviet parlance—and also to work energetically to fulfill the plan once it is finalized, then all of the detail planning can be devolved to the enterprise level. Moreover, the plan indicators—levels of inputs and outputs—transmitted to the center will be both accurate (reflective of specific local conditions) and based on the most ambitious yet realistic projection of the enterprise's possibilities. This conception avoids the gross inefficiencies that arise when the center sets the enterprise plan without adequate knowledge, as well as the problem of strategic behavior on the part of enterprises (concealing reserves of materials, labor, effort, etc.).

A typical baseline formulation of this problem defines the *enterprise share forming index*: a weighted average of any number of success indicators. Examples of the success indicators are indices of output and productivity growth, efficient use of financial resources, the degree to which target assortment of output is met. Others—crucially—measure the way in which the performance of the enterprise meets social targets, some of them essentially nonquantitative. Some of these may be evaluated by organizations outside the enterprise, which issue reports on the effects of the enterprise's activity on the society surrounding it. They may address issues such as the enterprise's impact on the environment (meeting of general and/or specific waste emission targets, for example), or its success in furthering social goals: progress in employing and promoting women and people from historically disadvantaged ethnic or cultural groups; the enterprise's ties to schools and provision of educational opportunities for children in the community where it is located; its success in drawing more of its workers into meaningful participation in management and planning; and so forth. Additional goals and measures could certainly be formulated.

The relative weights, which determine how important each success indicator is in shaping the overall outcome, are set by a political process. The important point to note here is that the overall measure of enterprise success can, in the socialist context, be made to depend significantly on qualitative indicators and evaluations that would simply not be available in any kind of spontaneous market system, whether capitalist or "market socialist." The outcome measure is therefore inherently different from a simple quantitative indicator of profit alone, as it would inevitably have to be in a spontaneous market framework. The *net realized rate of return* compares the value of enterprise net output (or perhaps net output minus base wages) to some measure of the stock of resources committed to use by the enterprise. This may be the best aggregator of the traditional economic indicators—output, productivity, sales, saving on raw materials, efficient use of productive stocks. Then the overall outcome measure may be determined as a weighted average of the realized net rate of return, plus two additional indicators: one to measure the enterprise's success at addressing the *negative* externalities missed by the rate of return (pollution, e.g.), and one to measure the *positive* externalities (the social indicators of the sort identified above). The outcome measure will then be the weighted sum of these three indicators.

The power of this conception lies in its possibilities: democratic involvement of numerous sections of the community in determining the outcome measure, and the instantiation of *social goals*, such as the progressive overcoming of the legacies of racism and sexism, in both the plan goals and in the measures of plan fulfillment on the basis of which enterprise income will be formed. The translation of qualitative social goals into quantitative indicators is not straightforward; this aspect of the problem requires much further study. These indicators, however, must be capable of prevision by the enterprise, which will want to try to maximize them. If, for example, progress in addressing problems of women workers, and other issues in the enterprise's relation to women in the community, is measured on a rating scale (0 to 10, e.g.), the enterprise must be able to meaningfully set a target (8, e.g.), and the appropriate evaluators similarly must be able to determine their view of the extent to which the target was in fact met. Clearly there is the possibility of political manipulation and distortion here, but that is to be expected, and addressed.

The final step in posing the problem is recognition that the outcome measure exists in two forms: first, the planned level (which will be published electronically and available for inspection by all interested parties), and its subsequent degree of plan fulfillment, the actual result.

Now the enterprise's income (again, only the discretionary portion of total income, with a base wage assured to workers on the basis of hours of labor performed) will be a share of its cash flow (the income beyond costs of materials, depreciation charges on equipment, and wages). There are several versions of the formulas for determining enterprise income, based on both its planned and its actual outcome measure. Arithmetic aside, the heart of the matter is to make it worthwhile for the enterprise to plan ambitiously, but also realistically: to set the highest possible achievable goals in all areas, qualitative and quantitative. This means that the enterprise will not conceal reserves, in order to get a relatively easy plan assigned to it, only to then *over*fulfill that plan by a large margin. It also means that the enterprise will not announce a grand plan that it has no hope of meeting. The share-forming formula relates the planned and the actual levels of the outcome measure in such a way that neither of these distortions will occur; it is in the enterprise's interest to set the most ambitious plan, but only among the set of plans that it can actually fulfill. The enteprise's income is greatest when the plan is both ambitious, *and* exactly achieved. (In a mature socialist economy, in which coordination and balance are essential and other sectors must count on accurate performance by the enterprise, no reward should obtain for *over*fulfillment of the plan, which results in unanticipated output, strain on storage and transport capacities, and related inefficiencies.)

The development of share-calculation formulas embodying these principles is a major step in the conceptualization of advanced socialism. It suggests that enterprise personnel can be drawn into the planning process, with due attention to both their material interest and their moral horizon; this, if possible, would be a major achievement of socialist democracy.

It turns out, however, that many of the actual formulas proposed to reward both ambitious planning and plan fulfillment result in contradictory signals being sent to the enterprises. This inconsistency is, I believe, due to a missing element in the concept set underlying the formulas. There are actually *three* concepts of the share-forming index (the outcome measure) to be distinguished: the two already defined—planned and actual result—plus one more: the *actual* level of *possibility*, which can be estimated by the enterprise, but is in principle unknown to the center. We may call this last measure the "possible outcome." To even estimate the possible outcome, an enterprise would have to mobilize all of its collectives, and enter into discussions with various community organizations and local government. The center's (and society's) goal is to urge the enterprise, in determining its own plan, to set the planned outcome as close as possible to the possible outcome, and *then* to implement the plan successfully: to achieve an actual outcome as close to the planned outcome as it can. In this more sophisticated version, the enterprise has an interest in setting both the plan and its actual achievement equal to its own perception of its best possibility, the possible outcome. Unfortunately, this version of the procedure is entirely nonoperational: since the center does not and cannot know the possible outcome, that variable cannot be used to determine the enterprise's reward.

This difficult situation has even been enshrined in an *impossibility theorem* (for one formulation, see Hurwicz and Walker 1990). Assuming that only the plan (once it is announced) and the results (once they are in), can be known by the center, there seems to be no way to link planning and achievements of decentral units into an efficient system of income formation. The only alternative appears to be the capitalist managerial approach, which would link bonuses or rewards directly to achievement alone (Ellman 1979). This abolishes planning altogether, and with it the advantages of prevision and coordination and de-alienation valued by socialists and linked to the planning process.

We seem, then, to be on the horns of a dilemma. Either the incentive regime for comprehensive planning is incoherent, requiring knowledge on the part of the center that it cannot reasonably possess, or the entire project must be abandoned.

My proposal to transcend the impossibility theorem rests on a simple idea, which is not unrelated to the notion of an efficiency wage. While the center does not know the possible outcome, the *members of the working collective do*, at least roughly. If the degree of technical and cultural development has placed enough knowledge and power in the hands of the rank and file, then their morale and feeling of engagement with the work of the enterprise come into play. Either wildly overambitious planning or severely underambitious planning will weaken the ability of the collective to put forward its own best effort. In short, there is, under advanced social and technical conditions, an objective relationship between the planned outcome and achievable levels of the actual outcome, which functions as a constraint, and prevents the collective's leadership from, for example, strategically misrepresenting its possibilities in a downward direction.

It is not difficult to specify this relationship. The actual outcome is plotted against the planned outcome, in such a way that actual is less than plan except when plan is equal to the possible level. The collective, in a word, can only get its own best effort out of itself if there is a shared perception that it is targeting its true possibility. If the plan is set at a level greater than the maximum genuine collective effort makes possible, the enterprise is pushing itself beyond reasonable limits; morale suffers, and results fall below plan. In the opposite case, the one feared by the impossibility theorists, the enterprise personnel collude to present to the center a plan that falls below the possible outcome level—a form of concealing reserves. Knowledge of this fact, however, pervades the enterprise and again morale sags; the actual output is again below the planned level, and enterprise income suffers.

The formula for the enterprise share coefficient is then quite simple, and need not contain a direct term rewarding taut planning; only a measure of plan fulfillment. Taut planning is, in effect, assured by the fact that in advanced social and technical conditions an ambitious plan is needed for the enterprise to harness its own creative possibilities, at a high level of morale. In this case, it turns out that enterprise optimization is consistent: the enterprise does best when achieving equality between the actual outcome and the planned outcome. The enterprise has a material as well as a moral incentive to plan up to its best possibilities (something the center does not know and cannot evaluate), and also to exactly fulfill the plan, once set.

The force of this argument, of course, depends on workers being very heavily invested in the quality of their work life within the enterprise. If, as was indeed the case in Soviet industrial culture, a large part of a worker's group identification, cultural life, and recreational activities takes place within the enterprise, so that workers have a large stake in the level of morale and the quality of the social life there, then we can expect the constraint of morale-based efficiency to function effectively and keep planned outcomes fairly close to possible ones. This constraint, however, would function less effectively to the extent workers' lives are oriented outside of the enterprise. If people find fulfillment and derive moral strength from activities and relationships that are unconnected with their work roles, the possibility of planning decentralization leading to strategic distortion is larger. This raises the intriguing possibility of a contradiction in socialist development; one might even speak of a low-level equilibrium trap. Maturing socialism presumably delivers a gradually falling amount of total working time; the work week might progressively fall to thirty-two hours, then to twenty-eight hours, for example, as rising productivity and stabilization of consumption expectations make that possible. But if this results in progressive loss of social orientation to the workplace, the resulting distortions in planning could result in productivity losses and hamper further evolution along the same lines. The core idea here is that socialist development requires and presumes a gradually widening *sphere of identification*, in which the enterprise is increasingly embedded in a larger social context to which the same advanced motivational principles apply.*

This discussion is, of course, merely illustrative of the types of procedures that can be developed to create parametric structures to assist enterprises in ambitious planning. The provisional conclusion is that share-forming formulas providing material incentives to decentral collectives to formulate and execute taut but realistic plans are in principle possible and consistent, once notice is taken of the relationship between principled leadership in a collective and effective action by that collective at all levels. This relationship, in turn, clearly has as presupposition that the levels of skill, education, participatory culture, individual autonomy, and collaborative interdependence within the enterprise are such that perceptions do matter; that both a sense and the reality of effective leadership are essential for the collective to function well.

---

*I am indebted to Tony Smith for suggesting this train of thought.

This idea of a principled, participatory enterprise collective is, in fact, a major instance of evolution of the PRs in conjunction with PFs that have evolved beyond levels appropriate for capitalist, or class-antagonistic, society. It also points beyond the crisis within the capitalist workplace site (chapter 4 of this book), in which in antagonistic conditions, the devolution index is crushed between an incentive floor and a control ceiling. The model of the socialist enterprise points beyond that structural crisis point, toward development of PRs in which ever-higher measures of devolution—socialist democracy—do not encounter barriers associated with exploitative control, and do not result in lagging effort and productivity.

The Problem of Democratic Income Distribution

A second illustration of parametric forms is provided by the problem of appropriate structuring of material incentives.

Economic democracy means, if it means anything, a *political* process determining the proportions of the economy. If I were asked to identity only the two most important of these proportions, they would be the division of the net product between consumption and growth, and the distribution of income among persons.

The capitalist market functions, among other things, as a narcotic: the pain of inequality is muted by the perception that distribution is determined not by any human agency, but by the impersonal, even god-like, force of "the market." Socialism, by contrast, insists on making society democratically responsible for this major aspect of its economic relations. This can be quite painful, and when attempted in premature conditions may create a temptation to replace the elemental market mechanism with authoritarian substitutes.

The politics of income distribution are daunting. Think of it: working people of every occupation and level of skill must sit down together (figuratively; perhaps literally), face each other across a table, and tell each other what they think each group ought to be earning. People's views on this are likely to be highly complex, and research into attitudes might produce some surprises. Most people in our society, for example, would, on reflection, agree that medical doctors should receive a significant income differential: we want competition for places in medical schools to be lively, so that the doctors who treat us have been selected from a pool of highly qualified candidates. But we would also want the differential to stay within reasonable bounds, so that the medical profession attracts people who are genuinely interested in healing, and not in material affluence (or power) alone. A final consideration is that we are influenced not only by our individual interests as workers, but also by those of our families; a production worker, for example, has a daughter or son in medical school. This sort of cross-fertilization will be greater, of course, the more progress has been made in eliminating the educational and professional stratification of families and communities that is characteristic of capitalist societies.

Even assuming, however, that there is a consensus against leveling as a matter of principle—a shared sense that in given conditions some inequality is desirable—it will be very difficult to reach agreement on the degree of inequality. Experiences of twentieth-century socialist construction widely report that, in these conditions, a tendency toward leveling or excessive equalization developed. In several countries of eastern Europe in the post–World War II decades, for example, there were widespread complaints about the consequences of excessive equalizing, and even about what were perceived to be reversals in the justified income distribution order, with, for example, professionals earning less than factory workers. (Imagine: *professors* earning less than mere laborers!) The Soviet "income revolution" of the 1960s and 1970s appears, in this light, as an example of possibly premature and excessive leveling.

Can parametric forms lessen the pain, and prevent tendencies toward overequalization, while simultaneously maintaining the political and democratic character of the income distribution process and avoiding relapse into elemental "market" determination (which, of course, is always ultimately an indirect register of more fundamental power relations)?

To get just a provisional fix on the highly complex problem of determining wage differentials among many diverse groups, imagine that there are just two groups of workers; imagine, further, that the boundary between the two groups is distinct, and that there is a consensus concerning the ordinal relationship between them—that is, it is known and agreed that group A will receive less than group B, or that the two groups will receive the same amount (the case of complete equality), but that in no conditions would group A receive more. A, then, are those with less skill, training, responsibility, or creativity, and B are those with more.

The income distribution problem amounts to determining a single parameter: the *ratio* of the wage received by B to the wage received by A. This ratio, together with the net wage income available for distribution, will determine the actual levels of the two wage rates. (It does not matter, for present purposes, whether this is conceived as taking place at the level of a single enterprise, a sector, or the economy as a whole.)

Now democracy suggests that a vote be taken. Since the numbers of individuals in the two groups are likely to be different, it would be appropriate to use the average vote of each group to represent that group. These are the distribution ratios that each of the two groups wants, and presumably the ratios that each group feels are justified by circumstances of skill and training, or of difficulty, danger and disagreeable-ness of work. We assume that the less-skilled group will opt for more equality than the more-skilled group.

If the actual ratio is determined as a simple average of the two groups' votes, each group will have an incentive to strategically exaggerate its true position. Is there a way to bring some honesty and dialog into the determination of the wage distribution ratio?

To do this, we would define two new variables: what group A *thinks* group B *thinks* the ratio should be; and what group B *thinks* group A *thinks* the ratio should be. We will want to reward each group for accurate perceptions of the thinking of the other group, and penalize each group for distorted perceptions of the other group. That way, we will get the two groups thinking about each other; perhaps even talking to each other. Each group will now declare its preferences, *and* its perceptions of the other group's preferences, knowing that it is in its interest to get these perceptions right. Each group's vote, then, is shaped to consider not just what that group intrinsically thinks the distribution should be, and certainly not its strategic interest in achieving a distribution most in its favor. The actual outcome will be favorable to a group to the extent that it has a correct perception of the position of the other group. The process then helps to shape an evolving consensus about the best degree of income inequality in any stage of the society's development; this helps to secure consensus, raise morale, and link working people to the process by which income distribution occurs (to demystify the one area that has been surrounded by the greatest amount of market and ideological mystification, reaching well back into the class-antagonistic era).

As in the previous illustration of parametric forms—the enterprise income-forming index—this discussion is intended only to illustrate the problem, and the possibilities. And as in the previous illustration, there is no intention that some sort of automatic device or formula serve as a *substitute* for a political process. On the contrary, the parametric forms force enterprises to deliberate, to confer, to analyze, in the first case, and different groups or strata in the labor force to enter into dialog, in the second. To the extent that the principles behind the parametric devices are progressively better understood over time, they help to deepen the socialist community's sense of a shared project. Enterprises arrive at plans that have the full moral backing of their members; income distribution evolves in a way that finds support in the working population, as well as a sense of collaboration and participation. The parametric forms also serve as a corrective against hyper-extension of the participatory machinery, and against political degeneration of the process (unprincipled bargaining, coalitions, etc.). Just as material and individual incentives must be promoted and supported, precisely in order to evolve most expeditiously toward their eventual transcendence, so parametric forms can be used to secure a path toward a situation in which labor is more and more freely forthcoming, and precise calculation of distributional ratios more and more irrelevant.

III. SOME CONCRETE SUGGESTIONS AND A CONCLUSION

Taking stock, I envision a maturing socialism with economic coordination (planning) elaborated at higher and lower levels, which are mutually en-abling and confirming, rather than in conflict. Participation is valued, but it is not hyperextended or treated as an absolute end; private space and "free evenings" are also features of the good life that we seek to develop, and are also essential aspects of democracy. Democratic input and control are rel-evant at *all* levels, from central to the most decentral. Autonomy of working and living collectives is also valued, but, like participation, is not reified into an absolute: genuine local autonomy needs society-wide coordination and structures that bring about a reality and sense of wider community and stability as well.

Comprehensive socialist coordination of economic activity requires parametric forms to assist in the democratic determination of working col-lectives' plans, and of crucial ratios governing enterprise income determina-tion, personal income distribution, and rates of growth. This should be, once again as it was in the past, an active area of research in socialist theory.

Price formation is a, perhaps the, crucial task of socialist economic coordination. The benchmark prices—social reproduction prices—afford a uniform rate of return across goods or industries, and are therefore distinct from the "vertically integrated labor coefficients," often referred to as the per unit direct plus indirect labor times, or labor values. This uniformity allows for cross-industry efficiency comparisons and assists both central and decentral bodies in their efforts to define and promulgate optimal growth paths, choices of technique, and other matters for decision. The uniform rate of return, however, will result in varying perceived rates of return among industries, as enterprises calculate their rates of return on the basis of stocks of resources only under their control and not on the basis of the entire stock of social resources used in their production activity. There is, then, no sense in which an industry's rate of return is a valid measure of its performance. The rate of return registered by an individual enterprise, on the other hand, is *one* of several indicators making up its performance index. It may be measured in comparison with the planned rate of return to the industry as a whole, to remove specific deviations from the economy-wide rate determined by features of production specific to the industry but unrelated to efficiency or performance.

An important advantage of socialist price formation is the stability of prices, which makes it possible to use prices as genuine sources of information. The usual neoclassical textbook ideal of continual marginal adjustment—which suggests that price planning would involve not only solving millions of equations, but also doing so hundreds of times every day—results in random noise and inability to perceive price centers of gravity, making prices essentially useless for rational calculation (despite the programmatic emphasis placed on rational calculation in this tradition). By contrast, the benchmark (social reproduction) prices of a socialist economy can become widely known, and used; they will be subject to periodic readjustment as underlying conditions change, but not to continual and unpredictable fluctuation.

Enterprises and industry centers may have the right to adjust market prices up or down, in cases where rapid shifts in demand conditions result in sudden inventory fluctuations. Short-run price adjustment may be a useful tool of coordination, in cases where rigid pricing might otherwise result in massive unanticipated increases in stocks of unsold goods or in severe shortages and queueing. In cases where transactions prices deviate from the benchmark prices, however, it is the benchmark prices that are used to calculate enterprise performance and form enterprise income. Excess revenues or deficits resulting from accidental and unforeseeable shifts in demand should go into, or be made up out of, the central budget; enterprises collectives should be neither rewarded nor penalized for fortuitous fluctuations over which they have no control.

The continual up-down flows of information and plan commitments, supplemented by horizontal contracts, are the basis for ongoing solution of the macro-coordination problem; here we need the best technology and mathematics that cyberplanners have to offer. Socialist coordination will require what might, perhaps somewhat fancifully, be called an "E-Coordi-Net," modeled after the Internet but restricted in function to registering and processing the continually shifting flows of economic data. The E-Coordi-Net would embody the increasing accessibility and efficacy of social information, making the PRs truly visible, for the first time. With simultaneous access on the part of all central and decentral bodies and individuals to the aggregate control figures, as well as to individual enterprise plans and positions, the distinction between up-down and side to side communication should gradually lose much of its force. The "central" functions gradually shed their associations with "height" and "power"; this attenuation of the coercive function of state bodies and their transformation into facilitation and service agencies is, in fact, the "withering away of the state" proposed in the classical Marxist literature (Marx 1933b).

As proposed above, the coordination system would operate on the basis of *provisional autonomy* of producer collectives. This means that these bodies may act on new information and new possibilities, and may enter into direct ties with suppliers and customers, *without* waiting for ex ante coordination and approval from above, so long as this is done within overall plan parameters (i.e., not suddenly branching into lines of production that are completely unrelated to the existing ones, and to the enterprises' mandate), and so long as the new directions are immediately posted on the E-Coordi-Net, so that central authorities can keep track of the aggregates affected and can intervene (again, according to mandate), should that be deemed necessary. This evolution of market relations into a means of executing democratic functions is in fact the *withering away of the market*. Note the transcendence of the old dichotomy, between market socialists who make "the market" permanent, on the one hand, and the hurrah socialists, who would "abolish" it with one wave of a magic wand, on the other.

I have mentioned my idea that democracy is important for all sites of the coordination process, including the central site (not to be confused with the central site in the capitalist crisis taxonomy; chapter 4). I almost wrote "levels" instead of "sites" here, and this points up both the difficulties with metaphors, and the degree to which socialism is a long-term, continual process of deepening democracy. The "up-down" metaphor clearly implies levels, and in one sense levels, or positions within a hierarchy, may in fact be the appropriate image. As noted above, I do not share the neo-anarchist abhorrence of all vertical structure and organization. However, we should not be misled by visual metaphors into reifying authority, especially when we are talking about maturing socialism! "Up-down," for example, could easily be replaced by "in-out," as a way of describing the two-way flows between central and decentral planning bodies. In the highly individuated political climate of debate and critique envisioned here, and given the massive access to information made possible and necessary in this conception, the aura of *power* that traditionally attaches to "high" bodies should rapidly attenuate, to be replaced by regular accessibility and frequent communication.

In maturing socialist societies one would expect to find new mechanisms for conveying the popular will to the center, including the use of referenda to register votes on such things as the growth-consumption trade-off and the distribution parameters. In fact, the E-Coordi-Net would make something like continuous referenda possible. After the fashion of the cult TV series "Max Headroom," set in a future in which television viewers' selections of networks to watch are continuously registered electronically, and instantly conveyed in the form of ratings to the TV moguls and to the public, popular votes on economic parameters could be registered and tabulated continuously—so long as a system of one vote per individual E-Coordi-Net id is maintained.

Aside from flights of electronic imagination, however, ultimate control over the central authority must rely on the democratic culture of a maturing socialist society, which would see to it that the evolving popular consensus prevails, through every means from election and recall to access to the media and input through community, workplace, and professional organizations.

Many investment decisions will be part of an enterprise's plan, and successful expansion of production capacity will certainly be reflected in its success indicators and its outcome measure. Parts of net investment, especially the start-up of large-scale projects and cutting edge technological breakthroughs, may well be the responsibility of central bodies—as always under intense public scrutiny and control, and following popularly expressed mandates. Something should be said, however, about the individual entrepreneur, especially given the widespread belief that socialist organization leaves little or no room for entrepreneurial activity.

Is the "entrepreneur" a myth (Dobb 1955a, ch. 1)? Undoubtedly, to some degree. The idea that economic progress in present-day conditions depends on the solitary eccentric infused with unique inspiration in her or his basement, or garage, is too redolent of the fantasies of Ayn Rand, especially in view of the huge infrastructure and integrated teamwork of advanced laboratory practice. Is the entrepreneur conception completely false, however? Undoubtedly not. We know of instances of genuine entrepreneurial creativity—most recently, perhaps, in the computer hardware and software industry—that have led to important transformations in production and in people's lives.

Theorists of maturing socialism must address this issue. Our standpoint should be that the *genuine* entrepreneur—the imaginative creator of new products and services—will be *more* at home under socialist conditions than under capitalist ones, where he/she is living in a sea of unprincipled sharks, "venture capital" departments of large banks and corporations as a case in point, waiting to descend upon promising inventions and rip them away from their creators.

The idea might run something like this. Out of central resources we create, as always by democratic mandate, an Entrepreneurial Fund. Any individual or group with an innovative idea can apply for Entrepreneurial Enterprise status. Those who do would receive a start-up budget, to be eventually repaid, perhaps with some nominal interest charge. For some fixed period of time, no benchmark price is set for the intended product. The individual or group keeps whatever income it receives from sales at prices set by themselves, subject of course to repayment of the budget loan and to a progressive income tax. The entrepreneurial enterprise is free to hire workers, subject to labor, safety and environmental laws, and to general wage legislation, as well as to existing forms of workplace organization and participation. After the honeymoon period (one year? five years?), the group must either fold or apply for regular enterprise status.

Notice the formulation above suggesting that *anyone* who applies will receive funding! Some preliminary screening might be necessary to rule out clearly incoherent proposals, but the goal is to avoid placing anyone in the powerful position of Bank Loan Officer. If the number of requests exceeds available resources, funds can be allocated by lottery among the extant proposals. If an Entrepreneurial Enterprise fails—either refusing to apply for or being denied regular enterprise status at the end of the trial period—the individual or group is barred from using the Fund again for a period of, say, five years. (An appeals process might be developed to adjudicate disputes over initial awards or enterprise status determination.) There should be sufficient incentive for prospective entrepreneurs to pre-screen their own projects, especially since there is always the alternate route of proposing novel ideas to existing enterprises. The heart of the matter is to find ways for society to reward, and benefit from, the sort of entrepreneurship that draws inspiration from the joy of creating new products and services, rather than from the twisted dream of acquiring vast power and wealth.

A final note. The term "planning" has often been used where I believe "economic coordination" is more accurate, as indicated above. This, however, does not mean that *planning* in its genuine meaning is not important. On the contrary, a maturing socialist economy will have a progressively longer time horizon, taking care of future generations, the planet, the future. Planning involves looking down the road: ensuring stable reproduction, ecologi-

cal balance, and widening social and personal opportunities. It means organizing democratic debate about what the built human environment of the
future should look like; whether production should be centered in production zones or dispersed among residential neighborhoods; whether development should concentrate in cities or should focus on dispersal to rural areas;
what forms social progress should take, and how rapidly it should proceed,
and so on. When we get the *coordination problem* progressively under control,
to the point where we have clearly transcended the narrow horizon of domination by the elemental "market," we will be ready for the *planning problem*,
which amounts to nothing less than finally placing human destiny under
democratic human control.

Chapter 7

THE SOVIET EXPERIENCE
AND THE THEORY OF FULL COMMUNISM

T he last chapter outlined a model of comprehensively planned, participatory socialism, which progressively transcends the alienating objectivity of the spontaneous market and uses modern information technology to combine coordination with autonomy. This vision, always a work in progress of course, represents the closing of the PF–PR circle with which we began. The most general premise concerning social evolution is the long transition, over many millennia, from a shared social existence based on poverty and ignorance, to one based on relative abundance and scientific knowledge. The transition, however, is marked by social antagonism and elementality, because these are, in the given conditions, essentially functional for the development of the productive forces, science, social organization, and cultural capacities necessary to eventually transcend them.

The present chapter adds to this story in several ways. First, it addresses a recent debate concerning the crisis and demise of the Soviet Union—the "Soviet interregnum" of chapter 5. To understand the fall of the USSR and its allied regimes in eastern Europe, at the end of the twentieth century, is to understand the nature of this first major postcapitalist experiment and the bipolar world to which it gave rise. The discussion of the Soviet experience is deeply interwoven with progress in socialist theory, and some aspects of that theory, presented in the last chapter, are further developed in this connection.

This leads into a wider speculation concerning the ultimate grounding of socialism in a new way of looking at the role of human needs fulfillment, and development, in promoting productivity growth and efficiency, at the postcapitalist level. I have proposed this idea, under the slightly mischievous label of "the Cherry Esplanade Conjecture" (explained below), but this playfulness is not intended to belittle the idea or suggest that it not be taken seriously.

The final section of the chapter turns to a topic that has been all but lost in recent discussion: Marx's higher stage of communism, toward which socialist development, once in place, is thought to be headed. We will want to see whether the PF–PR framework can get us just a little further into the foundations of this vision, which appears in only a few sentences in the classical Marxist writings (Marx 1933b), was reduced to a rather distant and unexamined projection in the thinking of the twentieth century Communist parties, and has been all but ignored in the "Western" Marxist tradition of the twentieth century and beyond.

I. SOCIALIST DEBATES ON THE SOVIET UNION: ITS REALITY, ITS DEMISE

Following the collapse of the Soviet Union in 1991, the left worldwide—after a period of shock and (at least in some circles) mourning—has begun a process of analysis, evaluation and reevaluation. The stakes are high; this is about nothing less than the long-term strategic vision of the left, and the place of socialism in that vision (where "socialism" means a determinate *system* that transcends capitalism, and not just a moral commitment to the cause of the oppressed and exploited).

I will use a recent book by Roger Keeran and Thomas Kenny (2004) to frame the issue. As its title—*Socialism Betrayed*—implies, the authors place the blame for the demise squarely on Mikhail Gorbachev and his collaborators, who are said to have followed a right-revisionist line that began with Nikolay Bukharin in the 1920s, and was continued by Nikita S. Khrushchev in the 1950s, until the latter's removal from power in 1964.

A review essay on the book, by Erwin Marquit (Marquit 2004), sets forth a different position. In Marquit's view, Keeran and Kenny's "betrayal" approach amounts to defense of an overcentralized and bureaucratic planning system, and of overpoliticized control by the Communist Party and its top leadership over all aspects of Soviet life. Marquit sees the *system*—the "model" of socialism in place—as the fundamental source of the crisis. He concludes that socialism must abandon "central planning," and must embrace markets, for the foreseeable future, as in the current Chinese and Vietnamese versions of a "market economy with socialist orientation." Both Keeran and Kenny and, on the opposite side, Marquit, thus see an inherent opposition between central-planning socialism and market socialism, and view the crisis and collapse of the USSR through the lens of this dichotomy.

I would like to propose a third alternative—based on the "comprehensive planning" model outlined in chapter 6—involving both the theory of socialism, and the interpretation of the Soviet demise. In my view, both

Keeran and Kenny and Marquit share the category error identified in the last chapter—unfortunately one that is quite common—which equates *planning* with *central planning*; equates *decentralization* with *markets*; and counterposes each of these pairs to the other. A related conceptual insufficiency is a tendency to speak of "the market," as though "the" market is a featureless entity that floats above the production relations underlying particular market phenomena. If the twentieth-century socialist experience, not to speak of the PF–PR model, has taught us anything, it is that "real existing" markets are never neutral embodiments of abstract principles (presumably the possessive individualism of rational individuals); they always contain and express social relations at a particular stage of evolution within a historically specific social formation.

This section seeks to sort out these issues. The first subsection (immediately below) addresses the argument in *Socialism Betrayed*. The second examines Marquit's critique, and sets forth the proposed alternative in more detail.

Gorbachev, Errors, and the Material Base of Revisionism

Keeran and Kenny, in successive chapters, tell the story of the Soviet Union at the level of state policy, very much in the style of the Kremlin-watching industry, which in fact supplies most of their sources. This literature speculates, among other things, on the experiences of the youthful Gorbachev, his early alliances, and how the personalities of the various Soviet leaders enter the story, from the beginnings of *perestroika* and *glasnost* through the political crises of the late 1980s and the events of late 1991. The broad picture that emerges is of a tendency within the Soviet leadership, beginning with Bukharin but taking significant form under Khrushchev, to promote policies that weakened both central planning and Communist Party control. Here is a key passage from their concluding chapter:

> What caused the Soviet collapse? Our thesis is that . . . it was triggered by the specific reform policies of Gorbachev and his allies. . . . [Gorbachev] replicated in an extreme way the Khrushchev policies of 1953–64 and even further back, the ideas espoused by Bukharin in the 1920s. Gorbachev's about-face [i.e., his reversal of the Andropov reform policies] was made possible by the growth of the second economy that provided a social basis for anti-socialist consciousness. Gorbachev's revisionism routed its opponents and went on to discard essential tenets of Marxism–Leninism: class struggle, the leading role of the Party, international solidarity, and the primacy of collective ownership and planning. Soviet foreign policy retreats and the eviscera-

tion of the CPSU soon resulted. The latter process occurred with the Party's surrender of the mass media, the unraveling of central planning mechanisms and resulting economic decline, and the end of the Party's role in harmonizing the constituent nations of the USSR. Mass discontent enabled the Yeltsin anti-communist "democrats" to capture control of the giant Russian Republic, and to begin to impose capitalism there. Separatists won out in the non-Russian republics. The USSR fell apart. (184–85)

Keeran and Kenny thus base their conception of the collapse on the willful choice of a wrong policy by Gorbachev. They are, however, sensitive to the problem this approach poses for anyone purporting to explain historical events in a serious, let alone Marxist, fashion. If wrong policies are enacted in an environment that contains healthy corrective potentials, it must be determined why the misguided leader did not see the error of his ways and change course; alternatively, why he was not replaced by others with a sound socialist perspective, once experience had made clear the dangers of the errant path. Keeran and Kenny therefore refer to the "second economy" as the material base for the revisionist policy direction that they trace.

The second economy, topic of their third chapter, consists of all economic activities, *both legal and illegal*, that take place outside of the central plan and Communist Party control. Keeran and Kenny insist on defining the second economy to include legal as well as illegal elements (52ff), both because this is how Western scholars defined it, and because, in their view, *all* private activity "fosters relations, values and ideas that are different from collective economic activity," and thus "can pose a danger to socialism" (52). Major sectors of the Soviet economy fit this definition, especially the entirely legal collective farm markets, which functioned spontaneously and provided a large proportion of agricultural produce to the population, after the obligatory quotas were delivered to the state. Provisions also existed for extra-plan activity in the service sector—another legal component of the second economy. There was also an underground economy, including spontaneous part-time service activity, and it is very hard to get reliable estimates of its size and importance. Here, and throughout the book, Keeran and Kenny pick up their source material from the long-established anti-Soviet publishing industry in the United States and other capitalist countries, much of which they cite uncritically. Since they are concerned to inflate the picture of the second-economy cancer, in order to demonstrate the folly of revisionist policy and bolster their argument positing a material base for that self-same policy, they are happy to draw upon a literature produced over many decades by writers who were concerned to demonstrate the insufficiency and impossibility of socialism *tout court*.

Progress on empirical estimation will undoubtedly have to wait until new rounds of data are examined by a new generation of scholars within the former Soviet countries. We can, however, consider the second-economy argument in its own terms—and herein lies a problem: *the second economy must itself be explained*. Keeran and Kenny must take one of two approaches. Either they must, in circular fashion, attribute the second economy to misguided revisionism on the part of certain Soviet leaders; or they must explain the vitality of the second economy by examining the "first economy" at its given stage of development in the USSR. The former tack suggests that the system of top-down central planning under highly politicized control by the Party, put in place under Stalin, was essentially non-problematic in and of itself—a rather indefensible position, to put it mildly, to which I return below. One notes, in any case, the circularity of this line of argument: Keeran and Kenny cannot explain revisionism by referring to the second economy, and simultaneously explain the second economy by referring to revisionism.

The second approach, then, must ask *why* the second economy could be so destructive for socialism—why the socialist sector, the "first economy," left such a huge vacuum, into which this polarizing, destabilizing and corrupting influence could pour. This points to weakness and insufficiency in the central authoritarian system, which are clearly related to the monumental internal historical limitations under which socialism was built in the Soviet Union, as well as to the impact of external factors—military intervention, economic and diplomatic isolation, and the arms race imposed by the hostile surrounding capitalist world. We may take external hostility for granted, but unless we succumb to some sort of inevitabilist dogma about the "impossibility" of socialism in one country, the focus returns to the internal, and here we need to understand the technological, material, and cultural limitations of the platform on which socialism had to be built in the USSR. Unfortunately for Keeran and Kenny's overall argument, this inquiry leads to the general conclusion that fundamental restructuring within socialism *was* required; that the very fact of the second economy and the failure of the "first" economy to absorb and contain it point to major weaknesses in the system inherited from the Stalin era; and that subsequent generations of the Soviet leadership, from Khrushchev forward, were correct to address this issue.

Throughout their discussion, however, Keeran and Kenny *imply* that the system of top-down Party-controlled central planning was essentially on track, and that if only misguided leaders such as Khrushchev and Gorbachev had not gone off the rails, socialism would be alive and well in the USSR. They see Brezhnev as weak and ineffectual, hobbled by age (perhaps true in his last years), Chernenko as unimportant and transitional, and Andropov—

Gorbachev's immediate predecessor—as a positive figure, whose reform program was socialist and nonrevisionist. I do not think these oppositions can be sustained. Brezhnev, in particular, requires much more respectful attention than he receives in the book.

Keeran and Kenny's attitude toward Stalin is—in the light of everything we know today about the brutal repression and criminality of the worst years, and about the inherited legacy of authoritarian political control that dogged efforts to move beyond it in the subsequent decades—strange, to say the least. They view with suspicion all expressions of opposition to Stalin, and speak, to give just one example, of "strident anti-Stalin campaigns" (155), placing "Stalinism" in quotes wherever the term is used. At one point (28) they state that Stalin did indeed do some bad things, but that the campaign against "Stalinism" was really a cover for anti-socialist sentiment (cf. 111, 119–120). While this may be true, it prompts one to ask what the authors' underlying view of Stalin, the Stalin era, and the Stalin legacy is. They provide a large amount of detail concerning Khrushchev's 1956 "secret speech," counting of the victims of imprisonment and execution, and related issues. Throughout, they imply that the usual accounts of the Stalin-era repression are exaggerated and duplicitous. As my interest is in basic socialist theory and the evolution and crisis of socialism in the USSR, I will simply cite, with approval, Marquit's judgment on this: "I cannot understand how it is possible for Keeran and Kenny to downplay or justify the murder of hundreds of thousands of Communists (not to mention ordinary citizens who were not in the Party) with phrases like 'alleged,' and 'difficult to believe' or even the suggestion that 799,455 instead of the figure of millions make these mass murders more acceptable" (Marquit 2004, 489).

The critique of Gorbachev proceeds to its ultimate conclusion, of course. By 1987, the word "socialism" drops out of his discourse, as Keeran and Kenny correctly note. They trace the evolution of language in the speeches of Gorbachev and his allies (especially Alexander Yakovlev), citing this as further evidence of apostasy. What they fail to see is that, in the burgeoning crisis atmosphere of 1987–91, Gorbachev could not have mounted a defense of socialism even if he had wanted to. He was an astute politician; it is possible that no one could have ridden out the stormy waves that engulfed the USSR in its final five years, and Gorbachev may have lasted longer than most would have done. The problem that Keeran and Kenny do not address is: Where was the base? Who would have responded to a call from the top to defend socialism and the USSR? Where was the Party rank and file? Where were the masses of working people, educated, and vigilant, prepared to defend socialist institutions? The simple truth is that the Soviet people

were demoralized and demobilized, by the *massive deformation* of Soviet socialism originating in the entire set of material and cultural circumstances
surrounding its emergence—and that cannot be explained by revisionism at
the top.

Put another way, if we were to accept the view that the Soviet crisis
was due to a revisionist program of emasculation of socialism, put over on
the Soviet people by a handful of demagogues corrupted by the second
economy, this would suggest that the mass base for socialism never existed;
that Soviet "socialism" contained nothing worth defending. This is possible,
of course, but I think it is refuted by the entire sweep of Soviet history,
beginning with the huge political mobilizations in the prerevolutionary
Soviets, the Revolution itself, the industrialization and collectivization movements, and the undeniably political character of the anti-Nazi war effort and
subsequent reconstruction. Are we to believe that the people who overcame
the extreme backwardness of their own economy and culture, beat back
military interventions by fourteen countries, defeated the Hitler onslaught,
and built and rebuilt their agriculture and industry on socialist foundations,
creating the world's second superpower in the process, were then led down
a garden path by a few misguided revisionists and cajoled into giving
everything away and returning to Third World misery, without resistance?
The explanation must run deeper than that.

Since collectivization of agriculture was mentioned above, an additional word may be in order. The drive to build collective farms began as a
genuine political movement in the countryside, designed to form a bloc of
landless, poor, and middle peasants against the wealthy stratum of labor-
employing landowners (the *kulaks*). It later was distorted by the cult of Stalin
(particularly severe in the countryside where the old authoritarian religious
consciousness had the deepest roots), and aggravated by stimulation of long-
dormant communal antagonisms. In the famine or near-famine conditions of
the early 1930s, the urgency of the campaign for collective-farm production
and meeting of quotas forced the collectivization movement to take on a
military character, which added fuel to the excesses and abuses committed in
its name. The point remains, however: the building of an agriculture sector
that could support industrialization and urbanization on the scale achieved in
the USSR was not carried out by a people who would easily give up everything they had built to a corrupt and careerist leadership.

Markets, Socialism, and "Market Socialism"

Erwin Marquit agrees that Gorbachev's errors or betrayal cannot explain the
Soviet demise. He sees the crisis as the necessary outcome of the socialist

system itself, as that system came to exist in the Soviet Union. ". . . growth of the second economy was the unplanned consequence of the utopian model of a centrally planned economy, which was introduced prematurely in the Soviet Union and which, in its necessary interaction with the world economy, proved unable to match the pace of market-driven technological development in the West" (Marquit 2003, 474). Later, Marquit writes:

> The goal of creating a communist society will be reached only through the replacement of production for private profit by production for need, through the creation of a productive base sufficient to allow distribution by need. Until this is reached, commodity production will continue. . . . A market economy with socialist orientation is characterized by commodity production for profit in the socialized sector as well as in the capitalist sector. . . . In view of the fact that socialist countries today do not have economies that are developed enough to cut themselves off from a world market dominated by capitalism . . . they must resort to mixed economies. . . . The state [can] guide the direction of economic development toward a growing dominance of the socialized sector. It is premature to speculate about the point at which the curtailment or absorption of the capitalist sector will occur. (503)

It is difficult to sort out all of the conceptual confusions abounding in these summary statements. Central planning is "utopian," but its introduction was "premature." Marx's lower phase of communist society, almost universally called "socialism" since the early twentieth century, completely disappears in this perspective, lost somewhere between the poles of a "communist society," at one end, and "mixed economies," at the other. "Market-driven technological development" implies that technological development can proceed under no driving force other that "the market." Over and over, "the market" is confounded with capitalism, as in "the capitalist sector" of a "market economy with socialist orientation." "The state"—here the implicit background is an image of China or Vietnam, with a strong Communist Party–headed state and some sort of "mixed" economy—can provide an overall socialist orientation to the market over which it presides, although it is not clear what the class character of this state may be, in an economy with a powerful spontaneous thrust toward development of a propertied wealthy class, or what characteristic, other than the traditional symbolic identification of Communist parties, validates definition of this state as a dictatorship of the proletariat.

But the main problem is the fact that, like Keeran and Kenny, Marquit simply cannot see in the Soviet experience anything other than the "centrally planned economy," on one side, and "the market," on the other. Both

sides therefore ignore—do not even evince awareness of—the *most* fundamental reality of the Soviet Union starting in the late 1950s, embodied in
a *massive* debate and literature, and culminating in major legislative transformations, beginning in the late 1960s: the process of *socialist economic reform*
that progressively changed the *planning* system from *central* to *comprehensive*
(for a useful survey of the literature up to the early 1980s, see Shaffer 1984).
As set forth in ch. 6, the latter term means an articulated combination of
central and *decentral* planning (planning at the local or enterprise level). In
1968, a Statute on the Enterprise became law in the USSR. This complex
document had at its core the devolution of a major part of the plan indicators (items targeted in the annual enterprise plan, with associated quantitative measures) to the enterprises themselves, with retention at the level of
the superior body of only a small number of aggregative indicators. As noted
earlier, this *Soviet* socialist innovation gave rise to large literatures in the
West, including the fields of "incentive design" (Tirole 1988; Campbell
1995) and planometrics (Zauberman 1967).

Throughout the 1970s, the reform process continued, with enactments
creating industrial associations (midlevel bodies between the Ministries and
the enterprises), the Shchekino experiment (an advanced experiment with
budgetary independence at the level of the work collective), and significant
improvement and sophistication of prices and other indicators. This came to
a head in July 1979—under Brezhnev, it must be noted—when a Council
of Ministers resolution approved a series of far-reaching changes: new plan
indicators that captured economic results more completely and helped in the
evaluation of the planning and plan-execution work of enterprises; extension
of plan responsibility to the level of the brigade, or team, within the enterprise; direct election of brigade councils; development of sophisticated
methods of personal evaluation and income formation, under the control of
the brigade councils; and direct election of enterprise managers. These
measures were more or less fully implemented by the mid-1980s, only to be
jettisoned in 1989, when they came into clear conflict with the then-
expanding idea of "private ownership."

In short, the Soviet Union pioneered the development of *democratic
planning*. To be democratic, this had to be *both* central *and* decentral. Good
planning at each level makes possible success at the other; they are complements, not alternatives. The culture of political democracy, including debate, openness, and responsibility, is essential for both levels to work, and to
work together. It should not be necessary to state that this crucial ingredient,
for essential cultural and historical reasons, was largely absent in the Soviet
Union—although I must disagree with Marquit's summary judgment that

rank-and-file Communists and mass organizations were denied *any* role; that the Party acted on behalf of the working class, but "without its participation" (501).

Decentralization must *not* be equated with the market. Planning inherently flourishes on both central and decentral levels, once it has evolved beyond its most primitive forms; markets, in turn—in many social conditions, especially capitalist ones—promote central power over decentral initiative. This crucial confounding—of democracy/decentralized/market, on one side, and totalitarianism/centralized/planning, on the other—is a cornerstone of capitalist ideology, and its transcendence a vital goal for socialist theory. It is disheartening, therefore, to find socialist theorists becoming enmeshed in it.

Marquit—and, needless to say, Keeran and Kenny—also largely ignore the Soviet literature on socialism and markets. By and large, this literature rejects the notion of "the" market, and treats commodity production as it should be treated, within a context of social relations. So various market forms existed in the USSR, from those expressing the sociopolitical independence of the collective-farm peasantry; to those emerging within the socialist (state) sector itself, reflecting the relative immaturity of enterprises in their ability to act and think as parts of a social whole, and their consequent need to receive confirmation of the social utility of their activity by selling the products of that activity to other parts of the same social whole; and finally, to market relations *within* plan formation, as a form of horizontal contact and contracting subordinate to the plan. The advanced socialist social forms outlined above came into existence only in the Soviet Union (and were, of course, abruptly terminated in the collapse). They had no counterpart in any other socialist country, despite the higher levels of technological development in Czechoslovakia, the GDR, and others. Marquit draws on his experience in several of these countries over a number of years, but by lumping the USSR together with the rest of eastern Europe, and Cuba, he misses this significant difference.

Markets thus *evolve*, along with the core socialist institutions surrounding them. As they do, they progressively come to represent increasingly socialist contents. If the abolition of markets after the NEP in the Soviet Union was "premature," this was because under the conditions then obtaining the more sophisticated possibilities of the planning system had not yet come into existence, and the material and human resources for both fully articulated (central and decentral) planning and incorporation of forms of market relations (other than the spontaneous forms associated with precapitalist or protocapitalist conditions) did not yet exist. Those conditions, including modern information technology, did begin to exist during the brief period of flowering of mature socialism, in the late Brezhnev/early

Gorbachev era, before that flowering was overcome by the accumulated hostility and disorientation resulting from the Stalin-era repression and the failure to address that deformation subsequently. They continue to exist today, with potentials symbolized by the E-Coordi-Net of the last chapter, although we await the political sea-change that can give them life.

I have proposed an alternative (see Laibman 2004, and chapter 6 above) to the utopian notion of abolition of markets, on one side, and capitulation to their eternal necessity (apart from transition to full communism, about which "it is premature to speculate"), on the other. In an analogy with the classical Marxist formulation regarding the state, markets are not abolished, nor are they permanent; *they wither away*. As in the case of the state, the withering away is the progressive transcendence of the repressive function. When the state withers away, society does not revert to formless anarchy or noncommunicating self-sufficient communes; there remains the democratic and nonrepressive, participatory administration of the common affairs of all members of society—a political process with new content. Similarly with markets. They remain within socialism, although increasingly subordinate to democratic planning. While they represent, first in their experienced reality and progressively in more atavistic fashion, the repressive content so well analyzed by Marx (fetishism, alienation, polarization, possessive individuation, instability, crisis), they gradually come to transcend those qualities, and to retain individual and horizontal initiative as a moment within a fully socialist process. The repressive core withers; the useful kernel of contribution to human fulfillment remains.

When Marquit speaks about China's and Vietnam's "market economy with socialist orientation," he is confusing socialism—the lower phase of communism—with a long process of transition, incorporating the developmental tasks of capitalism, to a *starting point* for socialism. The latter is important, and one wishes developing countries well in their efforts to achieve that foundation-laying; it is not, however, the building itself. It is one thing to recognize that at given levels of development the Asian countries whose leaderships proclaim a socialist orientation have much to do in creating the conditions for *eventual* transition to socialist construction, and that market relations, including even protocapitalist ones, will play an important role for a foreseeable period in achieving this development. It is entirely another thing to confuse this with socialist construction as such.

Summarizing: Implications for Socialist Theory.

Keeran and Kenny provide an "Epilogue," in which they consider six alternative explanations of the Soviet collapse, to which they, of course, prefer their own. The six are: flaws of socialism, popular opposition, external factors, bureaucratic counterrevolution, lack of democracy/overcentralization, and the Gorbachev factor (209). Marquit can, I think, be classified with "lack of democracy/overcentralization." It is, however, striking that the explanation preferred by the present writer is not on the list.

If this is a debate among socialists, we can immediately ignore mainstream versions of "flaws of socialism" and "popular opposition." In cold war mythology, socialism is of course inherently flawed: "the road to serfdom," as Frederick A. Hayek would have it. I agree with Keeran and Kenny that "popular opposition" does not accurately describe Soviet reality; the fall of the Soviet "empire" was unique in history in having taken place without significant popular mobilization against it, and almost with the acquiescence of its leading representatives. "External factors" can similarly be discarded; as noted above, these always play a role, but one conditioned by the more significant internal factors, which alone determine whether external pressure can be effective. "Bureaucratic counterrevolution" or "revolution from above" refers to the idea that top CPSU leaders deliberately sought to turn themselves into capitalists, and therefore undermined Soviet power. There are many reasons, in addition to those given by Keeran and Kenny, to discount this explanation. Finally, "the Gorbachev factor" refers to analyses that rely entirely on the characteristics of this single individual; Keeran and Kenny differentiate their view from this one by placing Gorbachev in line of revisionist succession, and rooting this trend in, first, the early difficult material conditions and then the second economy.

Incidentally, both Keeran and Kenny and Marquit implicitly assume that the Soviet collapse ushered in a new era of Russian "capitalism." This suggests that, against the background of Soviet socialist construction and presumed *de*-subsumption of labor to capital, a new primitive accumulation of capital in the hands of a capitalist class has been achieved. I will simply note here that the careful guidelines laid down by the PF–PR model, and especially the structure of capitalist relations outlined in chapter 3, show this conclusion to be superficial and misleading. The post-Soviet Russian social formation may be called "predatory-extractive," or even (with tongue in cheek) an instance of the "necrophagous mode of production" (Kotz 2001), for its reliance on plundering the wealth built up during the Soviet years. It is certainly not "capitalist" (for a full statement, see Kotz 2001, 2002; Laibman 2002b).

If the USSR fell without significant opposition by its people, however, it also failed, at the end, to attract popular support. The eerie quiescence of the Soviet working class, and the implosive character of the process, wherein rulers apparently stepped silently off the stage without resistance, are part of what needs to be grasped in an adequate theory of the collapse.

Here is explanation number eight (I am counting Keeran and Kenny's as number seven). Soviet socialism was a social formation that embodied a socialist mode of production within a deformed political shell. With some hesitation concerning designation of social realities by proper names, I think in this case the meaning can best be conveyed by referring to the *Stalin deformation*. "Stalin" here, of course, is also a "product of many other realities" (Fidel Castro); it is a matter of identifying the material-cultural base for the cult of the individual personality, the authoritarian incorporation of all social activity under the disciplined control of the CPSU, and the subordination of all scientific and cultural thought and practice to political ideology. Many of the roots of these phenomena are well studied: the conditions of underdevelopment and isolation, the anomie accompanying loss of the symbols of authority vested in the Tsar and Church, the profound backwardness of the peasant consciousness, the shortage of educated political cadre, and other factors.

I was able to observe firsthand the depth of the problem of "de-Stalinization" (moving beyond the authoritarian deformation) in visits to the USSR in 1969, 1974, and 1984. I was particularly interested in the economic reform: how would enterprise leadership now assume the responsibility of formulating their own plans? The question made some enterprise managers visibly uncomfortable. This generation was trained to follow orders from on high; in fact, that was how the people I met had survived. How could they now help develop a nonauthoritarian movement toward new forms of democratic planning? The limitations of the post-Stalin generation in this regard repeatedly undermined the reforms, which often came to be implemented mechanically, but not in substance. And the interlinking of generations assures that the simple passage of time will not remove this potent obstacle to realizing the potentials of the socialist economy. Thus, the paradox: an advanced, sophisticated, and novel system of social reproduction in place, and relatively poor actual results. Had the immediate post-Stalin generation of the Soviet leadership found the resources to address the painful legacy of the authoritarian deformation, at a time when the population, for both ideological and patriotic reasons, could be mobilized in support of socialist restructuring, the tragic outcome could possibly have been avoided.

So the socialist economy was not the source of the collapse; to the contrary, both central and decentral planning and plan execution were alive and well. Their potentials, however, could not be adequately realized without a thorough reckoning with the legacy of the Stalin-era authoritarian deformation. In these conditions, socialist reform was a razor edge, an unstable path between twin abysses: resurgent bureaucratic control, on one side, and a slide into anarchy and destruction of socialism as such, on the other. The source of the demise was indeed structural, but it was not the political *economy* of socialist planning, but the political *culture* that arose in the difficult circumstances of Soviet social construction that lay at its heart. One wants to say: don't blame Gorbachev; blame Stalin. But on reconsideration, it is at bottom not a matter of placing blame at all, but of understanding the real (material and cultural) roots of the distortion—which, after all, has counterparts in other recent historical experiences—so that the true potentials of a socialist economy can eventually be put to the test in a climate of critical and irreversible mass mobilization and participation.

II. THE CHERRY ESPLANADE CONJECTURE

Socialism, as depicted in the scenario under development here, appears as a set of intersecting *tensions*: between collective and individual principles in income distribution, between moral and material principles in income distribution, between enterprise autonomy and central coordination, between political coordination and market coordination, between core and informal sectors. Now, all social development takes place in the form of emerging tensions, which are then resolved into new levels. Socialism, however, is unique among modes of production in having conscious human action as its core regulating principle; the tensions, therefore, appear as conflict, making socialist progress appear to be an unending uphill battle. If a society does not evolve spontaneously, "behind the backs" of its own members, and if its growth does not rest on the fortunes of a ruling class but rather on those of all of its members as a democratic whole, must it necessarily appear resistant to change? Why must socialist development always seem to be a series of conquests, of battles against inertia?

We want to understand why socialism has seemed, in so many times and places, to require massive political mobilization to offset the spontaneous impulses of freely acting people. Socialism has been like a *guagua* (a small bus, in Cuban Spanish) without a steering wheel: the bus veers off the road into a ditch, and the passengers must periodically get out and physically lift it back onto the road, so that the next stretch of the journey can commence. Capitalist ideology claims that the spontaneous self-interest of individuals leads to capitalism. Much of our experience, it must be admitted, appears to bear this out: unless we intervene in massive and energy-consuming ways, people left to their own devices "spontaneously generate" polarization, domination, alienation, economic instability—in a word, the essential elements of capitalist social relations. We need now to consider why this has been the case.

Human progress can be described along two dimensions: objective and subjective. The objective dimension may be captured by the concept of productivity, but defined in a very broad sense: it is the total efficiency of our relationship to the external environment, as measured by ratios of output to input (the narrow component), but also by the effect of our productive activity on the environment and on living communities. It incorporates a suitably long time horizon, as well as the effects of human activity on the biosphere.

The subjective dimension is similarly broadly conceived: it measures the power of workers over their own lives, their rational understanding, the effectiveness and democracy of their forms of organization, and their autonomy—in the crucial double sense of absence of domination from outside *and* presence of inner capacity to act. It is the core quality of the labor process, insofar as that process impacts on people's working experience, and on their entire living experience.

The question now is: how do the two dimensions interact? In highly complex ways, undoubtedly; but I think we may be able to sift out two main links.

(A) FROM THE QUALITY OF LIFE TO PRODUCTIVITY. This link says that the quality of the work experience—the degree of autonomy and democracy in the workplace—shapes the level of productivity, in any given historical conditions of social consciousness. If we were to draw a curve showing the relationship between them, it would be a hardheaded, *Leninist* curve: drawn sloping downward to suggest that progress in *advancing* quality will carry a cost in *decreasing* productivity. Give people more equality and more participation, and productivity will suffer! This is, of course, what neoliberals say when they posit (without, it must be said, very much theoretical backing) an ineluctable trade-off between "efficiency" and "equity." Socialists need not accept the inevitability of this bleak picture, but we perhaps should give it some credence as a way of representing the hard choices facing socialism in its early stages of development.

(B) FROM PRODUCTIVITY TO THE QUALITY OF LIFE. A given level of productivity makes *possible* a certain quality of life, in both the narrow sense of standard of material well being and the broader one of putting into effect a rich, nonalienating and participatory structure of work and community organization—surely a major goal of socialist society. This is a direct relation, in which higher productivity is associated with the possibility of a higher quality of life; the point is fairly obvious and should not require much elaboration.

The two relations between productivity and quality (I will use these terms as shorthand for the two concepts) determine a consistent possibility for any society at a given stage of development. In the socialist context, productivity cannot result in a surplus that is siphoned off to a ruling class; the possibility of raising productivity therefore depends on the use of the rising living standard it secures, in a manner that is consistent with the motivation constraint. Raising living standards, according to the hard-boiled inverse trade-off between quality and productivity, will lead to a fall in productivity. The society therefore has to find levels of quality and productivity that are consistent with one another, when both causal directions are taken into consideration. Productivity is at a level that affords a quality of life which, in turn, and at the established levels of motivation and consciousness, is consistent with the given level of productivity.

If a political push is made, a higher quality of work/living at each given level of productivity can be achieved, clearly a result of education, organization, and struggle. The cost, however, is a lower level of productivity, given the inverse trade-off. This trade-off then represents the anti-socialist critique: we can achieve a higher quality of life—read: higher living standards, more equal income distribution, greater participation, less alienation—only by lowering productivity. The even higher levels of productivity associated with sweated labor, inequality and authoritarian workplaces are a constant temptation and drag on the maturation of socialist consciousness. We can hear the siren song of the capitalists: "Just submit to our domination and we will give you 'first-world' levels of consumption!" This is perhaps why socialists have to mobilize politically all the time just to keep the *guagua* out of the ditch.

Now, the Cherry Esplanade Conjecture (named, with tongue in cheek, after the Cherry Esplanade at the Brooklyn Botanic Garden, where the author first conceived it): Suppose the quality-to-productivity relationship is not always inverse. Suppose, specifically, that rising quality leads *for a time* to falling productivity, as we have been supposing, but that if quality continues to rise, beyond a certain point, far from causing productivity to fall, it now becomes essential for productivity to rise further. The relation between quality and productivity stops being a negative trade-off at a certain point, and turns into a positive relation; we have never before found this crucial turning point, because social evolution has not progressed that far. The core logic is this: without a high sense of commitment, principle, responsibility, and creative fulfillment, workers and their collectives cannot (or will not) achieve the productivity increases that are latent in the most recent stages of technical development. Both the level of production and its dynamic evolution, says the Conjecture, come to depend on a motivation structure of a qualitatively new type. It should be clear that the Cherry Esplanade Conjecture embodies the core historical materialist insight: development of the PFs must proceed, through stages, on the basis of ever-more-sophisticated PRs. In class-antagonistic contexts, this means the periodic replacement of one form of surplus extraction by a more sophisticated one. The transition to the socialist–communist MP is provided with a foundation in human development when a point is reached at which even the most sophisticated form of exploitation runs up against advanced forms and possibilities of production, which require nothing less than uncoerced, principled, critical, and voluntary participation by cooperating (and therefore equal) workers.

Now suppose we are building socialism, in a low stage of development: forcing up the quality of life at a cost of falling productivity. It has not been my custom to quote extensively from Marx in this book, but I cannot resist citing this remarkably prescient passage:

> Of course, in the beginning, this cannot be effected except by means of despotic inroads on the rights of property, and on the conditions of bourgeois production, by means of measures, therefore, which appear economically insufficient and untenable, but which, in the course of the movement, outstrip themselves, necessitate further inroads upon the old social order, and are unavoidable as a means of entirely revolutionizing the mode of production. (Marx and Engels 1998, 39)

I consider this insufficiency and untenability to characterize production in the full early stage of socialism, in which inroads on property are no longer the issue, but inroads on old, long-established values, levels of consciousness, and capacities for collective action most certainly are. This is the source of the relative truth in the long-standing neoliberal critique of socialism, and of the perception that gains for the people in a socialist context can only be achieved at great cost, in both productivity and in the effort involved in political mobilization.

The Conjecture, however, suggests that a great reward follows upon pursuit of this course toward greater democracy and equality, even when that course involves momentarily restricting productivity and productivity growth. Along that path of development, a crucial turn is eventually achieved: people's experience now begins to show them that the improvement in quality does not come at the expense of productivity—and living standards—but rather that it now makes possible *higher* levels of these goods. As this new reality sinks into social consciousness, the political task of moving further along the same path is greatly eased. Without further political effort, the spontaneous self-interest of working people takes over. The goals of raising productivity and improving the overall quality of work life and consumption, from their historical relation as opposites, now become complementary. It is as though we no longer need to tell ourselves, or have our political institutions constantly remind us, that we need to pursue productive growth in our long-term interest, or "for our own good," or "in the interests of future generations." Rather, the stimulus to productive development now coincides with people's self-interest, as this has itself evolved—to a point far beyond the norms of capitalist society, which do indeed connect productivity and self-interest, but by means of negative and distorted incentives (fear of unemployment and poverty, and the goal of acquisition of wealth to secure invidious status).

In socialist conditions, at the Cherry Esplanade turning point the movement toward high and stable levels of both productivity and life quality thus becomes self-sustaining. Spontaneous activity—which may be individual, but also undoubtedly involves many collective forms of organization: teams, community organizations, etc.—now works not in the direction of dissolution of socialist relations, but the opposite. At a critical level of maturation, involving political organization, democratic structures, and sound scientific management, building socialism no longer seems like swimming upstream; it harnesses the spontaneous impulses of diverse individuals and collectives, instead of opposing them. The result is evolution to high and stable levels of productivity and life quality that both may be justified by global ecological constraints and permit continued qualitative evolution of social relations toward full communism.

Is this just a pipe dream? Let's see whether the Cherry Esplanade Conjecture can tell us anything about actual problems, and possibilities.

The major implication, of course, is that although capitalism (the "free market," through the ideological lenses of today's neoliberalism) may seem natural at a given stage of social development, the natural property may migrate to socialism at a higher stage. We thus have every reason to "hang in there," and continue to grapple with the enormous problems of socialist construction in a few places such as Cuba, and of building (or rebuilding) the working-class social and political alternative everywhere else.

The Conjecture also tells us something about the long-standing debate concerning market vs. plan. Critics of "market socialism" insist that socialism must be about more than spontaneous individual self-interested activity, combined with institutional constraints preventing accumulation of wealth in private hands—and I think they are right. The sort of activity envisioned beyond the critical turning point postulated by the Conjecture is self-interested in an almost tautological sense; but it is an enlightened self interest, with long time horizons, deeply interpersonal and collective, both creative and responsible. This part of the vision embodied in the

Conjecture requires the evolution of human motivation through the experience of socialist construction, and the stable reproduction of the high forms of consciousness evolved.

So much for the "market." What about planning? Clearly, the stages of evolution in which the productivity-quality relation progresses toward its turning point require both central and decentral planning, and solid democratic controls at both levels. But good planning means high levels of initiative at the "micro" level of the workplace and community—as the vast literature on economic reform in the former Soviet Union and eastern European socialist countries attests. Now one stage of development crucially absent in the Soviet experience was the emergence of horizontal ties among enterprises. This absence was undoubtedly due to the authoritarian deformation, discussed earlier, that overlay the economic process there, with roots in earlier cultural and material conditions and external factors.

But the potential was present: to develop horizontal contracting relations, without the cumbersome requirement of communicating only through the vertical chains of authority. These relations are, in principle, socialist: they are entirely visible, both to central planners and to the public; they are subject to evaluative criteria involving qualitative assessment of their total social contribution, criteria that are not accessible to spontaneous markets; they involve unprecedented degrees of democratic participation. They are progressively incorporated into the plan, and become part of a larger vision of where the society is going, but they are not "planned" in the narrow sense of involving pre-envisioned instructions from above.

In short, the spontaneous yet principled relations and activities I have in mind transcend the narrow distinction between "market" and "plan"; this perhaps gives us a means of going beyond what increasingly appears as a constraining limitation on the terms of the discussion. Not "market," in the sense of atomistic, private self-seeking; not "plan," in the sense of a completely predetermined set of coordinated activities. Rather, empowered and enlightened individuals and collectives, working in a climate and culture of democratic scrutiny, debate, and controls, but confident in their fundamental freedom to create, and to grow.

This, of course, is but an invitation to *begin* the massive work on details. These details, however enriched by the creative socialist imagination, must in fact draw heavily on the vast practice of socialist construction and transformation in the twentieth century. I have tried to avoid the sort of "recipes for the cookshops of the future" that Marx decried. My hope is that the Conjecture, and the vision to which it gives rise, may contribute to the development of a socialism that is both inspirational—because it points the way toward realization of transcendent human potentialities—and realistic in allowing full scope to the complexities of social organization, given the high degree of individuation and the intricacies of communication, coordination and motivation inherent in modern life.

III. THE HIGHER STAGE OF COMMUNISM

In the stadial spirit, we must now consider the postulate, going back to Marx's *Critique of the Gotha Programme* (Marx 1933b), that the evolving socialist economy in the lower stage that has widely come to be called "socialism" eventuates in a higher stage, for which we now reserve the "communism" designation. It is noteworthy that this stadial conception of the society transcending capital and class has been largely eclipsed in the relevant literatures. In the Soviet Union and its allied states, after an early flirtation with enthusiastic predictions of "laying the foundations for communism in ten years," and so forth, the subject was relegated to brief sections of the standard political economy texts, but was not actively elaborated. In the West, Marxists have almost totally ignored the stadiality of postcapitalist society, other than some consideration of issues of transition, when the state machinery is in the hands of the working class and its allies but the old ruling class (and *its* allies) still exist and still contest for power. One (perhaps the) notable exception to this neglect is an article by Howard Sherman, "The Economics of Pure Communism" (Sherman 1970), on which I will draw in many ways in the following discussion.

Maturing socialism has already eliminated any remnants of capitalist restorationist forces, and has brought about gradual blurring of remaining distinctions among strata and cultural groups within the working population. Wages—real living standards—have been rising, income differentials have been gradually and purposefully reduced. Skill levels have been increasing; indeed, we can imagine a slow approach to the vision of a working population with the intellectual, cultural, and scientific horizons previously associated only with the stratum of professional intellectuals. Ecological and population growth issues are being sorted out; the demographic transition is being completed. Work is constantly in progress on the core socialist mechanism of central-decentral coordination, as outlined above, and the balance between community and autonomy is evolving (in different ways, undoubtedly, in different countries and cultures). The culture of democracy and solidarity is striking ever deeper roots, so that we may even speak of the transformation to socialism being now irreversible—at least, barring any ecological or extraterrestrial catastrophes (I am thinking not of extraterrestrial intelligence; only of the more mundane possibility of a damaging meteor strike, or something similar). There would be no possibility of a return to capitalist wage-slavery, any more than to chattel slavery.

With this as background, proceed to the definition of a "pure" communist economy. The central feature of this conception is the total absence of money and prices, and therefore of money income. Goods are distributed to consumers either as free goods, in which case there is no constraint on the quantity obtained for consumption purposes by any individual, family, or group; or under a system of rationing, which would presumably apply only to "large-ticket" items, such as one's residence, or vouchers for vacation (holiday) travel. (Other large-ticket items that meet intrinsic needs and therefore would not be subject to inordinate demands from consumers, such as education and health care, are in the free goods—zero price—category.) With zero prices on food, for example, to give this conception a concrete feel, consumers would take items off of supermarket shelves, proceed to checkout counters (where, we assume, they will run the bar codes through scanners so that the store can keep track of inventory), and walk out with them, without "paying" (there would be nothing that could be used to "pay" with, in any case).

One must first be struck by the enormous power of this conception. Marx once defined money as "the alienated power of humanity." It is the last great form of coercion, and enforced inequality. Freeing consumption from the income constraint would allow people's genuine needs to shape consumption, and conversely. One might even say that this unalienated, uncoerced consumption at last enables us to find out *who we really are*.

Having said that, the idea of pure communism seems to run up against insuperable obstacles. Sherman identifies three of these, and I will follow his discussion here. First, without prices, it would be impossible to value goods, either as inputs or as outputs. This presses against the entire tradition of price theory in economics—including both the "neoclassical" view (orthodox in capitalist societies) and a classically grounded conception of benchmark prices for a socialist economy. Valuation, according to some social criterion, would seem essential to an advanced society that must make highly complex decisions. It is doubtful whether the increasingly advanced technology of a maturing socialist society could be so advanced as to move "beyond scarcity" in some sense that would make sophisticated calculation and evaluation unnecessary—especially in view of the need to address the pressures imposed by population and increasing aspirations, against a backdrop of the finite reproducible resources available on our really existing planet.

I will address this issue before mentioning the other two. In brief, the answer is that the absence of actual money prices used in transactions to acquire goods does not imply the absence, or impossibility, of *shadow prices*: valuations, in terms of one or several comparison goods or baskets of goods, that result from compilation of optimal plans. Modern information technology, applied to the economic coordination problem, suggests emergence of a network of enterprise intranets, which I have called the "E-Coordi-Net" (refer to the discussion in chapter 6). A central task of the Net is the ongoing computation of social reproduction prices. It is not germane to the project of this book to pursue this matter in technical detail; it is enough to endorse the observation of W. Paul Cockshott and Allin F. Cottrell (2002, 55n) that, while the techniques needed to perform this sort of computation did not exist in the middle of the twentieth century, "they do now." In this sense, the electronic revolution is a major instance of the undermining of capitalism by its developing PFs: it establishes the *possibility* of capitalism's decisive transcendence. For the present, we simply note that the absence of *transaction* prices in the pure communist economy does not entail absence of computed shadow prices or analytical prices that can be used for evaluation, comparison of alternatives, and so on.

We can then turn to the two major objections to the possibility of pure communism, as we are defining that system. The first refers to the problem of unlimited demand for consumer goods. Zero prices means no constraints on the quantities of goods that people can acquire; all goods are "free," and people would therefore seek to acquire vast quantities. The total demand (no longer "effective demand"; *all* demand is "effective") for each good would exceed any reasonable assumption about the amount available. The second looks at the supply side of the same problem. If goods are free, then no meaning can be attached to the concept of "income"; without money, there would be no payment—"compensation"—for work performed, and indeed work would not be necessary in order to acquire consumer goods. With the link between work and income thus broken, the incentive to work would be absent; very little work would be done, and work that is done would be of poor quality and low productivity. The supply of goods, against which the insatiable demand is measured, would be meager, only exacerbating the problem and increasing the sense that the pure communist model is utterly unworkable.

Sherman's response to these two issues, which I will consider together, is to suggest that the pure communist model is best considered as the endpoint of a long period of transition—surely the appropriate approach in the spirit of the stadial model. Suppose, for example, that prices of *some* goods are reduced, so that there *gradually* emerges a sector of consumer goods with prices that are effectively, and eventually actually, zero. There already are public goods, in both capitalist and socialist contexts; the idea here is that the sphere of public goods be *gradually* enlarged. To the traditional ones of free public restrooms and water fountains—we focus on goods suitable for individual consumption, and therefore ignore major items such as parks, roads, and other nonexcludable goods—might be added some staple or subsistence food items, with relatively low elasticity of demand: bread, potatoes. The question is, as these goods' prices are dropped, so that they become effectively free, and as additional goods enter into the free sector, at what point will problems of insatiable demand or irrational use arise?

The point is, first of all, one of education, of steadily raising the level of public consciousness. If certain goods suddenly became free, irrational use might be encouraged, such as feeding bread made for human consumption to livestock, or children taking and playing with food items (potatoes would be great fun at baseball practice). Borders between countries also create problems for this idea; we must imagine progress toward communist distribution occurring more or less simultaneously in all countries, or at least in adjacent ones.

The problems become more severe when we consider luxury goods—those with, in standard economic parlance, high income elasticity of demand. If clothing and durables were free, for example, wouldn't everyone want (the equivalent of) $700 Brooks Brothers suits? Sixty-five inch plasma injector TVs? Caviar and champagne, on a daily basis? The answer is not precise, but it is, I believe, convincing; it relies, again, on the progressive, gradual evolution of communist distribution.

The first point is that, in a free-distribution system, no one can acquire or display *social status* by means of ownership of consumer goods. To the contrary: if your acquisition of clothing, cars, personal computers, bottles of champagne, etc. exceeds social norms, you would be to that extent an object of derision, not admiration. An individual could acquire, say, ten television sets. But since this exceeds all possible reasonable actual need, it would be seen as an irrational act, subject to informal social sanction. One must remember that the goods in question cannot be resold; their intrinsic usefulness, within consumption activity that has a significant social component, is all that matters.

The role of social sanction applies, in particular, to goods that are subject to improvement over time. Would everyone scrap his/her one-year-old computer, to immediately acquire the latest model, which is a bit bigger, faster, and more sophisticated than last year's? This would indeed create a problem of insatiable demand. Cultural norms, therefore, will strongly urge people to respect an informal queueing process when it comes to goods of this sort. I allow my computer to depreciate over a period of years, from normal use and in relation to the improved properties of the latest models.

When appropriate, I will acquire the latest model, thus leaping over the models between my old one and the latest, and thus for a time I will take my turn as possessor of the most advanced, as others will in their turn.

There will undoubtedly be some loss, some waste, measured against the age-old system in which all goods are rationed through prices. But when this loss is set against the gains—one may think, for example, of all of the sales, bookkeeping, legal, and other labor saved from the absence of prices—the net gain is still impressive. Above all, we must consider what consumption can become if it is, finally, freed from the encumbrances of social status, "power consumption" (see chapter 4), envidious competition, and so forth. When we consume, we do so for the intrinsic contribution to our own development, as individuals and within families, associations and communities. Consumption increasingly evolves from an end in itself into a means of social and personal growth.

We turn next to the other side of the problem: the absence of labor incentive due to breaking the link between work and income. Here, again, the stadial conception is a useful starting point. If we suppose that the transition to communism is 75 percent complete, in the sense that three-quarters of the consumer goods (however measured) are in the free category, that still leaves 25 percent, presumably the most high-ticket, high-elasticity items, that can only be acquired through income earned by working. The social security and enhancement of consumption quality in the 75 percent sector are hard at work, while the 25 percent sector keeps the flame of incentive alive in the workplace. We could do much worse than this.

Now, here is the rhetorical question about what happens as this picture progresses, and the 75–25 division slowly moves toward 80–20, and so on. At what point will workers, facing increasing size of the free-goods sector, and decreasing weight of the remaining priced sector, withdraw their labor, or begin to work less efficiently? Of course, the answer is that there is no such point. Labor, in a technologically dynamic economy, proceeding from the levels that we can envision today, in the midst of the electronic revolution and at the dawn of the robotic revolution, promises to be generally creative and rewarding, with a large intellectual component and a small and diminishing role for physical exertion. The hard physical labor and mindless repetition of tasks have been largely overcome. Workplaces are democratic, in a degree that we can only begin to imagine: the creative and managerial components of labor are widely shared; the control ceiling and incentive floor of chapter 4's workplace site have receded, making new workplace relations possible. All labor, in short, is polytechnical and professional; jobs are careers (although not necessarily *one-track* careers; learning and evolving through a lifetime would be encouraged). Workers would have "balanced job complexes" in which, to the extent culturally possible and taking into account individual variation, elements of managerial, creative, skilled, and caring labor are all present (see Albert and Hahnel 1991a, 1991b, 2002; Devine 1988, 2002). In addition to all of these considerations, the *formal* work week—the number of hours per week a worker is customarily expected to provide—would be short, and increasingly so as productivity rises, population stabilizes, ecological sustainability is secured. In a word, the goal is for every person to have work she/he looks forward to. This work is an important life-defining aspect of her/his activity; it is an important site for solidarity and connection to a collective, or team, whose support and judgment are essential to one's self-esteem. In this society, the question, "so, what do you do?" takes on whole new meaning, precisely because whatever it is that you do you do not do because you have to, to "make a living." You do it because it is a major part of what and who you are.

Now, we can ask again: at what point would workers withdraw their labor, if it is increasingly the case that that labor is not necessary as a means of access to consumer goods? And again, while there is no precise answer, the goal of achieving a state of social maturity in which sufficient labor would be freely forthcoming, having become, in Marx's phrase, "life's prime want," certainly cannot be dismissed out of hand as unrealizable.

Before taking leave of this very speculative foray into the possible future, I must address one observation in Sherman's 1970 article. Sherman presents his conception of a socialist price system evolving toward pure communism, with prices falling toward zero while money wages remain constant. He then asks whether existing socialist societies, in particular the Soviet Union, are in fact moving in this direction (in concert with their programmatic insistence on "laying the foundations for communism"). His conclusion, in 1970, is that they were *not* doing so, for the simple reason that prices in the Soviet Union remained relatively constant, with no tendency to fall, whereas money wages were subject to slow but steady increase. This appeared to Sherman to be moving in the opposite direction from communist distribution. On reflection, however, I think it should be clear that this is not the case, and this leads to an important insight. If money wages rise against a backdrop of a constant price level—what amounts to an increase in the real wage rate—this is precisely the same as a decrease in prices against a constant money wage rate. When a price falls from ten dollars per unit to one dollar per unit, against my income of one hundred dollars, this has *exactly* the same effect on the degree of compulsion surrounding my acquisition of the good in question as does a rise in my income to one thousand dollars, against a price of ten dollars per unit. Put another way, against an income of one thousand dollars, the price of ten is as "close to zero" as is the price of one, against an income of one hundred. This leads to the following conclusion: *the approach to communist distribution is inherent in rising real wages (incomes)*. This is the real meaning of the maximum wage rate barrier in the workplace site of chapter 4's discussion of capitalist crisis, and brings into focus the inexorability of socialist development into communism. The final meaning of the PF–PR model is this: development of the productive forces must, sooner or later, bring in its train a level of living standards that is incompatible with exploitative and antagonistic social relations. The eventual transition to the higher stage of communism, far from being just a creative product of the imagination, is the embodiment of this central direction in social development.

I once suggested this formulation of an answer to the question of inevitability in social evolution: *Communism is inevitable because it is possible* (Laibman 1984, 1992, ch. 12). Inevitability is clearly conditional—upon survival, which is not guaranteed (as I have insisted throughout this book). But the line of development is increasingly clear.

BIBLIOGRAPHY

Abouchar, Alan, ed. 1977. *The Socialist Price Mechanism*. Durham, NC: Duke University Press.

Adamson, Walter L. 1985. *Marx and the Disillusionment of Marxism*. Berkeley, CA: University of California Press.

Aglietta, Michel. 1979. *A Theory of Capitalist Regulation: The U. S. Experience*. London: New Left Books.

Albert, Michael and Robin Hahnel. 1991a. *The Political Economy of Participatory Economics*. Princeton, NJ: Princeton University Press.

———. 1991b. *Looking Forward: Participatory Economics for the Twenty First Century*. Boston, MA: South End Press.

———. 1992. "Participatory Planning." *Science & Society* 56, 1 (Spring): 39–59.

———. 2002. "In Defense of Participatory Economics." *Science & Society* 66, 1 (Spring): 7–21.

Albritton, Robert, Makoto Itoh, Richard Westra, and Alan Zuege, eds. 2001. *Phases of Capitalist Development*. Basingstoke, England: Palgrave Macmillan.

Amin, Samir. 1985. "Modes of Production, History, and Unequal Development." *Science & Society* 49, 2 (Summer): 194–207.

———. 2004. *Obsolescent Capitalism*. London and New York: Zed Books.

Anderson, Perry. 1978. *Passages from Antiquity to Feudalism*. London: New Left Books.

———. 1979a. *Lineages of the Absolutist State*. London: New Left Books.

———. 1979b. *Considerations on Western Marxism*. London: Verso.

Aptheker, Herbert. 1960. *The Nature of Freedom, Democracy and Revolution*. New York: New Century.

Ardrey, Robert. 1967. *African Genesis: A Personal Investigation into the Animal Origins and Nature of Man*. New York: Dell Publishing.

Aronson, Ronald. 1995. *After Marxism*. New York: Guilford Press.

Arrighi, Giovanni, and Beverly J. Silver. 1999. *Chaos and Governance in the Modern World System*. Minneapolis, MN: University of Minnesota Press.

Aston, T. H., and C. H. E. Philpin, eds. 1985. *The Brenner Debate*. Cambridge, England: Cambridge University Press.

Auerbach, Paul and Peter Skott. 1993. "Capitalist Trends and Socialist Priorities." *Science & Society* 57, 2 (Summer): 194–203.

Baltzell, E. Digby. 1964. *The Protestant Establishment: Aristocracy and Caste in America*. New Haven, CT: Yale University Press.

———. 1989. *Philadelphia Gentlemen: The Making of a National Upper Class*. New Brunswick, NJ: Transaction Publishers.

Baran, Paul A. and Paul M. Sweezy. 1966. *Monopoly Capital*. New York: Monthly Review Press.

Barrett, Michele. 1980. *Women's Oppression Today: Problems in Marxist Feminist Analysis*. London: Verso.

Becker, Ernest. 1971. *The Birth and Death of Meaning: An Interdisciplinary Perspective on the Problem of Man*. New York: Free Press.

Bell, Daniel. 1965. *The End of Ideology: On the Exhaustion of Political Ideas in the Fifties*. New York: Free Press.

Blackledge, Paul and Graeme Kirkpatrick, eds. 2002. *Historical Materialism and Social Evolution*. London/New York: Palgrave Macmillan.

Blaut, James M. 1993. *The Colonizer's Model of the World: Geographical Diffusionism and Eurocentric History*. New York: Guilford Press.

Bois, Guy. 1985. "Against the Neo-Malthusian Orthodoxy." In *The Brenner Debate*. Edited by T. H. Aston and C. H. E. Philpin, 107–118. Cambridge, England: Cambridge University Press.

Böhm-Bawerk, Eugen von. 1966. *Karl Marx and the Close of His System*. Edited by Paul Sweezy. New York: Monthly Review Press.

Bortkiewicz, Ladislaus von. 1966. "On the Correction of Marx's Fundamental Theoretical Construction in the Third Volume of *Capital*." In *Karl Marx and the Close of his System*. By Eugen von Bohm-Bawerk. Edited by Paul M. Sweezy. New York: Augustus M. Kelley.

Bourdieu, Pierre. 2003. *Firing Back: Against the Tyranny of the Market 2*. New York: New Press.

BGW. Bowles, Samuel, David M. Gordon and Thomas E. Weisskopf. 1983. *Beyond the Waste Land: A Democratic Alternative to Economic Decline*. Garden City, New York: Anchor Press/Doubleday.

Braverman, Harry. 1974. *Labor and Monopoly Capital*. New York: Monthly Review Press.

Brenner, Robert. 1976. "Agrarian Class Structure and Economic Development in Pre-Industrial Europe." *Past and Present* 70: 30–70.

Brody, Andras. 1970. *Proportions, Prices and Planning: A Mathematical Restatement of the Labor Theory of Value*. Chicago, IL: American Elsevier.

Bronfenbrenner, Martin. 1965. "*Das Kapital* for the Modern Man." *Science & Society* 29, 3 (Fall): 419–38.

Burbach, Roger and William I. Robinson. 1999. "The Fin de Siecle Debate: Globalization as Epochal Shift." *Science & Society* 63, 1 (Spring): 10–39.

Cammett, John. 1967. *Antonio Gramsci and the Origins of Italian Communism*. Stanford, CA: Stanford University Press.

Campbell, Donald E. 1995. *Incentives: Motivation and the Economics of Information*. New York and Cambridge, England: Cambridge University Press.

Carchedi, Guglielmo. 1984. "The Logic of Prices as Values." *Economy and Society* 13, 4.

Carling, Alan. 1991. *Social Division*. London: Verso.

———. 2002. "Analytical Marxism and the Debate on Social Evolution." In *Historical Materialism and Social Evolution*. Edited by Paul Blackledge and Graeme Kirkpatrick, 98–123. London/New York: Palgrave Macmillan.

———. 2006. "*Karl Marx's Theory of History* and the Recovery of the Marxian Tradition." *Science & Society* 70, 2 (April): 252–274.

Carneiro, Robert L. 2000. *The Muse of History and the Science of Culture*. New York: Kluwer Academic/Plenum Publishers.

Carnoy, Martin, Manuel Castells, Stephen S. Cohen, and Fernando Henrique Cardoso. 1993. *The New Global Economy in the Information Age.* University Park, PA: University of Pennsylvania Press.

Childe, V. Gordon. 1969. *What Happened in History.* New York: Penguin.

Clarke, Simon. 1990–91. "Overaccumulation and Crisis." *Science & Society* 54, 4 (Winter): 442–467.

Cockshott, W. Paul and Allin F. Cottrell. 1993. *Towards a New Socialism.* Nottingham, England: Spokesman Books.

———. 1997. "Value, Markets and Socialism." *Science & Society* 61, 3 (Fall): 330–357.

———. 2002. "The Relation Between Political and Economic Instances in the Communist Mode of Production." *Science & Society* 66, 1 (Spring): 50–64.

Cohen, G. A. 1978. *Karl Marx's Theory of History: A Defence.* Oxford, England: Clarendon Press.

Cohen, G. A., ed. 1988. *History, Labour, and Freedom: Themes from Marx.* Oxford, England: Clarendon Press.

Cohen, Joshua. 1982. Review of G. A. Cohen, *Karl Marx's Theory of History: A Defence. Journal of Philosophy* 79, 5: 253–273.

Cornforth, Maurice. 1954. *Historical Materialism.* New York: International Publishers.

Das, Raju J. 1996. "State Theories: A Critical Analysis." *Science & Society* 60, 1 (Spring): 27–57.

Davidson, Paul. 1972. *Money and the Real World.* New York: Wiley.

———. 1994. *Post Keynesian Macroeconomic Theory: A Foundation for Successful Economic Policies for the Twenty-First Century.* Aldershot, England; Brookfield, VT, USA: Edward Elgar.

Deacon, Terrence W. 1997. *The Symbolic Species: The Co-Evolution of Language and the Brain.* New York: W. W. Norton and Co.

de Brunhoff, Suzanne. 1978. *The State, Capital and Economic Policy.* London: Pluto Press.

Devine, Pat J. 1988. *Democracy and Economic Planning: The Political Economy of a Self-Governing Society.* Boulder, CO: Westview Press.

———. 2002. "Participatory Planning Through Negotiated Coordination." *Science & Society* 66, 1 (Spring): 72–85.

de Waal, Frans B. M. 2001. *The Ape and the Sushi Master: Cultural Reflections by a Primatologist.* New York: Basic Books.

Diamond, Jared. 1997, 1999. *Guns, Germs and Steel: The Fates of Human Societies.* New York: W. W. Norton and Co.

Dobb, Maurice. 1947. *Studies in the Development of Capitalism.* New York: International Publishers.

———. 1955a. "The Entrepreneur Myth." In *Economic Theory and Socialism.* Edited by Maurice Dobb. New York: International Publishers.

———. 1955b. "A Note on the Transformation Problem." In *Economic Theory and Socialism.* Edited by Maurice Dobb. New York: International Publishers.

Domhoff, G. W. 1967. *Who Rules America?* Englewood Cliffs, NJ: Prentice-Hall.

dos Santos, Theotonio. 1970. "The Concept of Social Classes." *Science & Society* 34, 2 (Summer): 166–193.

Duchesne, Ricardo. 2001–02. "Between Sinocentrism and Eurocentrism: Andre Gunder Frank's *Re-Orient.*" *Science & Society* 65, 4 (Winter): 428–463.

———. 2003. "The Post-Malthusian World Began in Western Europe in the Eighteenth Century: A Reply to Goldstone and Wong." *Science & Society* 7, 2 (Summer): 195–205.

Duménil, Gérard. 1983–84. "Beyond the Transformation Riddle: A Labor Theory of Value." *Science & Society* 47, 4 (Winter): 427–450.

Dussel, Enrique. 2001. *Towards an Unknown Marx: A Commentary on the Manuscripts of 1861–63*. London: Routledge.

Edwards, Richard. 1979. *Contested Terrain: The Transformation of the Workplace in the 20th Century*. New York: Basic Books.

Ehrenreich, Barbara and Janet McIntosh. 1997. "The New Creationism: Biology Under Attack." *The Nation* (June 9).

Ellman, Michael. 1973. *Planning Problems in the USSR*. London: Cambridge University Press.

———. 1979. *Socialist Planning*. London: Cambridge University Press.

Elson, Diane, ed. 1979. *Value: The Representation of Labour in Capitalism/Essays*. Atlantic Highlands, NJ: Humanities Press.

———. 1991. "The Economics of a Socialized Market." In *After the Fall*. Edited by Robin Blackburn. New York: Verso.

Elster, Jon. 1985. *Making Sense of Marx*. New York: Cambridge University Press.

Engels, Friedrich. 1964. *The Origin of the Family, Private Property, and the State*. New York: International Publishers.

———. 1966. *Herr Eugen Dühring's Revolution in Science (Anti-Dühring)*. New York: International Publishers.

Fast, Howard. 1946. *The American: A Middle Western Legend*. New York: Duell, Sloan and Pearce.

Federici, Sylvia. 2004. *Caliban and the Witch: Women, the Body and Primitive Accumulation*. Brooklyn, New York: Autonomedia.

Fine, Ben, ed. 1986. *The Value Dimension: Marx versus Ricardo and Sraffa*. London: Routledge and Kegan Paul.

Foley, Duncan. 1982. "The Value of Money, the Value of Labor Power, and the Marxian Transformation Problem." *Review of Radical Political Economics* 14, 2 (Summer): 37–47.

———. 1986. *Understanding Capital: Marx's Economic Theory*. Cambridge, MA: Harvard University Press.

Foster, John Bellamy. 1986. *The Theory of Monopoly Capitalism: An Elaboration of Marxian Political Economy*. New York: Monthly Review Press.

Foster, John Bellamy, and Henryk Szlajfer, eds. 1984. *The Faltering Economy: The Problem of Accumulation Under Monopoly Capitalism*. New York: Monthly Review Press.

Fox, Bonnie, ed. 1980. *Hidden in the Household: Women's Domestic Labor Under Capitalism*. Toronto: Women's Press.

Frank, Andre Gunder. 1998. *Re-Orient: Global Economy in the Asian Age*. Berkeley/LosAngeles, CA: University of California Press.

Freeman, Alan. 1995. "Marx Without Equilibrium." *Capital and Class* 56 (Summer): 49–89.

Freeman, Alan, and Guglielmo Carchedi, eds. 1996. *Marx and Non-Equilibrium Economics*. Aldershot, England: Edward Elgar.

Freeman, Alan, and Andrew Kliman, eds. 2004. *The New Value Controversy and the Foundations of Economics*. Aldershot, England: Edward Elgar.

Friedman, Milton. 1962, 2002. *Capitalism and Freedom*. Chicago, IL: University of Chicago Press.

Garegnani, Pierangelo. 1991. "Some Notes for an Analysis of Accumulation." In *Beyond the Steady State: A Revival of Growth Theory*. Edited by Joseph Halevi, David Laibman and Edward J. Nell. London: Macmillan; New York: St. Martin's.

Gettleman, Marvin E., and Stuart Schaar, eds. 2003. *The Middle East and Islamic World Reader*. New York: Grove Press.

Goldstone, Jack. 2003. "Europe Vs. Asia: Missing Data and Misconceptions." *Science & Society* 67, 2 (Summer): 184–195.

González, Marcial. 2004. "Postmodernism, Historical Materialism and Chicana/o Cultural Studies." *Science & Society* 68, 2.

Gordon, David M., Richard C. Edwards, and Michael Reich. 1982. *Segmented Work, Divided Workers*. Cambridge, MA: Cambridge University Press.

Gordon, David M., Thomas E. Weisskopf, and Samuel Bowles. 1983. "Long Swings and the Nonreproductive Cycle." *American Economic Review* 73, 2 (May): 152–157.

Gottlieb, Roger S. 1984. "Feudalism and Historical Materialism: A Critique and a Synthesis." *Science & Society* 48, 1 (Spring): 1–37.

———. 1987. "Historical Laws, Social Primacy." *Science & Society* 51, 2 (Summer): 188–199.

Gramsci, Antonio. 1971. *Excerpts from the Prison Notebooks*. Edited and translated by Quintin Hoare and Geoffrey Nowell Smith. New York: International Publishers.

———. 1992. *Prison Notebooks*. Edited with an introduction by Joseph A. Buttigieg. New York: Columbia University Press.

Habermas, Jürgen. 1975. *Legitimation Crisis*. Boston, MA: Beacon Press.

Hahnel, Robin. 2002. *The ABCs of Political Economy: A Modern Approach*. London: Pluto Press.

Harris, Donald J. 1978. *Capital Accumulation and Income Distribution*. Stanford, CA: Stanford University Press.

Harris, Marvin. 1979. *Cultural Materialism: The Struggle for a Science of Culture*. New York: Random House.

Hayek, Friedrich A. 1935. *Collectivist Economic Planning*. London: Routledge and Kegan Paul.

———. 1945. "The Use of Knowledge in Society." *American Economic Review* 35, 4 (September): 519–530.

Heilbroner, Robert. 1985. *The Nature and Logic of Capitalism*. New York: W. W. Norton Co.

Heller, Henry. 1985. "The Transition Debate in Historical Perspective." *Science & Society* 49, 2 (Summer): 208–213.

Herrnstein, Richard J., and Charles Murray. 1994. *The Bell Curve: Intelligence and Class Structur in American Life*. New York: The Free Press.

Hilton, R. H. 1979. *The Transition from Feudalism to Capitalism*. London: New Left Books.

Hobsbawm, Eric J. 1964. "Introduction." In Karl Marx, *Pre-Capitalist Economic Formations*. New York: International Publishers.

———, ed. 1982. *The History of Marxism*. Bloomington, IN: Indiana University Press.

Hodgson, Geoff. 1980. "A Theory of Exploitation Without the Labor Theory of Value." *Science & Society* 44, 3 (Fall): 257–273.

Hoffman, John. 1985–86. "The Dialectic of Abstraction and Concentration in Historical Materialism." *Science & Society* 49, 4 (Winter): 451–462.

Holloway, John, and Sol Picciotto, eds. 1978. *State and Capital: A Marxist Debate*. Austin, TX: University of Texas Press.

Howard, M. C., and J. E. King. 1989. *A History of Marxian Economics*. Volume I, 1883–1929. Princeton, NJ: Princeton University Press.

———. 1992. *A History of Marxian Economics*. Vol. II, 1929–1990. Princeton, NJ: Princeton University Press.

Hunt, E. K., and Mark Glick. 1987. "The Transformation Problem." In *The New Palgrave*. Edited by John Eatwell, Murray Milgate and Peter Newman. New York: Stockton.

Hurwicz, L., and M. Walker. 1990. "On the General Non-Optimality of Dominant-Strategy Allocation Mechanisms: A General Theorem that Includes Pure Exchange Economies." *Econometrica* 58: 683–704.

Itoh, Makoto. 1980. *Value and Crisis*. New York: Monthly Review Press.

Jay, Martin. 1973. *The Dialectical Imagination: A History of the Frankfurt School and the Institute of Social Research, 1923–1950*. Boston, MA: Little, Brown and Co.

Jessop, Bob. 1990. *State Theory: Putting the Capitalist State in Its Place*. Cambridge, England: Polity Press.

Kaldor, Nicholas. 1960. *Essays in the Theory of Growth and Distribution*. London: Duckworth.

Kalecki, Michal. 1968. *Theory of Economic Dynamics*. New York: Monthly Review Press.

Katz, Claudio J. 1994. "Debating the Dynamics of Feudalism: Challenges for Historical Materialism" *Science & Society* 58, 2 (Summer): 195–204.

Keeran, Roger, and Thomas Kenny. 2004. *Socialism Betrayed: Behind the Collapse of the Soviet Union*. New York: International Publishers.

Kelso, Louis O. and Mortimer J. Adler. 1958. *The Capitalist Manifesto*. New York: Random House.

Keynes, John Maynard. 1961. *The General Theory of Employment, Interest and Money*. London: Macmillan.

Kirsch, Leonard Joel. 1972. *Soviet Wages: Changes in Structure and Administration Since 1956*. Cambridge, MA: Massachusetts Institute of Technology Press.

Khudukormov, G. N., gen. ed. 1967. *Political Economy of Socialism*. Moscow: Progress Publishers.

Kliman, Andrew. 1996. "A Value-Theoretic Critique of the Okishio Theorem." In *Marx and Non-Equilibrium Economics*. Edited by Alan Freeman and Guglielmo Carchedi. Aldershot, England: Edward Elgar.

Kliman, Andrew, and Ted McGlone. 1988. "The Transformation Non-Problem and the Non-Transformation Problem." *Capital and Class* 35.

Kluckhohn, Clyde. 1950. *Mirror for Man: The Relation of Anthropology to Modern Life*. London: G. G. Harrap.

Kotz, David. 1990. "A Comparative Analysis of the Theory of Regulation and the Social Structure of Accumulation Theory." *Science & Society* 54, 1 (Spring): 5–28.

———. 2001. "Is Russia Becoming Capitalist?" *Science & Society* 65, 2 (Summer): 157–181.

———. 2002. "Is Russia Becoming Capitalist? Reply." *Science & Society* 66, 3 (Fall): 388–393.

Krader, Lawrence. 1975. *The Asiatic Mode of Production: Sources, Development and Critique in the Writings of Karl Marx*. Assen, Germany: Van Gorcum.

Krause, Ulrich. 1982. *Money and Abstract Labour: On the Analytical Foundations of Political Economy*. London: New Left Books.

Kurz, Heinz D., and Neri Salvadori. 1995. *Theory of Production: A Long-Period Analysis*. Cambridge, England: Cambridge University Press.

Kuusinen, Otto V., gen. ed. 1960. *Fundamentals of Marxism–Leninism*. Moscow: Foreign Languages Publishing House.

Laibman, David. 1973–74. "Values and Prices of Production: The Political Economy of the Transformation Problem." *Science & Society* 37, 4 (Winter): 404–436.

———. 1978. "Price Structures, Social Structures and Labor Values in a Theoretical Socialist Economy." *Economics of Planning* 14, 1: 3–23. Republished as chapter 15, "Socialism: Prices, Social Structures and Labor Values." In *Value, Technical Change and Crisis*. By David Laibman. Armonk, NY: M. E. Sharpe, 1992a.

———. 1983. "Capitalism and Immanent Crisis: Broad Strokes for a Theoretical Foundation." *Social Research* 50, 2 (Summer): 359–400.

————. 1984. "Modes of Production and Theories of Transition." *Science & Society* 48, 3 (Fall): 257–294.

————. 1984–85. "Value: A Dialog in One Act." *Science & Society* 48, 4 (Winter): 449–465.

————. 1987. "Modes and Transitions." *Science & Society* 51, 2 (Summer): 179–188.

————. 1992a. *Value, Technical Change and Crisis: Explorations in Marxist Economic Theory.* Armonk, New York: M. E. Sharpe.

————. 1992b. "Market and Plan: The Evolution of Socialist Social Structures in History and Theory." *Science & Society* 56, 1 (Spring): 60–91. Republished as chapter 16, "Toward a Working Theory of the Socialist Economy." In *Value, Technical Change and Crisis.* By David Laibman. Armonk, New York: M. E. Sharpe, 1992a.

————. 1995. "An Argument for Comprehensive Socialism." *Socialism and Democracy* 9, 2 (Fall–Winter): 83–93.

————. 1997. *Capitalist Macrodynamics: A Systematic Introduction.* London: Macmillan.

————. 1998a. "Accumulation, Technical Change, and Prisoners' Dilemmas: A Rejoinder to Frank Thompson." *Review of Radical Political Economics* 30, 2 (Spring): 87–101.

————. 1998b. "Value Theory: Beyond Gridlock. *Utopia* 28 (Athens, in Greek) (January–February): 29–47.

————. 1999a. "The Cherry Esplanade Conjecture: A Contribution to Conceptual Foundations for Socialist Renewal." *Science & Society* 63, 3 (Fall): 373–379.

————. 1999b. "Revisioning Socialism: The Cherry Esplanade Conjecture." In conference volume, *Contemporary Economic Theory: Radical Critiques of Neoliberalism.* Edited by Andriana Vlachou, 113–132. London: Macmillan; New York: St. Martins.

————. 1999–2000. "Capitalism as History: A Taxonomy of Crisis Potentials." *Science & Society* 63, 4 (Winter): 478–502.

————. 2000. "Rhetoric and Substance in Value Theory: An Appraisal of the New Orthodox Marxism." *Science & Society* 64, 2 (Fall): 310–332.

————. 2001. "Contours of the Maturing Socialist Economy." *Historical Materialism* 9: 85–110.

————. 2002a. "Value and the Quest for the Core of Capitalism." *Review of Radical Political Economics* 34, 159–178.

————. 2002b. "Is Russia Becoming Capitalist? Comment." *Science & Society* 66, 3 (Fall): 381–388.

————. 2004. "From the Ashes of the Old." Interview. *Political Affairs* 83, 9 (September–October): 40–45.

Landes, Joan. 1977–78. "Women, Labor and Family Life: A Theoretical Perspective." *Science & Society* 41, 4 (Winter): 386–409.

Lange, Oskar. 1956. *On the Economic Theory of Socialism.* Minneapolis, MN: University of Minnesota Press.

————, ed. 1962. *Problems in the Political Economy of Socialism.* New Delhi: People's Publishing House.

————. 1963. *Political Economy.* Volume I: *General Problems.* New York: Macmillan.

Lebowitz, Michael. 2003. *Beyond Capital: Marx's Political Economy of the Working Class.* 2d ed. Basingstoke, England: Palgrave Macmillan.

Lembcke, Jerry. 1991–92. "Why 50 Years? Working-Class Formation and Long Economic Cycles." *Science & Society* 55, 4 (Winter): 417–445.

————. 1995. "Labor History's 'Synthesis Debate': Sociological Interventions." *Science & Society* 59, 2 (Summer): 137–173.

Lenin, V. I. 1933. *Imperialism, the Highest Stage of Capitalism: A Popular Outline.* New York: International Publishers.

————. 1967. *The Right of Nations to Self-Determination*. 4th ed. Moscow: Progress Publishers.

Lilley, Samuel. 1966. *Men, Machines, and History*. New York: International Publishers.

Lipietz, Alain. 1982. "The So-Called 'Transformation Problem' Revisited." *Journal of Economic Theory* 26, 1: 59–88.

————. 1987. *Mirages and Miracles: The Crisis in Global Fordism*. London: Verso.

Lundberg, Ferdinand. 1968. *The Rich and the Super Rich: A Study in the Power of Money Today*. New York: L. Stuart.

Luxemburg, Rosa. 1976. *The National Question: Selected Writings*. New York: Monthly Review Press.

Mage, Shane. 1963. *The "Law of the Falling Tendency of the Rate of Profit": Its Place in the Marxian Theoretical System and Relevance to the United States*. Ph.D. Diss., Columbia University.

Maler, Henri. 1998. "An Apochryphal Testament: Socialism, Utopian and Scientific." In "Friedrich Engels: A Critical Centenary Appreciation." Edited by Joost Kircz and Michael Löwy. Special issue, *Science & Society* 62, 1 (Spring).

Mandel, Ernest. 1975. *Late Capitalism*. London: New Left Books.

Marquit, Erwin. 2004. "The Need for a Balanced Appraisal of the USSR—A Review Essay." *Nature, Society, and Thought* 16, 4: 473–506.

Marx, Karl. 1913 (1859). "Preface." *A Contribution to the Critique of Political Economy*. Chicago, IL: Charles H. Kerr.

————. 1928. *The Eighteenth Brumaire of Louis Bonaparte*. New York: International Publishers.

————. 1933a. *Wage-Labour and Capital / Value, Price and Profit*. New York: International Publishers.

————. 1933b. *The Critique of the Gotha Programme*. New York: International Publishers.

————. 1935. *Value, Price and Profit*. New York: International Publishers.

————. 1963 (1852). *The Eighteenth Brumaire of Louis Bonaparte*. New York: International Publishers.

————. 1967. *Capital*. Vols. I, III. New York: International Publishers.

Marx, Karl, and Friedrich Engels. 1998 (1848). *The Communist Manifesto*. New York: Monthly Review Press.

Mavroudeas, Stavros. 2004. "Review of Albritton, Hoh, Westra, and Zuege." *Science & Society* 68, 1 (Spring).

McDonough, Terrence. 1995. "Lenin, Imperialism, and the Stages of Capitalist Development." *Science & Society* 59, 3 (Fall): 339–367.

McIntosh, Janet. 1998–99. "Symbolism, Cognition, and Political Orders." *Science & Society* 62, 4 (Winter): 557–568.

McLennan, Gregor. 1986. "Marxist Theory and Historical Research: Between the Hard and Soft Options." *Science & Society* 50, 1 (Spring): 85–95.

Meek, Ronald. 1956. *Studies in the Labor Theory of Value*. New York: Monthly Review Press.

————. 1967a. *Economics and Ideology and Other Essays*. London: Chapman and Hall.

————. 1967b. "Some Notes on the 'Transformation Problem.'" In *Economics and Ideology and Other Essays*. London: Chapman and Hall, 1967a.

Meyer, Gerald. 2002. "Frank Sinatra: The Popular Front and an American Icon." *Science & Society* 66, 3 (Fall): 311–335.

Mills, C. Wright. 2000. *The Power Elite*. New York: Oxford University Press.

Milonakis, Dimitris. 1993–94. "Prelude to the Genesis of Capitalism: The Dynamics of the Feudal Mode of Production." *Science & Society* 57, 4 (Winter): 390–419.

———. 1997. "The Dynamics of History: Structure and Agency in Historical Evolution." *Science & Society* 61, 3 (Fall): 303–329.

Minsky, Hyman P. 1982. *Can "It" Happen Again? Essays on Instability and Finance.* Armonk, New York: M. E. Sharpe.

Moore, Barrington. 1966. *Social Origins of Dictatorship and Democracy: Lord and Peasant in the Making of the Modern World.* Boston, MA: Beacon Press.

Morishima, Michio. 1973. *Marx's Economics: A Dual Theory of Value and Growth.* London: Cambridge University Press.

Morishima, Michio, and George Catephores. 1975. "Is There an 'Historical Transformation Problem'?" *Economic Journal*, 86, 342–347.

Moseley, Fred, ed. 1993. *Marx's Method in Capital.* Altantic Highlands, NJ: Humanities Press.

———. 1993. "Marx's Logical Method and the 'Transformation Problem.' " In *Marx's Method in Capital.* Edited by Fred Moseley. Atlantic Highlands, NJ: Humanities Press.

Needham, Joseph. 1969. *The Grand Titration: Science and Society in East and West.* London: Allen & Unwin.

Nicolaus, Martin. 1967. "Proletariat and Middle Class in Marx: Hegelian Choreography and the Capitalist Dialectic." *Studies on the Left* 9, 1 (January–February): 22–49.

Nolan, Paul. 1993. *Natural Selection and Historical Materialism.* Watford, England: Glenfield Press.

———. 2002. "A Darwinian Historical Materialism." In *Historical Materialism and Social Evolution.* Edited by Paul Blackledge and Graeme Kirkpatrick, 76–97. London/New York: Palgrave Macmillan.

———. 2006. "Why G. A Cohen Can't Appeal to Charles Darwin to Help Him Defend Karl Marx (But Why Others Can)." *Science & Society* 70, 2: 155–179.

Nove, Alec. 1969. *The Soviet Economy.* New York: Praeger.

———. 1983. *The Economics of Feasible Socialism.* London: Allen & Unwin.

O'Connor, James. 1994. "Is Sustainable Capitalism Possible?" In *Is Capitalism Sustainable?* Edited by Martin O'Connor, 152–175. New York: Guilford Press.

Okishio, Nobuo. 1963. "A Mathematical Note on Marxian Theorems." *Weltwirtschaftsliches Archiv* 91, 2: 287–299.

Ollman, Bertell. 1996. "Market Mystification in Capitalist and Market Socialist Societies." Paper presented to American Political Science Association, San Francisco, August 29–September 1.

Ollman, Bertell, James Lawler, David Schweickart, and Hillel Ticktin. 1998. *Market Socialism: The Debate Among Socialists.* New York: Routledge and Kegan Paul.

Pasinetti, Luigi. 1977. *Lectures in the Theory of Production.* New York: Columbia University Press.

Peterson, Janice, and Margaret Lewis, eds. 2003. *The Elgar Companion to Feminist Economics.* Cheltenham, UK: Edward Elgar.

Pevzner, Ia. 1984. *State Monopoly Capitalism and the Labor Theory of Value.* Moscow: Progress Publishers.

Pirenne, Henri. 1939. *Medieval Cities: Their Origin and the Revival of Trade.* Princeton, NJ: Princeton University Press.

Polanyi, Karl. 1957. *The Great Transformation.* Boston, MA: Beacon Press.

Postan, Michael M. 1975. *The Medieval Economy and Society.* London: Penguin.

Postan, Michael M., and John Hatcher. 1985. "Population and Class Relations in Feudal Society." In *The Brenner Debate.* Edited by T. H. Aston and C. H. E. Philpin, 64–78.

Cambridge, England: Cambridge University Press.

Ramos, Alejandro, and Adolfo Rodriguez. 1995. "The Transformation of Values Into Prices of Production: A Different Reading of Marx's Text." In *Marx and Non-Equilibrium Economics*. Edited by Alan Freeman and Guglielmo Carchedi. Aldershot, England: Edward Elgar.

Robinson, Joan. 1942. *An Essay on Marxian Economics*. New York: St. Martin's Press.

———. 1962. *Essays in the Theory of Economic Growth*. New York: Macmillan.

Robinson, William I. 1996. *Promoting Polyarchy: Globalization, U.S. Intervention, and Hegemony*. Cambridge, England: Cambridge University Press.

Robinson, William I., and Jerry Harris. 2000. "Towards a Global Ruling Class: Globalization and the Transnational Capitalist Class." *Science & Society* 64, 1 (Spring): 11–54.

Roemer, John E. 1982. *A General Theory of Exploitation and Class*. Cambridge, MA: Harvard University Press.

———. 1988. *Free to Lose: An Introduction to Marxist Economic Philosophy*. Cambridge, MA: Harvard University Press.

———. 1994. *A Future for Socialism*. Cambridge, MA: Harvard University Press.

Roosevelt, Frank, and David Belkin, eds. 1994. *Why Market Socialism? Essays from Dissent*. Armonk, New York: M. E. Sharpe.

Rorty, Richard. 1992. "The Intellectuals at the End of Socialism." *The Yale Review* (Spring).

Rosenthal, John. 2000–01. "On Two 'Models' of Capitalism." *Science & Society* 64, 4 (Winter): 424–459.

Ross, Andrew, ed. 1996. *Science Wars*. Durham, NC: Duke University Press.

Rudra, Ashok. 1987. "Lessons for Third World Marxists." *Science & Society* 51, 2 (Summer): 170–178.

Samuelson, Paul A. 1971. "Understanding the Marxian Notion of Exploitation: A Summary of the So-Called Transformation Problem Between Marxian Values and Competitive Prices." *Journal of Economic Literature* 9, 2 (June): 399–431.

Schor, Juliet. 1991. *The Overworked American: The Unexpected Decline of Leisure*. New York: Basic Books.

Schorsch, Louis L. 1980–81. "Direct Producers and the Rise of the Factory System." *Science & Society* 44, 4 (Winter): 401–442.

Schumpeter, Joseph A. 1951. *Ten Great Economists, From Marx to Keynes*. New York: Oxford University Press.

Schweickart, David. 1992. "Economic Democracy: A Worthy Socialism that Would Really Work." *Science & Society* 56, 1 (Spring): 9–38.

———. 1996. *Against Capitalism*. Boulder, CO: Westview Press.

Science & Society. 1977. *The Transition from Feudalism to Capitalism: A Symposium*. With Paul M. Sweezy, Maurice Dobb, R. H. Hilton, H. K. Takahashi, and Christopher Hill. New York: S&S Quarterly. Republished as Hilton, 1979.

———. 2002. "Building Socialism Theoretically: Alternatives to Capitalism and the Invisible Hand." Special Issue, edited by Pat Devine. 66, 1 (Spring).

Sekine, Thomas T. 1975. "Uno-*Riron*: A Japanese Contribution to Marxian Political Economy." *Journal of Economic Literature*. Vol. 13.

———. 1984. *The Dialectic of Capital*. Vol. I. Tokyo: Yushindo Press.

Sememov, V. 1980. "The Diary of Socio-Economic Formations and World History." In *Soviet and Western Anthropology*. Edited by E. Gellner. New York: Columbia University Press.

Seton, Francis. 1957. "The 'Transformation Problem.' " *Review of Economic Studies* 24, 3 (June): 149–160.

Shaffer, Harry G., ed. 1984. *The Soviet System in Theory and Practice: Western and Soviet Views.* 2d ed. New York: Frederick Ungar.

Shaikh, Anwar. 1977. "Marx's Theory of Value and the 'Transformation Problem.' " In *The Subtle Anatomy of Capitalism.* Edited by Jesse Schwartz. Santa Monica, CA: Goodyear.

———. 1978. "An Introduction to the History of Crisis Theories." In *U.S. Capitalism in Crisis.* New York: Union for Radical Political Economics.

Shandro, Alan. 2001. "Reading Lenin: Dialectics and Eclecticism." *Science & Society* 65, 2 (Summer): 216–225.

Sherman, Howard. 1970. "The Economics of Pure Communism." *Soviet Studies* 22 (July): 24–36; *Review of Radical Political Economics* 2 (Fall): 39–50.

———. 1972. *Radical Political Economy: Capitalism and Socialism from a Marxist-Humanist Perspective.* New York: Basic Books.

Singer, Daniel. 1999. *Whose Millennium: Theirs or Ours?* New York: Monthly Review Press.

Skillman, Gilbert. 1996–97. "Marx's Theory of Value and the Labor–Labor Power Distinction." *Science & Society* 60, 4 (Winter).

Smith, Adam. 1976 (1759). *The Theory of Moral Sentiments.* Oxford: Clarendon Press.

Smith, Paul. 1978. "Domestic Labor and Marx's Theory of Value." In *Feminism and Materialism: Women and Modes of Production.* Edited by Annette Kuhn and Annmarie Wolpe. Boston, MA: Routledge and Kegan Paul.

Sokal, Alan. 1996. "Transgressing the Boundaries: Toward a Transformative Hermeneutics of Quantum Gravity." *Social Text* (Spring–Summer).

Sokal, Alan, and Jean Bricmont. 1998. *Intellectual Impostures: Postmodern Philosophers' Abuse of Science.* New York: Profile Books.

Sraffa, Piero. 1960. *Production of Commodities by Means of Commodities.* London: Cambridge University Press.

Steedman, Ian. 1977. *Marx After Sraffa.* London: New Left Books.

Steedman, Ian, and Paul M. Sweezy, eds. 1981. *The Value Controversy.* London: Verso.

Steindl, Joseph. 1952. *Maturity and Stagnation in American Capitalism.* Oxford: Blackwell.

Stigler, George. 1965. "Ricardo and the 93% Labor Theory of Value." In *Essays in the History of Economics.* Chicago, IL: University of Chicago Press.

Sweezy, Paul M. 1956. *The Theory of Capitalist Development.* New York: Monthly Review Press.

———. 1977. "The Transition from Feudalism to Capitalism." In *Science & Society* (Symposium).

———. 1986. "Feudalism-to-Capitalism Revisited." *Science & Society* 50, 1 (Spring): 474–485.

Tawney, R. H. 1926. *Religion and the Rise of Capitalism.* New York: Harcourt, Brace and Company.

Timasheff, Nicholas. 1976. *Sociological Theory: Its Nature and Growth.* New York: Random House.

Tirole, J. 1988. *The Theory of Industrial Organization.* Cambridge, MA: Massachusetts Institute of Technology Press.

Toynbee, Arnold. 1972. *A Study of History.* New York: Oxford University Press

Uno, Kozo. 1980. *Principles of Political Economy: Theory of a Purely Capitalist Society.* Translated and edited by Tom Sekine. Sussex, England: Harvester Press.

Veblen, Thorstein. 1975. *The Theory of the Leisure Class.* New York: A. M. Kelley.

Vogel, Lise. 1983. *Marxism and the Oppression of Women: Toward a Unitary Theory.* New Brunswick, NJ: Rutgers University Press.

———. 1986. "Feminism Scholarship: The Impact of Marxism." In *The Left Academy.* Vol. 3. Edited by Bertell Ollman and Deward Vernoff. New York: Praeger.

Wallerstein, Immanuel. 1974. *The Modern World System I: Capitalist Agriculture and the Origins of the European World-Economy in the Sixteenth Century*. New York: Academic Press.

———. 1977. "Rise and Future Demise of the World Capitalist System." *Comparative Studies in Society and History* 16, 4 (September): 387–415.

Walsh, Vivian. 1996. *Rationality, Allocation, and Reproduction*. Oxford, England: Clarendon Press.

Webber, Michael J., and David L. Rigby. 1996. *The Golden Age Illusion: Rethinking Postwar Capitalism*. New York: Guilford Press.

Weber, Max. 1998. *The Protestant Ethic and the Spirit of Capitalism*. 2d ed. Los Angeles, CA: Roxbury Publishers.

Weeks, John. 1981. *Capital and Exploitation*. Princeton, NJ: Princeton University Press.

White, Leslie A. 1959. *The Evolution of Culture*. New York: McGraw-Hill.

———. 1969. *The Science of Culture*. New York: Farrar, Straus, and Giroux.

White, Lynn Townsend. 1964. *Medieval Technology and Social Change*. London: Oxford University Press.

White, Robert W. 1975. *Lives in Progress: A Study of the Natural Growth of Personality*. New York: Holt, Rinehart and Winston.

Wicksteed, Philip H. 1933. *The Common Sense of Political Economy*. Vol. I and II. London: Routledge and Kegan Paul.

Wilson, Edward O. 2000. *Sociobiology: The New Synthesis*. Cambridge, MA: Belknap Press of Harvard University Press.

Winternitz, J. 1948. "Values and Prices of Production: A Solution of the So-Called Transformation Problem." *Economic Journal* 58 (June): 276–280.

Wittfogel, Karl. 1957. *Oriental Despotism: A Comparative Study of Total Power*. New Haven, CT: Yale University Press.

Wolff, Rick, Antonio Callari and Bruce Roberts. 1984. "A Marxian Alternative to the Traditional Transformation Problem." *Review of Radical Political Economics* 16, 2: 3.

Wong, R. Bin. 1997. *China Transformed: Historical Change and the Limits of European Experience*. Ithaca, New York: Cornell University Press.

———. 2003. "Beyond Sinocentrism and Eurocentrism." *Science & Society* 67, 2 (Summer): 173–184.

Wood, Ellen Meiksins. 1999. *The Origin of Capitalism*. New York: Monthly Review Press.

Wright, Erik Olin, Andrew Levine, and Elliott Sober. 1992. *Reconstructing Marxism*. London: Verso.

Wright, Erik Olin, ed. 1996. *Equal Shares: Making Market Socialism Work*. John E. Roemer and Contributors. London/New York: Verso.

Zauberman, Alfred. 1967. *Aspects of Planometrics*. New Haven, CT: Yale University Press.

INDEX

211